Planet Google

Randall Stross is a professor of business at San José State University. He writes the *New York Times* column 'Digital Domain', and is the author of a number of critically acclaimed books, including *The Wizard of Menlo Park*, *eBoys*, and *The Microsoft Way*. He lives in Burlingame, California.

Planet Google

How One Company is Transforming our Lives

RANDALL STROSS

Atlantic Books
LONDON

First published in hardback in the United States of America in 2008
by Free Press, a division of Simon & Schuster, Inc.,
1230 Avenue of the Americas,
New York, NY 10020.

First published in paperback
in Great Britain in 2009 by Atlantic Books
an imprint of Grove Atlantic Ltd.

1 3 5 7 9 10 8 6 4 2

A CIP catalogue record for this book is available from
the British Library.

ISBN: 978 1 84354 982 6

Printed in Great Britain by CPI Bookmarque, Croydon

Atlantic Books
An imprint of Grove Atlantic Ltd
Ormond House
26–27 Boswell Street
London WC1N 3JZ

www.atlantic-books.co.uk

For H. Joy Stross

Contents

Planet Google

Introduction

Google began with a grand aspiration: organize the world's information. Lofty aspirations alone are not noteworthy—they are commonplace in every tiny start-up in Silicon Valley. What sets Google apart is the rapidity of its growth since its founding in 1998, growth that has, in turn, provided the company with the capital, smarts, technology, and brand to make its founders' extravagant wish to organize the world's information seem like a practical, one-item to-do list.

In the course of quickly becoming a ubiquitous presence—by 2003, a mere five years after the company's founding, the popularity of *google,* the verb, was formally recognized by the American Dialect Society—Google has undertaken initiatives to attain comprehensive control of information. It has made great progress in expanding in numerous directions, doing so well ahead of our ability to notice the details or the cumulative impact. This book explores how Google has grown up and out, how early technology choices enabled it to extend its reach without limit, how its pursuit of information of all kinds has brought it unrivaled power, and how its power affects the general interests of everyone, for better or for ill.

Google version 1.0 searched Web pages. Google 2.0 has been reaching outward beyond Web pages, omnivorously. Books, news, and videos are three of many categories of information that Google has added to its storehouses, bringing it into conflict with entire industries: book publishing, newspapers, and television entertainment.

In other industries, it has acted at times as provocateur, and at other times as a friendly ally of everyone. In the wireless industry, for example, it had sufficient cash on hand in early 2008 to indulge in a playful multibillion-dollar game with Verizon, AT&T, and other bidders in the federal government's spectrum auction. Google put $4.71 billion on the line for spectrum that it did not really want. (A Google manager later described his team's anxiety that it might win: "We kept hitting the 'refresh' button on the browser" to see if other companies had bid higher, which eventually they did.) Google also has befriended a sizable and still growing segment of the wireless industry since it decided to organize and lead a coalition of companies that will introduce new cell phone handsets based on software that Google designed.

Google's growth has not been held back by pride: when it has failed in its efforts to gain new markets that it desires, it will spend the large sums needed to acquire the companies that possess what it seeks. YouTube essentially owned the online video market, and cost Google $1.65 billion to acquire in 2006. DoubleClick essentially owned the dominating advertising network that places banner advertising on Web sites, and cost Google $3.1 billion to acquire in 2008.

As Google has expanded well beyond Web search, introducing new services developed in its own labs and absorbing market-leading companies that it acquired, the company has managed for the most part to maintain an appearance of benign innocence. Its senior executives do not speak in the militaristic language common in business—the lexicon of raw ambition, conquest, and mastery. Instead, they speak in the bland language of science and engineering, and the uplifting language of public service. The company was fortunate during its rise to acquire a patina of historical inevitability. Every age—coal, steel, oil—has a raw material that defines its historical moment. In ours it is information, and Google has become its preeminent steward.

The sense of historical predestination is illusory, however, an artifact of hindsight. Google's power derives from its financial base, which was built upon an accidental discovery, two years after the company's founding, that plain text advertisements on its search results pages produce enormous profits. Neither Larry Page nor Sergey Brin, the company's cofounders, who met as graduate students in computer science at Stanford University, predicted—nor did anyone else—that those unobtrusive ads would form the foundation of a business that within seven years would be accorded by investors a historic high valuation, in early November 2007, of $225 billion.

The ad giveth, and the ad taketh away, too. Bright future prospects for those ads drove Google's share price up to its historic peak, and when future prospects for continued growth in ad revenue dimmed, investors' interest cooled. In the last quarter of 2007, Google enjoyed 30 percent annual growth in the number of clicks on its paid ads, but the growth disappeared in early 2008. When evidence surfaced that the number of clicks in the first two months of 2008 was flat, and when dark economic clouds gathered, portending a global recession and a difficult market for ad sales for Google by mid-March 2008, investors sent Google's share price down 45 percent from its historic peak of $747. Then, when Google reported in April that its ad sales in the first quarter of 2008 had remained strong, its shares soared 20 percent in a single day.

Google's dependence upon text ads is especially remarkable given that advertising was entirely absent in the original business plans of the founders. When the Google search engine was first made available to the public, visitors noticed superior search results, but they also noticed the service was entirely free of commercial messages. Google spared them the irritating pop-ups, flashing banners, and other mutating forms of advertisements that at that time were competing in an escalating arms race for a visitor's attention on the Web.

Brin and Page were hostile to the very notion of permitting advertising on a search site. In an April 1998 academic paper prepared when they were still students, they criticized "advertising funded search engines," which they believed would be "inherently biased towards the advertisers and away from the needs of the consumers." They argued that for a search engine to remain immune from the temptation of biased results, it would have to remain "in the academic realm."

Even after Google moved from its first home, a Stanford dorm, to a rented garage off campus, Brin and Page moved cautiously in permitting advertising on their site. They decided to introduce advertisements as an experiment, restricting the format to three very short lines of text and a Web address, which were placed on the right margin of the search results page and displayed only if the advertisement was directly relevant to the search term. This was sufficiently unorthodox that even some withinaogle were skeptical that plain text ads would succeed in attracting attention. Marissa Mayer, a Google vice president and early employee, later recalled that a colleague leaned over at the meeting that settled on the details of the text-only advertising and predicted, "You wait, in a month, we'll be selling banners."

When Google offered the ads on a trial basis in 2000, prospective advertisers were invited to spend a modest sum to see if plain text ads, matched to the keyword phrase used in a search, would draw customers. The effectiveness of the ads was easy to measure: only if a user clicked on the ad was it deemed successful. Google's offer was risk free for advertisers: they would pay only when users clicked.

Initially, the text ads were displayed so sparingly that they went largely unnoticed. The self-imposed requirement that advertisements had to be meaningfully related to the search phrase meant that in 85 percent of all Google searches in 2000, no advertisements were shown at all because the search phrase had no relation to any commercial product or service offered by Google's advertisers. Brin said in an interview at the time that he heard Google visitors report that they never saw an advertisement. Even in 2001, the advertisements were still so unobtrusive that how Google made money remained a mystery to journalists and analysts. The founders showed no indication that they foresaw how important advertising would be to the company: Google also earned money from licensing its search engine technology to other companies, like Yahoo, and that seemed to everyone at Google to be as promising a source of revenue as any other.

As late as 2002, four years after the company's founding, Google's text advertisements seemed, at least to some informed observers, to be so insignificant that the company's ability to ever turn a profit seemed uncertain. The *New York Times* ran a story whose headline preserved the prevalent view that Google still lacked a means to make money: "Google's Toughest Search Is for a Business Model." Yuri Punj, an analyst at UBS Warburg, said, "The Internet advertising model has been shown not to work. We all know in business that free doesn't work. I think Google will realize that they have to go to some paid search capability." Indeed, Google's own Omid Kordestani, a senior vice president who oversaw sales, wondered aloud whether Google might charge for its service in the future.

Those unprepossessing text ads, however, were providing advertisers one of the most cost-effective ways of reaching desirable customers ever devised in the history of advertising. It took a while before this was noticed. Achieving a one-to-one match between an advertiser and a receptive viewer is not only feasible, but relatively easy, because the very act of submitting a search term provides precise information about what a user is currently thinking about—permitting a highly educated guess about the user's likely interest in an advertiser's product. Freed of the inefficiencies of broadcasting a message to those who may or may not happen to be in a receptive frame of mind, Google's advertisers are happy. And by setting up an auction system, in which interested advertisers bid against one another for the price they are willing to pay Google if a user clicks on their advertisements, Google is happy.

By 2002, Google's revenue passed $400 million and then grew even faster—to $1.4 billion in 2003, $6.1 billion in 2005, $16.5 billion in 2007. Net income increased apace, growing from $100 million in 2002 to $4.2 billion in 2007.

Ninety-nine percent of its revenue still is generated by those simple text ads, many of which now appear on the Web pages of affiliates, companies with whom Google has arranged to place ads and receive a share of the advertising revenue. No annoying visual gimmicks are needed. Just a handful of words, placed before the right online audience in the right frame of mind at the right time, works wonders.

As Google reached out to affiliates, it relaxed its text-only rule, permitting advertisers to use display, banner, and video ads on the non-Google sites in its affiliate network. But for years Google resisted pressure from advertisers to tamper with the plain text format on its own search results pages. The text format had been instrumental in Google's earliest growth and remained the sentimental favorite of veteran Google employees.

In early 2008, however, Google began a trial experiment that placed links to video ads on its own search results pages. It vowed it would not introduce the noise of the arcade, nor would it force any viewer to watch a video ad involuntarily. The online commercials do not roll—and Google is not paid—unless a user clicks on a plus sign that accompanies the otherwise ordinary text ad. The company said the video ads have to conform to the same principle applied when text ads are selected for placement on search results pages: all ads, of whatever format, must be directly relevant to the search. "If you search for golf clubs," Marissa Mayer explained, "you get ads for golf clubs, not a banner ad about Pepsi that you may drink on the golf course."

The best minds at Yahoo, Microsoft, and Google's smaller rivals have spent years trying to replicate Google's ad-placing formulas and all have failed to do so. Each advertisement Google places is so much more likely to attract a click and generate revenue that Yahoo in June 2006 struck an agreement with Google to outsource a portion of its own search advertising. Assuming the deal were to pass antitrust review, it was expected to generate $250 million to $450 million in increased cash flow for Yahoo in the first year of the four-year agreement, even after Yahoo shared the advertising revenue with Google. Jerry Yang, Yahoo's CEO, expressed the rather fanciful hope that "the financial benefits of better monetizing our search traffic" by relying on Google would help to strengthen Yahoo's "independent search business."

The profits generated by its ads have provided Google with ample means to add to its collection of Web pages, adding indexes of published items in a variety of formats, including news, books, scholarly journals, street maps, satellite images, corporate financial information, patents, and more. Google has also started collecting personal information about its users. If you so choose, Google stores your photos, videos, e-mail messages, calendar, word processing documents, spreadsheets, presentation slides, bookmarks to your favorite Web pages, online discussion groups, personal blog, instant messaging chats, social network messages, and stock portfolio. No category is too personal to be deemed unsuitable for Google's organizing—one's medical records can also be included, with the launch in May 2008 of Google Health. And Google's reach extends right into the home: the files that sit on your personal computer can be indexed by Google software, if you give it permission to do so.

Personal data will be collected by other software developers, which Google has invited to build applications on top of Google's infrastructure. In April 2008 when Google introduced its new program the Google App Engine, its pitch to developers highlighted three features: No assembly required. It's easy to scale. It's free to get started.

Google's expansion has been smoothed by its disarmingly anticorporate persona, the one known for its self-assigned "Don't Be Evil" mantra and the one that gives its home page over to the primary colors in its company name, lots of unused white background, and the button that asks whether one is feeling lucky. When the *New York Times* published a story in 2006 with the headline "Planet Google Wants You," it ran in the Fashion & Style section, not in business. It was a light piece on Google's popularity, not an alarm raised about Google's push for what the article called global ubiquity.

As Google has pushed outward, all has not gone smoothly. The colonization of Planet Google has taken it to places in which host governments restrict the access of citizens to Google's services. In 2006, Google had to decide whether to set up a Google site located in China that would filter out search results deemed sensitive by the Chinese government, or operate outside of China, as it had been doing, which made it easy for the Chinese government to block access to Google completely. Constructing what it called an "evil scale" to weigh which course of action was less evil, it decided to set up in China, which it viewed as a step toward the eventual goal of providing full, unfiltered access to information. Its critics saw the move as craven and "Don't Be Evil" as hollow.

Google still wears a white hat, at least in the eyes of those who see Microsoft as the Evil Empire. Google's ambition now includes persuading customers to adopt a new model for personal computing, one that directly threatens Microsoft. The company known for search already has much of the necessary infrastructure, it turns out, to perform more tasks than search, such as creating documents like those that Microsoft Office's Word, Excel, and PowerPoint applications produce. Google has begun to offer "software as a service," using its own software and storing and processing users' data on remote servers run by the company. The more that users rely upon Google's Office-like software, the less need they will have to purchase and maintain software for a desktop computer.

The computer industry has adopted a newish phrase, *cloud computing*, for this model of highly centralized computing. A user's documents will seem to float in cyberspace, accessible from anywhere with an Internet connection. The vision is not new—Sun Microsystems and a number of other computer companies had attempted a decade earlier to proselytize network computing, but the network was not ready and their marketing efforts failed. Today, the idea refurbished now as cloud computing seems feasible in all the ways it hadn't earlier. But new complications have come to the fore. Some environmental critics see the "cloud" as a gauzy euphemism for data centers that sit not on a diaphanous cloud but solidly on earth, consuming enormous amounts of scarce energy. By 2006, data centers already consumed more power in the United States than did television sets.

When Google was founded in 1998, broadband Internet connections were not in place and cloud computing simply was not possible. Google's search business certainly posed no possible threat to Microsoft's profitable Windows and Office businesses. Yet today, Google, with its multifarious interests, constitutes the most formidable challenger that Microsoft has ever faced. Google is still a much smaller company—its $16.5 billion in sales in 2007 are dwarfed by Microsoft's $51 billion. In terms of market capitalization, Google was the tenth largest U.S. company ($180 billion in June 2008) when Microsoft was the third largest ($270 billion). But Microsoft realizes which of the two is best positioned for the future, and its bid for Yahoo was widely interpreted as an expression of its fear of competing against Google alone.

For years Microsoft has tried to match Google by improving its own search and online advertising capabilities, and investing in its own nascent services in the cloud. Failing to make much headway, it decided to make its hostile bid for Yahoo. By offering a 62 percent premium on Yahoo's share price at the time of its offer in January 2008, Microsoft revealed the extent of its desperation. Michael Cusumano, a professor at MIT's Sloan School of Management, described Microsoft's bid as a pursuit of "an old-style Internet asset, in decline, and at a premium." Microsoft's merger offer was rebuffed and withdrawn in May, but it drew a fair amount of mockery, perhaps most colorfully described by Dan Lyons, in his *Secret Diary of Steve Jobs* blog: "It's like taking the two guys who finished second and third in a 100-yard dash and tying their legs together and asking for a rematch, believing that now they'll run faster."

In May 2008, Google fielded 68.3 percent of all U.S. Internet searches, up from 58.3 percent in March 2006. Second-place Yahoo's share was only 20 percent—and Microsoft's MSN Search's share was 5.9 percent.

If Google were content to prosper with Web search, and only Web search, its story would be compact. It is Google's pursuit of all information, in any form, that has made its story larger, more complicated, and more interesting. Yet it is an ambition that has remained unexamined for the most part. Google has been determined to "organize the world's information and make it universally accessible and useful" since June 1999, when the company released its first press release on the occasion of its receiving $25 million of equity financing from two venture capital firms. Until then, Google had used a modest statement of company mission that the founders had hastily put on Google's Web site at the time the site was launched: "To make it easier to find high-quality information on the web." Once the company dropped this limited aim seven months after its founding and adopted the goal of organizing all the world's information, its outsized ambition has been a matter of public record.

Google executives do understand that the further the company advances toward this ultimate goal, the more people are unsettled by the prospect that a single company controls an increasing share of precious information assets. In 2006, an unknown person at Google prepared a PowerPoint presentation that included an offhand remark in the slide's comments that Google at that point had collected only 5 percent of the information it seeks. Another slide's comments emphatically added: "We plan to . . . get all the world's information, not just some." The slides were posted on Google's corporate Web site, but apparently someone thought better of it, because they were soon removed.

Google's quest to organize all the world's information originates in the founders' engineering view of the world and their original work as graduate students in computer science. In the early 1990s, computer science was trying to come to the aid of library science, using computer technology to make the information in books searchable. Among those attracted to the intellectual challenge were Page and Brin. It was research that was based on the side of Stanford's campus that housed its School of Engineering, not its Graduate School of Business.

Page and Brin have nothing in common with the business generalists that ran IBM for decades, nor the computer hobbyists that launched the early personal computer companies. Both born in 1973, they represent more than a new generation of founders in the computer industry. Having passed through the formal programs of computer science as undergraduates at the University of Michigan and the University of Maryland, respectively, they went on to doctoral programs in computer science at Stanford. They had not completed their dissertations in 1998 when they founded Google, but their extended period of academic socialization imbued them with the optimistic notion that any problem can be solved. Design and build a suitable system, and anything can be accomplished.

They have continued to favor engineering over business. When the two young men sought a CEO with more business experience, they looked for someone of a similar persuasion. In Eric Schmidt they found that person: a seasoned industry executive (Sun

Microsystems, then Novell) who was also a computer scientist (Ph.D., University of California, Berkeley). Schmidt arrived at Google in 2001. Three years later, in 2004, on the eve of the company's initial public offering (IPO), the three men committed to working together for the next twenty years—a feat of unfathomable corporate comity for a troika, should it endure.

Google employees who sit in on meetings with the executive team see on a daily basis that these three work so closely together that their shared sense of company priorities is all but indistinguishable. They communicate their priorities in unison throughout the company so that even teams at the lowest level of the hierarchy know what principles guide their decision making and what projects will be deemed most helpful in fulfilling Google's mission.

The most visible difference distinguishing members of the trio is that Schmidt steps forward as the public spokesperson, and Brin and Page step back. Schmidt, who is eighteen years older than Brin and Page, is described in the general press as the person who supplies the "adult supervision," but it is his skill at controlling what is said publicly, saying little without appearing to do so, that is most valuable to the executive team. In describing what Google is doing, or not doing, Schmidt has a more shrewd sense of what phrasing the world outside will receive in the most positive way. When Brin was asked in 2008 about why consumers should trust Google to protect their personal data, he responded in a tone that suggested the very question was absurd: "How many people do you think had embarrassing information about them disclosed yesterday because of [using Google]? Zero. It never happens. Yet I'm sure thousands of people had their mail stolen yesterday, or identity theft." Schmidt, by contrast, regularly handles the same question calmly, without betraying irritation, acknowledging the concern about privacy and gently pointing out that Google is fully aware that its entire business relies upon maintaining the trust of its users.

Occasionally, though, Schmidt will blurt out a thought that has not passed through his internal review filter. When this happens, he sounds indistinguishable from the cofounders. One such instance was in May 2006. He was talking about Google's strategic model,

11

which he said is "designed to scale to no boundary. We don't see today any limit to this model of continuing to grow. I'm sure there are limits, but we don't see them today. This limitless-growth model is very exciting." Exciting for Google, yes. What the prospect of growth without limit means for the public is something more complicated than a pure thrill. It's a prospect that has appeared so quickly, historically speaking, that we have not really had time to take a good look at what Google has become, let alone to consider what comes next.

It is possible that Google is currently using as many as a million computers for its operations, harnessed together to create effectively a supercomputer, the world's largest. Google will not disclose the number of computers nor say much about the data centers that house them. When Schmidt was asked in April 2007 how many data centers Google had, he replied, "I don't actually know." And then, anticipating that the answer would sound coy—how could the CEO not know such a thing?—he allowed that there were "dozens" of centers, including some of immense size. Then he added, cheerfully, "In a year or two the very large ones will be the small ones because the growth rate is such that we keep building even larger ones." He was oblivious to the possibility that such growth might strike some as ominous.

Schmidt, Page, and Brin were also slow to appreciate that Google's technical achievements would not necessarily be praised. When Google's ambitious plan to digitize entire university libraries brought upon it legal difficulties and furious criticism from book publishers and authors, the company was utterly surprised. It had viewed book scanning as a practical matter of addressing engineering issues "at scale." It had not realized that the problems on the engineering side were the easy ones; those concerning intellectual property and the law, far more difficult.

The company's allegiance to the engineers' ethos came through one day when I attended a weekly all-hands meeting at the Googleplex, the main corporate campus, in Mountain View, California. Schmidt, Page, and Brin all appear at the Friday afternoon meetings whenever they are in town. Within the company, they are not reclusive in the least. Their offices are on a busy floor, small, and in the case of Brin and Page, still shared. The TGIF gathering is a combination of official briefing, informal question-and-answer session, and party. Only a few hundred employees can pack into the atrium where the meeting is held, but live video feeds are sent to all Google offices around the world.

When I inquired about attending a TGIF, I was told that they were for employees only. Gaining admittance took a while. After five months of conversations with the company's corporate communications staff, however, I sat down with Eric Schmidt for a heart-to-heart chat (or, more accurately, knee-to-knee; the room was no bigger than a closet). There I put directly to him my wish to see more of the company than my interviews with individual employees afforded. He brought up the TGIFs before I did and suggested that I attend. He did not have to ask me twice.

On the Friday that I chose in early May 2007, Schmidt and Brin were out of town and Larry Page was the sole emcee. He led off with a set of unremarkable announcements, a short demo of a new product, and then he dove into the real business of the day, fielding employee complaints.

Of all workplaces in the world, this would seem to be the place least likely to find employee unhappiness of any kind. Every conceivable condition that might impinge on workplace productivity seems to have been attended to. The company famously provides free meals—breakfast, lunch, and dinner—that make a gourmet's heart flutter. For those who work at the Googleplex in Mountain View, a free shuttle service covering the entire Bay Area is available. Free on-site medical care is provided by two full-time doctors who are on staff. Subsidized massages are available on the premises. A company child care center is nearby and various services are provided, for a fee, right at the workplace: personal trainers, haircuts, a laundry, dry cleaning pickup, bike repairs, and car wash and oil-change services. Larry Page in 2004 had told Google's shareholders in an "Owner's Manual" to "expect us to add benefits rather than pare them down over time," and so the company had. Little wonder that Google would be named in 2007 and again in 2008 by *Fortune* magazine as the Number One Best Company to Work For.

And yet, at the Friday meeting, complaints do come in. The machines that software developers use are too slow. An internal online calendar for scheduling massages is balky. Nearby traffic lights seem mistimed, causing irksome delays in the daily commute. Google's maps for Japan lack English translations for place-names. As Page listens to each grievance, he is good-humored and patient, even when the pettiness of the grievance should embarrass the complainant. If Page agrees that the company should take action, he tries to fix the problem on the spot. When an employee complains that the legal department has decreed that every outgoing e-mail message from the sales team must include a long disclaimer in legalese, a very "un-Googley practice," Page looks out over the crowd. "Who's responsible for that?" A hand is raised. "All right. Don't do it." The audience laughs. (Whether corporate counsel will back down without a fight will be determined only later.) Page is ready to move to the next question, but he can't resist adding, "It does seem kind of ridiculous."

In the very middle of the meeting, Page fields a more hard-hitting question. It concerns Google's recent hiring of so many newly minted MBAs. "How do we insure we don't hire too many of them?" an employee asks him in an e-mail message. The question is greeted by approving applause. Page stops reading and asks for a show of hands to find out how many MBAs are present in the room. Almost no hands are raised. He tries, halfheartedly, to make the case that MBAs are "equally helpful to the world, too"—which provokes some derisive laughter. So he moves on quickly to say that he and the senior managers have taken measures to make sure that the company's high ratio of engineers to nonengineers will remain constant.

Google goes after not just the well educated, but the very well educated. Among the company's first hundred engineers, forty were Ph.D.'s. The company's emphasis on Ph.D.'s was not shared universally in the software industry. Microsoft mostly recruited computer science majors who had only a bachelor's degree; the company eschewed those with advanced degrees ("We're huge believers in hiring potential," Kristen Roby, Microsoft's director of recruiting at colleges in the United States, said in 2004). In contrast, Google sought those with the most academic training possible. A typical

Google job listing featured a three-word phrase rarely seen outside of academe: "Ph.D. a plus."

At Google, management and staff use the empiricism of science to guide their business, developing hypotheses, collecting data, revising hypotheses, and repeating the cycle. Kevin Scott, a senior software engineering manager who worked at Google, described the iterative process: "Ideas at Google do not burst forth from the heads of geniuses and then find their way unimpeded to huge audiences of receptive users. Rather ideas emerge, are torn to shreds, reformulated, torn to shreds, prototyped, torn to shreds, launched to internal users, torn to shreds, rebuilt and relaunched, torn to shreds, refined some more . . . and launched, whereupon they are torn to shreds by bloggers, journalists, and competitors."

Google has been in the enviable position of being able to afford additions to its information collections that may not produce profits, and may not even produce revenue. It is even dabbling in genomics as well as software, with an investment in 23andMe, a Silicon Valley start-up that offers individuals the ability to browse their individual genome. "Information," if interpreted as broadly as possible, encompasses many kinds of businesses, and Google has shown an eagerness to try many things.

In 2005, Schmidt explained at a public forum, "We often do things that don't make any sense from traditional norms. And we're proud of that, and we talk about that. The founders have set the mission of the company—that we work on big problems that affect people at scale that have not been solved before." That phrase *at scale*—a shortened form of *on a very, very large scale*—is heard often around campus.

Building at scale is not so much a business quest as an imperative that is dictated by Google's core search technology, the software that makes judgments about the quality of Web pages based on what other Web pages have to say about them. Its software is self-teaching. The more data it massages, the more sophisticated the software becomes. "More data is better data" is a favorite maxim of Google's engineers. Building systems at scale is the way to gather the data to create ever-smarter software.

There is no limit to the kinds of data that would help improve the software. A corollary of more-data-is-better-data is that any information not in a digital form that the software can process must be digitized. During a visit to London in May 2007, Schmidt was asked what Google might look like five years hence. He said that the total amount of information that Google possessed was still at an "early" stage. By broadening and deepening its information collections, he explained, Google will be able to provide search results better tailored to a particular user. He said the ultimate goal was to provide Google's software with enough personal detail about each of its visitors that it could provide customized answers to the questions "What shall I do tomorrow?" and "What job shall I take?"

One need not squint hard to picture a computer being able to answer such questions: it's the HAL 9000, whose omniscience made it the most disturbing and memorable character in *2001: A Space Odyssey*, the 1968 film adaptation of Arthur C. Clarke's saga. Sergey Brin told an interviewer in 2002 that HAL was "what we're striving for," with its ability to stitch together all of the information it was fed and, in Brin's words, "rationalize it." He said, "Hopefully, it would never have a bug like HAL did where he killed the occupants of the space ship."

Were Google able to endow its own supercomputer with the power of HAL—Brin had said, "I think we've made it a part of the way there"—it would command a system that is the stuff of an advertiser's dream; the more it knows about each visitor, the more precisely it can target the advertising. The better the customer response, the greater the company's profits.

Brin, Schmidt, and their Google colleagues have felt free to imagine a world in which their company will hold, in a very literal sense, all the world's information. Yet as the company proceeds, it must spend less time in dreamy ruminations about the big vision and more time on the prosaic details that, until recently, had seemed unimportant or, in the giddy rush of Google's hypergrowth, seemed to take care of themselves.

If Google's shares do not fully recover after falling steeply in early 2008, Google will no longer be able to assume that stock options for its employees will serve to ensure loyalty. Its veteran employees, having received all of their options that were granted when the strike price was extremely low, are leaving in significant numbers. It's an exodus that is natural and expected, but some of its most able talent are heading for Facebook, which indirectly competes with Google. In March 2008, Facebook hired Google's Sheryl Sandberg to be its chief operating officer; by one account, almost 10 percent of Facebook's employees were ex-Googlers.

Google's ability to pursue its most ambitious ventures depends on its continuing to have access to top technical talent, and recruiting is bound to become ever more difficult. Companies that have not yet had their own IPO and that can offer new employees both greater responsibilities and a much greater possibility of a financial windfall—like Facebook—vie with Google in the marketplace for engineers.

The company's ability to recruit the most highly qualified new employees will be diminished further should it experience a disappointing quarter and decide that the generous employee benefits that Larry Page had said in 2004 he expected to expand indefinitely would have to be pared after all. The unthinkable, a rollback of benefits, was already visible in 2008 when subsidized child care was dropped from the list of employee perquisites. Then in June 2008, Google announced that rates for new child care centers near the Googleplex would jump 70 percent (to $2,290 a month for a toddler; more for an infant). Although it also introduced at the same time a "child care scholarship program" for those for whom the rates would create a financial hardship, the very idea that an employee would have to apply for a scholarship in order to afford company-provided daycare was an unsettling reminder that Google employees belonged to one of two classes: employees who had been hired early enough to receive stock options before the IPO and were wealthy—in many cases, extremely wealthy—and employees hired since the IPO, who had the same workaday concerns about living in high-cost-of-living areas as anyone else.

Or worse, what happens to Google's golden aura when a difficult quarter or two forces its senior executives to decide that instead of hiring at a furious pace, the company must reverse course for the time being and trim its head count? There have not yet been layoffs of regular Google employees, but in March 2008, when Google completed its acquisition of DoubleClick, it did immediately terminate the employment of three hundred of DoubleClick's twelve hundred U.S. employees. This produced a headline on the Bloomberg financial news service that referred to the firings as Google's "biggest staff cuts." Even with the qualification that these involved DoubleClick employees, it was jarring to see "Google" anywhere in the vicinity of "staff cuts." But it served as a reminder that Google should not be regarded as permanently protected from encounters with the same kinds of adversity that other companies experience.

Is Google likely to be the primary beneficiary of the shift to cloud computing, or will it be supplanted by other companies, perhaps by one that has not yet been founded? Will Google's cloud be popularly embraced, as users enjoy the benefits, or is it more likely to be rejected, as fear of misuse of personal information becomes a matter of great concern? Google's future will be determined to no small degree by the view that its users hold of the company itself. Google has enjoyed mostly favorable public notice in its first ten years, but maintaining a cuddly, anticorporate image when it stands among the U.S. companies with the largest market capitalization may pose an increasingly difficult challenge.

The company that seems to be everywhere, deeply embedded in our daily lives, actually has a smallish physical presence. *Googleplex* brings to mind an architectural monstrosity the size of the Pentagon. In reality, the signature buildings are not much bigger than those of a single suburban high school. The core consists of four eccentrically ornamented two- and three-story buildings that had served previously as the home of computer manufacturer Silicon Graphics. These are arranged around a swath of shared space: young shade trees; tables protected from the almost always present sun by umbrellas in the Google colors of red, green, blue, and yellow; a grassy knoll and circular volleyball court; an outdoor garden; and "Stan," a bronze Tyrannosaurus Rex skeleton. Depending on the time of day, many or few Googlers pass among the buildings. As a group, they have one striking attribute: they are a very young workforce, even for Silicon Valley.

At the end of 2003, the last year before its IPO, Google had 1,628 permanent employees; only four years later, at the end of 2007, the number had grown tenfold, to 16,805. Given its ambition, Google could not remain small. A reminder of this came up in May 2007, before the company's annual shareholders' meeting began, when Page and Schmidt met with a small group of reporters, including me. Page was asked how he felt about seeing so many new faces on campus and watching the company grow so large. He protested that Google was not large—not when measured by what it sought to do, to provide "all the world's information to everybody in the world, and do a really good job of it." He countered, "That's just not a small company, right?"

Indeed. That is not a small company.

CHAPTER 1

Open and Closed

War, hyperinflation, breakdowns in public utility services. None of these elements of an adverse business environment have fallen into Google's path. The company has had the good fortune to enjoy a most hospitable business environment. It is not widely appreciated, however, how dependent Google is upon an environment remaining free of not only major disruptions, particular to the online world, but also other problems that would bring its business to a standstill as surely as a war would. Google needs the Internet to remain open and true to its founding spirit, without (pay) walls, without (subscription) fences, without (proprietary software) barriers, without any other impediments to the unrestricted exchange of information.

The credo that holds that "information wants to be free" has always faced an opposing school of thought: "Information is too valuable to be free." From this latter perspective, information is a commercially valuable asset, to be hoarded, not shared. Access to information is unimpeded in the open camp, and severely restricted in the closed camp. The epitome of open is "wiki" sites, which are completely open to anyone to edit, as well as read. Their opposites are social networking sites like Facebook, which permit only members to enter, limiting access to information to subsets of a member's web of friends.

Google's search engine needs access to the entire Internet, not merely the patches that remain outside the walled gardens of social networking sites. The company's very existence depends upon the advocates of an open online environment holding at bay the threat of encroachment by their opponents.

Contention between open and closed is also the defining issue roiling the world of software development. Microsoft achieved its success as a practitioner of the closed approach to software development, keeping its source code secret and using its control of the operating system to extend its reach into other sectors of the software business. It treated industry standards that belonged to no single company as competitors to Microsoft's own proprietary software. The company follows a strategy of what it calls "embrace and extend," that is, begin with industry standards but "extend" them by attaching Microsoft's own proprietary additions to them.

Microsoft's self-aggrandizement antagonized many companies and software developers in the industry, and ultimately it created a backlash, the open-source software movement, which has become a potent challenge to Microsoft's closed approach to software. Open-source software permits software developers to see all of a program's source code, something that Microsoft would never allow. The movement depends upon software developers' willingness to volunteer their time and skills, without remuneration, but hatred of Microsoft and all it stands for has provided ample motivation.

Google uses open-source software extensively for its own operations. It has not, however, placed its own proprietary search formulas into the public domain. It's a company that is attached to its own secrets and will not win any contests for corporate transparency. Still, compared to Microsoft, Google is more closely aligned to those in the industry clustered around the open model. The two companies represent not just the interests of their own firms but also the interests of two ideologically opposed camps, open and closed. It was fitting that it was Microsoft that won the privilege in late 2007 of investing in Facebook: the two companies manifest the greatest comfort with closed over open. Their alignment unites them in fighting their principal ideological rival, Google.

The social networking phenomenon attracts inordinate attention now because of its recent popularity. The World Wide Web, Google's original domain, has been a presence for so long that it has receded into the background. But as long as open and closed models contend for favorable position, the Web's founding principles remain as relevant to the present moment as ever. The Web was conceived as an alternative to closed communications systems. It was built as an open medium—open to anyone to publish or read, designed not only to make information easy to access, but also to make tracing the origins of an idea easy, as simple as clicking on a link. No geographic boundaries, no fences, nothing to impede the researcher from zipping across the Internet, link by link, to find information that was both useful and free, wherever it happened to be, anywhere in the world.

It was conceived by an academic for fellow academics, and the only place the Web existed at first was on servers that belonged to research laboratories. Tim Berners-Lee, a computer scientist who was on the staff of CERN, the European Organization for Nuclear Research, in Geneva, Switzerland, came up with the essential concepts in 1989 and built the first servers for holding Web pages in 1990. From CERN, the Web spread to other particle physics laboratories. The Web browsers at that time worked only on scientific workstations, and the Web could easily have remained what it was then, a tool used within the closed world of physicists. In 1993, however, CERN announced that its Web technologies could be used by anyone, without paying royalties. It set in motion the creation of the world's largest open network—and ultimately the creation of Google, the most valuable company to be built upon that open network.

The combination of *open* and *network* was an oxymoron in the 1990s, when commercial-grade networks were closed, by design. Cellular phone networks and cable television networks, for example, ensured quality by using a strong central authority to exert close control and restrict who and what had access to the network. In contrast, the Web lacked a central authority and also lacked built-in mechanisms for Web site publishers to collect revenue, so initially the Web appeared to be the place for academics, amateur authors, and others without interest in commercial pursuits to share information without concern about remuneration.

In its openness and radically decentralized design, the Web mirrored the design of the underlying technical standards for the Internet, the networking technologies that are used to transfer digital bits of information. But the Web was not an instant success. In June 1993, two years after it was introduced, less than one-half of 1 percent of all Internet traffic was used for Web pages—the rest of the traffic was for e-mail, file transfers, and discussions in "news groups." There were not many places on the Web to go: only 130 or so sites were in existence then. In 1994, a year after the introduction of Mosaic, the first popular Web browser, there were twenty-seven hundred sites, but Web traffic still was only 6 percent of all Internet traffic. The Web remained a curiosity.

The Web would have remained a place for academics with very specialized information needs were it not for the willingness of more and more individuals outside of academe to place information on the Web for free. Today's Google employees and shareholders should be eternally grateful to the Web's early contributors, because later demand for Google's search service came about only because so many people decided, one by one, to give information away without charge on the Web.

Before the Web, information was available online, but one had to pay dearly for access. The first generation of digital information services were commercial information providers, such as Lockheed's Dialog service, which began in the 1970s and charged high prices to business clients. The second generation of pre-Web information services were sold to consumers by American Online (AOL), CompuServe, and Prodigy. They offered customers access to their private networks, reached with a dial-up modem using the household's phone line, and information that was available only to their members.

No one in the early 1990s could have predicted that the Web would attract abundant information that was both of high quality and free. The only business model for information services that seemed practical was to build a walled garden around information and then charge users to enter the garden. Google enjoyed a huge advantage arriving when it did in the late 1990s, as a latecomer to the digital information business. It was conceived outside the walled garden and never had to pass through a painful transition, as did its forebears, replacing the core business model based on a closed network for one based on an open one.

Microsoft had the ill luck to become interested in information services later than incumbents like AOL but not late enough to grasp the competitive threat to closed networks that the Web would soon pose. Six years before Google's founding, Microsoft began planning, in 1992, to offer its own information service, which would eventually appear as MSN (Microsoft Network) in 1995. It naturally followed the closed-network model of AOL and the others. Nathan Myhrvold, Microsoft's research chief at the time, likened MSN's future role to that of a shopping mall landlord. Other companies would be invited to sell information or goods within the Microsoft Network, and Microsoft would retain 10 to 30 percent of the revenue. When the growth of the Internet loomed as a free alternative to the walled garden, he held out hope that Microsoft could still set up a toll booth outside MSN's garden by inserting Microsoft's proprietary software into all e-commerce purchases on the Internet, and exact a transaction fee of 1 or 2 percent, just as Visa or MasterCard did.

The one company that seemed to be ideally positioned to profit from the advent of the Web was Netscape Communications, whose Netscape Navigator Web browser became sensationally popular upon release in 1994. The company grew so fast that in August 1995, only eighteen months after its founding, it had one of the most successful initial public offerings for any company in the technology industry. Netscape declared itself to be the faithful guardian of "openness," the foundation of the Internet's architecture, and the company placed the internal source code for its browser into the public domain in 1998. It learned that giving away its Web browser for free was easy. Collecting revenue from paying customers, however, was far more difficult: it required offering a product that embodied intellectual property that was not freely available, and when Netscape tried to sell Web server software to corporate customers, it found that sales came slowly. It attempted, in vain, to have its proprietary additions to Web standards adopted as a new industry standard. As a chronicle of

Netscape's history summed up, Netscape was "open, but not open."

Almost every information technology company claims to be a champion of open standards—even Microsoft did so, too, touting Windows as an open platform, that is, open to any software developer who wished to create Windows applications, without having to secure Microsoft's permission and without having to share the revenue with Microsoft (in contrast to game system manufacturers likes Nintendo, which control their own closed software systems and force game developers to share revenue from game sales). When Microsoft added its own proprietary code to the industry's Internet standards, such as internal Web page tags that its Internet Explorer would recognize, but Netscape's browser would not, it euphemistically called the changes "extensions" to preserve the appearance of adhering to open standards.

When Google was founded in 1998, it did not have to fight against Microsoft's extensions, nor did it have to displace Microsoft's operating system or push back Microsoft's browser. It had the advantage of a better field position than previous Microsoft challengers had ever enjoyed—it floated above the fray. Any browser, running on any operating system, could reach Google.

Google was fortunate in another respect: the sheer mass of pages placed on the Web overwhelmed the abilities of Yahoo and others in the first generation of Web navigation and search businesses to develop search techniques that grew in sophistication as fast as the Web was growing. Their failure created the opportunity for Google.

Craig Silverstein, the first Google employee hired in 1998 by the two founders, later said that had the company been founded two years earlier, or even one year earlier, it surely would have failed. Before 1998, the Web was still small enough that almost any search method served well enough, producing a list of sites with matching Web pages that was short enough to be easy to scan in its entirety. By 1998, however, the Web was much larger and a need had arisen for a search engine that could do more than simply match the text of the search term with that of all Web pages that contained the phrase. Silverstein said it also had to "discriminate between good results and not-so-good results."

Google would have no search service to offer if Web pages were inaccessible to its "spider," the software that systematically "crawled" the Web, collecting copies of Web pages that were then indexed and analyzed, in readiness for matching when a visitor to Google later submitted a search request. (As fast as Google's software appears to perform a search, it should be remembered that when Google receives a search request, its search does not at that moment check the world's Web sites, but rather checks the copies of those sites that were collected earlier and stored on Google's servers.) When the crawling software was written in unsophisticated form, as Google's initial version was, it caused many problems for the Web sites it crawled. In some cases, where bandwidth was limited, the Google crawlers' visits resulted in a spike in traffic that the Web site could not accommodate. The software that ran the Web site would freeze, closing the site to all visitors. This did not endear Google to the sites' owners, some of whom sent Brin and Page angry e-mail messages or phoned them to convey their objections.

The upset passed. The code embedded in the Google spider was improved, which reduced the time that it spent on each site and also reduced the likelihood that it would crash the system it was visiting. At the same time, Web hosts became accustomed to the visits of automated software programs and understood spiders' visits would, in turn, make their sites visible to the search engines and could serve in the future to draw in visits by actual humans.

The Web's original designers agreed upon a piece of code Web site hosts could use to signal that a spider or any other kind of "robot" software was not welcome to visit. It was Google's very good fortune that the Web grew without Web site owners' electing to use this option to block visits by Google's spider. The relevance of Google's search results are dependent upon having access to the broadest possible range of Web pages. These provide the essential materials used in calculations that go into Google's ranking of search results, placing Web pages with the greatest presumed authority at the top of the list.

To calculate authority for any given page, Google's software looks at its database of links for the entire Web and notes which Web sites link to that page, providing, in effect, a recommendation. This provides only a beginning. The sites that provide recommendations have to be examined carefully, in order to determine whether the recommendation should be weighted heavily or lightly or disregarded entirely. The software returns to the database of links to see who recommends the recommending sites, and when those are found, to see who recommends *those* sites, and so on. The process works backwards, recursively. Checking who points to whom may seem as endless a process as going up a stairway in an Escher print, but the long chain of calculations eventually produces a distillation of relative authority for every page on the Web, which is expressed as a number, 1 to 10. It sums up whether editors at other Web sites regard any one Web page as authoritative and worthy of recommending to others. Google refers to the number as PageRank (the *Page* officially refers to Larry Page, who developed the original formula, but his surname permits the term to work nicely even if its paternity remains unknown to the reader). PageRank wasn't the first system devised to analyze the Web's structure—Cornell computer scientist Jon Kleinberg's mid-1990s work at the IBM Almaden Research Center is generally credited as a landmark in the field—but PageRank was the one that made it out of the lab first.

With its near-endless tracing of links and cross-references, Page-Rank relies upon a complete database of all links found on pages in the entire Web, and that in turn requires that Google's crawler be able to range freely across an open ecosystem. Google can utilize the judgments embodied in links without having to purchase rights to use them because of the open ethos of the Web. If even a small number of owners of Web sites with high PageRank scores and presumed high authority were to exclude Google's spider—demanding, perhaps, that Google share revenue earned by indexing their sites—then Google's ability to operate as it has would end.

The advent in the 1990s of an open model for publishing information on the Web did not immediately spell doom for the closed model of walled gardens. Novice users of e-mail and the Web were slow to venture out beyond the carefully manicured garden of their Internet service provider. This gave the service provider considerable leverage in negotiating deals with prospective tenants who wanted to set up shop within the proprietary network. The most sought after real estate online was screen space within the gated world of AOL, a fact that AOL exploited to the fullest in negotiations with prospective commercial tenants.

AOL was the widely acknowledged gatekeeper to online information in the place that its members found most convenient to access. The fact that the area within its garden was finite and merely a subset of what was available on the Web did not seem to bother its members. An observation that Vic Gundotra, a former Microsoft manager now at Google, made about Windows applied to AOL too: "At Microsoft, our view was that if the walled garden was big enough, it was indistinguishable from something that was open."

When AOL customers sought faster Internet service than AOL's dial-up service and switched to cable or DSL broadband service, they also began to see the limitations of AOL's information services. AOL's members began declining after 2001, falling from about 28 million membership in the United States to 9.3 million at the end of 2007. As it lost members, AOL executives realized that its wall prevented it from relying more heavily on advertising revenue to replace shrinking subscription revenue. In 2005, Michael Kelly, an ad-sales executive placed in charge of all of AOL's Web properties, complained, "My biggest problem is the walled garden. The world can't see the good stuff we do every day." AOL edged closer to the outside world when it announced a strategic alliance with Google in late 2005. The next year, AOL finally tore down its own garden wall.

The opening of AOL's closed network seemed to mark the permanent end of an era. Small vestigial gardens offering content from a single source, open to subscribers only, could be found here and there, but one by one, they, too, acknowledged the greater attractiveness of an advertising-based business model open to all visitors. The *New York Times*'s site experimented for a year with a "pay wall" that was placed around some of its columnists, and decided to remove the wall in 2007. The *Wall Street Journal*'s Web site remains the last major outpost of a gated, subscribers-only community.

At the same time, however, that the triumph of the open network model seemed complete, Facebook demonstrated that a closed network model could still work well—very well, indeed. In 2007, it grew into the second-largest social network site in the United States, with more than 42 million members by October—only MySpace, the sensation of 2006, was larger, with more than 100 million active users. For Google, Facebook's growth was somewhat worrisome. When Facebook members logged on, their online communications and activities were fenced off from outside view. The more members that Facebook signed up, and the more time that they spent within its cozy but closed confines, out of reach of Google's spider, the slower the pool of searchable information for Google to find on the open Web grew.

Google did not immediately respond to the steep climb in Facebook's membership in early 2007. Orkut, Google's own social network site, named after Orkut Büyükkökten, a Google engineer, remained on the periphery of Google's core services and priorities. The service had been launched three years before, in January 2004, and left to make its way by word-of-mouth promotion. It had become hugely popular in Brazil and in India, but not in the United States. This was not a matter of concern to Google—until May 2007, when Facebook became more than a fast-growing irritant. Overnight, it changed into a potently self-sufficient secessionist from the open Web when it invited outside software developers to create mini software applications that would run within Facebook. The company shrewdly sweetened the offer by letting the developers retain all advertising revenues that their application generated. Developers rushed to accept the offer.

In a twinkling, Facebook became a miniature Web universe—behind a wall, inaccessible to Google. As Facebook became more fully furnished with software from the outside, Facebook members had fewer reasons to ever leave the site. This development brought back to life the once-discredited notion that "if the walled garden was big enough, it was indistinguishable from something that was open."

For Google, Facebook's creation of a flourishing closed world was of much more concern than the growth of MySpace, whose walls were more porous, permitting Google's spiders to enter. Google had also struck an exclusive advertising deal with MySpace's parent, Fox Interactive Media, the year before, so it was able to profit by MySpace's growth. Facebook, however, had not struck a similar advertising deal with any search engine and had grown without building out an advertising system at the same time. To its rivals, Facebook's self-contained world was a violation of the Web's founding ethos of openness and free flow of information. Steve Rubel, an executive with Edelman, the giant public relations firm whose client list included MySpace, complained about Facebook on his blog: "Facebook gives nothing back to the broader web. A lot of stuff goes in, but nothing comes out. What happens in Facebook, stays in Facebook."

How Google should respond to the social networking phenomenon in general, and to Facebook in particular, was not clear to Google's executive troika, but they understood that the question was a pressing one. In June 2007, shortly after Facebook invited software developers in, Google appointed three executives in its applications group, Joe Kraus, Graham Spencer, and David Glazer, to organize an internal team that would provide an answer to the question, what would Google do about (in the new shorthand) "social"?

The first step was recruiting other members of the team. This did not require hiring new employees—scattered across different groups within Google were plenty of individuals who were working in one way or another on projects that could conceivably contribute to Google's social networking initiative. Kraus and his fellow team leaders could not reassign these Google employees—they had to be persuaded. This called for a "sales process," Kraus said. He had a printout of an e-mail message from the most senior executives, who bestowed their imprimatur on the "social" team. He brandished it when making the rounds of Google offices on his sales calls: "I really need your help, and your team needs to redirect because—as you see—this letter, from three levels up, says this is the project everyone should focus on." The initial response was, in many cases, a shrug. Google may appear, on the outside, to be a monolithic organization that acts with terrifying efficiency and concentrated purpose when entering new markets. On the inside, however, it is a federation of autonomous teams, staffed by feisty individuals who have no compunction about slamming the door on fellow employees and the company's top priorities.

Once a full team for the social networking initiative was signed up—and was able to secure office space, which required pushing out another group—it took up the question of whether it should try to make a success of Orkut in the United States, either retaining its name or creating a fresh brand identity and relaunching it. There was no enthusiasm for retaining the Orkut name, but there were some who believed that Google should introduce a new social network of its own. Kraus, however, was not enthusiastic. "At this point in the marketplace," he said, "do people want to join yet another social network?" He almost was convinced otherwise by another team member, who argued, "Look, social networks are one of maybe only three communications media to gather hundreds of millions of users—you have e-mail, you have instant messaging, you have social networking. How can you actually believe that you don't want to start another social network?"

Kraus's position, which eventually prevailed, was that Google should not try to persuade users to create a brand-new habit but rather should try to make all Google services more social, that is, connected to one's network of friends. Compared to starting a new social networking site, this marked a substantial shrinking of the initiative's ambitions. After a little while, the team decided it did not want to settle for modest changes to existing services. It changed course again, seizing the opportunity to make what Kraus called "the bigger play": attempting to make every site on the entire Web more social, recognizing that the way users searched for information was changing. "Information discovery is evolving," he said, "from a solitary exercise to one that involves what your friends are up to, and discovering things based on what your friends like."

Google was set up to help the solitary user find information. A socially oriented approach to search did not play to Google's traditional strengths. What Kraus and his team thought would be a wise course was to eschew anything that would appear to further Google's own proprietary interests and instead lead an industry-wide alliance to adopt standards that would make social networking data universally available to software developers for use at all Web sites. The story Google would tell itself was that this was an altruistic project, helping everyone use their social network to find the information they were seeking, even if they weren't using Google's products. If there was any self-interest at stake, Google would say only what it always said—that Google's interests were tied indirectly to the health of the Internet. Anything that induced people to spend more time on the Web is good for Google because, sooner or later, online users end up using Google's services.

Another way of viewing Google's initiative, however, was to see it as a move to try to preserve the open Web as new fences like Facebook's were erected. And still another view was that Google was acting in desperation, trying to address what it internally referred to as "the Facebook Problem" and find some means of counteracting Facebook's influence. It was remarkable that a company of Facebook's size, with only about three hundred employees, was a cause of concern at Google, with about sixteen thousand—or a bit fewer, thanks to Facebook's maddening ability to poach some senior Google engineers. In this view Google declined to promote Orkut in the United States not because it preferred a more noble cause—making the entire Web more socially aware—but because it understood it was too late for it to have a chance to compete head-to-head with Facebook.

When Facebook finally aligned with a larger partner, it was with Google's old rival Microsoft. In October 2007, Microsoft announced that it was making a $240 million investment in Facebook, which was accorded a valuation of $15 billion and reciprocally bestowed upon Microsoft the rights to serve as the exclusive intermediary selling advertising for the site to third parties. Reserving rights to sell advertising itself, Facebook prepared to unveil its own advertising system two weeks later.

The business press was filled with coverage of the Facebook-Microsoft deal, of the astounding valuation of a company with paltry revenues, and with speculation about how Facebook planned to convert its intimate knowledge of its members' lives into advertising dollars. Google decided that in the few days remaining before Facebook's next announcement it should try to reclaim some attention and make a formal public announcement of its own social initiative.

One problem: Google had little to announce, other than a name—"OpenSocial." The initiative's software standards were far from complete, and Google's efforts to assemble a roster of the most influential social networking sites as participants had not produced much. Two days before the OpenSocial announcement was to be made public, the list of participants was composed of social networking also rans: Orkut, of course, and Bebo, Six Apart, Hi5, Friendster, LinkedIn, Ning, and some others that were not social networking sites, like Salesforce.com. Conspicuously missing were MySpace and Facebook. At the end of the week, the initiative received a badly needed injection of credibility when MySpace joined in, too. But the fact that Google had earlier that week felt it had no choice but to unveil the coalition without a major anchor tenant suggested the OpenSocial team's belief that it could not wait to try to slow Facebook's momentum.

The primary competitive weapon that Google possessed was semantic: it used *open,* and all the positive connotations associated with it, to attack Facebook at what appeared to be Facebook's most vulnerable spot, the closed nature of its software universe. It was not a hypocritical ploy. From its birth, Google had been a devotee of the creed of *open.* More than any other company, Google had depended upon unrestricted access not only to the Web, but also to the software created as open source, which it used for its search engine and other services, and to which it contributed new code. It created a free hosting site for open source projects. It hired as Google employees a number of coders who were leaders in prominent open source projects. And each year, it organized a Summer of Code, in which it paid hundreds of computer science students to work on open source projects. Google's credentials as an advocate of an open approach to software development were in good order.

When *open* was used to apply to a social networking model, however, the adjective's meaning was ambiguous. The most fundamental way that the social networking world could be opened would be by endowing all social network sites with interoperability, permitting a member's data and web of relationships that were originally collected at one site to move with the user to other sites, too—what publisher and commentator Tim O'Reilly calls "data mobility." OpenSocial had a grand-sounding name, but in its initial announcement, it spoke of no such ambition. More modestly, it would attempt to provide software developers the standards for writing mini applications designed to work within all social networking sites, making life easier for the developers by eliminating the need to customize software for each site. It was not designed to make social network data truly mobile.

When Joe Kraus was asked on the eve of his announcement of OpenSocial why Google had not yet implemented OpenSocial capabilities on its own Web properties to demonstrate the initiative's promise, he readily conceded that its absence was embarrassing. He added that his team was concerned about increased risk of privacy breaches and was moving slowly to ensure the integrity of the company's privacy protections. "Trust builds up over a very long time," he said, "and can be lost very quickly."

A week before Facebook would tell the world about its new advertising system, Kraus predicted that "because they're a start-up" Facebook would take on privacy risks that a publicly traded company like Google could not accept. He drew a surprising analogy when he offered up YouTube—by then a part of Google—as an example of a start-up that early in its history had made a critical bet that an established company would not have made. "They decided early on they didn't care about copyright issues. Huge risks," Kraus said. It turned out well for YouTube, when it was acquired for $1.65 billion, but it was the exception. For most start-ups, the assumption of large risk does not turn out so well.

The next week, on November 6, 2007, Facebook founder and CEO Mark Zuckerberg ascended a stage in New York and portentously began, "Once every hundred years media changes" and offered Facebook's new advertising systems as a once-every-hundred-years media revolution. Unlike the previous century's advertising, based on "broadcasting messages," Facebook's was based upon "getting into the conversations between people." Facebook's new Beacon program offered advertisers the opportunity to track what Facebook members did on their Web sites and automatically inform the members' friends what they had purchased. Another part of Facebook's new advertising program would match advertisements to the interests that members disclosed on their profiles. Facebook members were not asked to grant permission for Facebook to send information about their online purchases to their friends, nor were they asked whether they were comfortable having advertisers use their most personal information on their profile to guide advertisers' pitches. Zuckerberg had no sympathy: "There is no opting out of advertising."

Beacon drew the most immediate attention, and little of it was favorable. Facebook tried to explain that Beacon had been designed for the convenience of its members, who, in Zuckerberg's words, "wouldn't have to touch it for it to work." Many users did not want it to work, however. They were upset that their purchases were broadcast to their friends, whether they wanted that or not. The criticism was so intense that the company had to backpedal. Over the next few weeks, Beacon's design was changed, and changed again. At the time it was introduced, Beacon was activated automatically and reported on the purchases of all members at the forty participating sites, unless the member specifically opted out and asked that his or her purchases at a particular site be excluded. Initially, no one could opt out of all Beacon sites with a single click, but under pressure, Facebook provided an option that allowed members to opt out completely. Then Beacon became opt-in only, ensuring that only those who wished to participate would have their purchases broadcast.

Facebook executives were loath to change because they were convinced that consumers would, as one put it, "fall in love" with Beacon once they became familiar with it. After damage to Facebook's public image was widely commented upon, Zuckerberg publicly apologized for the company's handling of the controversy. But the next month, when *60 Minutes* featured Zuckerberg and Facebook, his contrition had disappeared and he was again depicting Beacon as a service that members should appreciate. He said, "I actually think that this makes it less commercial. I mean, what would you rather see, a banner ad from Bloomingdale's or that one of your friends bought a scarf?" Facebook's own sponsors, however, were not as certain as Zuckerberg that this service would be welcomed by Facebook members, and some backed out.

Google was saved from committing a blunder identical to that of Facebook because it did not possess the information about who its users' friends were. In Google's early years, when it offered just Web search and nothing more, the company was the target of criticism from some privacy advocates for permanently storing information about what users searched for. In retrospect, the alarm was premature, before Google really knew anything much about its users. Searching the Web at Google was done anonymously, so in Google's records, search terms were accompanied only by a computer's Internet address, such as 172.16.254.1, not by a person's known name.

The only circumstances in which a Google user had cause to regret conducting a search were highly unusual, such as a 2003 murder case in North Carolina in which police seized computers at the suspect's house and found that Google searches had been submitted from one of the household's computers for *neck, snap,* and *break,* and for *rigor mortis* and *body decomposition.* The victim was the suspect's wife, who had been found dead, floating in a nearby lake. (The jury found the defendant guilty after only two hours of deliberation.)

In a strange way, the murder case and run-of-the-mill advertising on Google's search pages were similar: they used what was typed into the Google search box as the next best thing to seeing what was actually on the user's mind at that moment. For advertisers, Google offered a way of making a pitch with a precision never before possible: the advertisement was displayed only when the user had indicated an interest in that topic, such as "hotels Maui." The interest might not have been present five minutes before, and it might not be present five minutes later. But at the moment that the search for "hotels Maui" was submitted, it was highly likely that the user, whoever she or he was, would be interested in hotels on Maui. That close association between what was being searched for and the user's receptivity to advertising messages that were very closely linked to the search term held true so reliably that advertisers quickly realized that advertising on Google was a very efficient way of reaching prospects.

The general public did not appreciate what Google had stumbled upon: a way to serve up highly individualized advertising to an audience of one at the best moment—when a relevant topic was on the user's mind, not later—and achieving this without having to know anything about the personal identity of the user. Age, gender, income, nationality, zip code—none of it mattered to Google's advertising engine. Google had all it needed to know—a search phrase—in order to match up the advertisement with the greatest likelihood of eliciting a response.

Google's advertisements worked so well, in fact, without access to the identity of the person conducting the search, that Google executives thought Google would be able to brush off any criticism that its service placed its users' privacy at risk. As late as 2003, Google saw itself as a search company that had no reason to collect personal information. When Urs Hölzle, a senior Google engineer, was asked at a talk about how Google safeguarded an individual's privacy, he explained that Google users did not log on to use the service, so nothing could be known about who they were. To illustrate the difference between Google and other search sites, Hölzle pointed out that Google did not offer e-mail, so user concerns about privacy were "a little bit less of an issue than, let's say, if you had an email service." Of course, within a year, Google introduced Gmail, and a host of new services followed that required a Google user to identify him- or herself. Earlier, Google had claimed it had no personal information about its users, so there was no way that information could be leaked. Now it did have that information, and it could no longer claim that a leak was an impossibility.

What turned out to cause the most trouble for Google, however, was not a leak but a deliberate decision by Google managers to apply a technical shortcut to accelerate its attempts to catch up with Facebook. Google suffered a public relations mishap in December 2007, a month after Facebook introduced Beacon, when it added a social-network-like feature to its Google Talk program, which provided instant messaging and Internet-based telephone service. Google decided to automatically define anyone who had received a call from a Google Talk user to be, ipso facto, the user's "friend." Google now began sending to these recipients items from another service, Google Reader, that were supposed to go only to people whom the user had explicitly designated as personal friends. Critics drew comparisons between this new Google feature and Facebook's Beacon (the *Motley Fool* wrote, "Everyone's following Facebook these days, even down to its missteps"). Like Facebook, Google had placed the onus on users to take action to opt out, rather than attempt to persuade users to participate through an opt-in system. Indeed, Google was so eager to create an instant social network for its users that it had made the foolish assumption that any online conversation—even with a former employer—could be treated as equivalent to induction into one's inner circle of confidants.

The lack of readiness that had been apparent at the time of the announcement of OpenSocial continued to hurt the initiative. Google had released what it called "Version 0.5," which was far from being sufficiently complete to even be called "beta." Developers who tried to build applications with the software discovered it wasn't usable. Kraus attempted to defend the OpenSocial software as merely a first version. "We didn't call it 1.0. We called it 0.5," he said. "We want our partners helping us to figure out what else it's missing and continue to develop it."

In the meantime, Facebook had put the Beacon messiness behind it and moved on to present a new challenge to Google and the OpenSocial alliance: it played the *open* card itself and annouced it was opening up the Facebook architecture, offering to license its standards for third-party software applications to other social networking sites. This move placed it in direct competition with OpenSocial as Facebook vied to have its standards adopted across the entire social networking industry. Taking a page from Microsoft's dog-eared playbook, Facebook was reclaiming the adjective *open* for its own use, even though the source code remained firmly in Facebook's hands.

The tussle between Google and Facebook over who could claim to be more open than whom was initially a matter of interest only to the digerati and software developers. But in early May 2008, MySpace and Facebook made announcements about steps that would allow their users' personal data to be used a little bit more widely than before. Then Google followed with its own announcement of the launch of Google Friend Connect, which went the furthest in opening up social networks so that users' data could be utilized elsewhere around the Web. By utilizing the programming information that Facebook had made available to software developers, Google introduced a service that would let Facebook members pull their own data out of Facebook for use elsewhere. It was a brilliant move on Google's part, putting Facebook's commitment to openness to a very public test.

Facebook failed the test. Claiming that it had to "look out for the privacy of our users," Facebook blocked Google Friend Connect from accessing Facebook data. The decision drew the ire of many commentators. TechCrunch founder Michael Arrington wrote, "How dare Facebook tell *me* that I cannot give Google access to [my] data!"

The slippery adjective *open* was used in different ways by friend and foe in another competitive battle that Google launched in November 2007 in another industry dominated by closed networks, the wireless phone business. Google announced the formation of the Open Handset Alliance, with thirty-four inaugural members, who would jointly work on the development of a new mobile phone standard, Android. The announcement sounded the theme of openness at every opportunity: "Open Software, Open Device, Open Ecosystem." Google also announced it would bid in an upcoming FCC auction of spectrum that could be used to establish a wireless network that would compete directly with the wireless incumbents.

The wireless carriers treated the Google announcements as harbingers of change and all but conceded the need to open, or at least appear to open, their networks in ways they would never have permitted earlier. The year before, Chris Sacca, a Google manager in charge of special projects, had received numerous complaints from the wireless carriers because Google had circumvented the carriers' tight controls on third-party software and directly offered customers its own software, Google Mobile Maps, for free, and without having asked the carriers' permission. Sacca had embarrassed the carriers publicly when he was speaking at Oxford University and extemporaneously told the audience in detail about the carriers' attempts to keep their wireless networks closed. He said, "They're inserting themselves in between you and an application that you want. I think that has scary, scary implications." Sacca's remarks were picked up by news media around the world and many of his Google colleagues were upset with him, fearing that the wireless carriers would exact retribution. He described his position at Google then as "in the doghouse."

Sacca discovered, however, that some Google colleagues shared his interest in breaking the hold of carriers, and a group of volunteers within Google began meeting; their work would eventually become the Open Handset Alliance. The prospect of having any impact at all on the wireless carriers still seemed remote. In the summer of 2007, Google proposed that the FCC require that users be permitted to choose their own phones to use on a new network that would be created by the winning bidder in the upcoming spectrum auction. But Verizon Wireless had immediately brushed Google's proposal aside, arguing that opening a network to phones that it did not sell itself could compromise the network's integrity. It had even resorted to claiming that use of non-Verizon phones would weaken the nation's defense, "in an era of heightened national security concerns."

Yet shortly after the Open Handset Alliance was announced, Verizon decided, in November 2007, that opening up its network to phones purchased elsewhere did not present a problem after all. In a dramatic change of its position, it announced a new "Any Apps, Any Device" slogan. By the end of 2008 it planned to permit its consumers to purchase cell phones from any store and permit them to run any software they wished. There were a couple of qualifications—Verizon would still insist that the devices meet "the minimum technical standard," which was not yet defined, and it appeared that it would treat its new "bring-your-own" customers differently from "full-service" customers. Still, its embrace of *open*, even if it turned out to be mainly rhetorical, signaled that the incumbent carriers no longer could easily defend their closed systems. Although Verizon had not agreed to join Google's Android initiative, Verizon did confer privately with Google, seeking advice about how to open its network, and Eric Schmidt declared the Verizon announcement to be "a great step forward" and used it to extol the virtues of the open network model, which creates "better services for consumers," he said, "as the Internet has demonstrated."

Google's chief executive frequently pointed to the Internet as the world's most robust working model of an open network. He readily acknowledged Google's own indebtedness to the ethos of openness that had created the foundations of Google's own success, the Internet's infrastructure, and the open source software that Google relied upon in its own operations. But Google could not claim that among information providers it best embodied the Internet's spirit of openness. That honor would more properly be conferred upon Wikipedia, which organized information in a system far more radically open than Google's—open to any contributor and to revisions by any editor.

As Wikipedia grew, its articles showed up prominently in many Google searches. A 2006 study of a thousand randomly selected topics covered by Wikipedia showed that the encyclopedia showed up either once or twice among the top ten results in 88 percent of Google searches, and in a majority of cases was placed in first, second, or third position. Google became increasingly unhappy with the fact that it was sending its users off to a site that was strictly noncommercial, open editorially but closed to advertising. Google's AdSense network, which placed advertisements on non-Google sites, could not penetrate Wikipedia, and that rankled. In December 2007, Google announced a new initiative, which invited anyone to submit to Google articles he or she had authored on any subject. The articles would be called *knols*—a neologism meaning units of knowledge. Google's Knols experiment was another instance of moving beyond indexing information hosted at other sites to hosting the information on its own site. Google's Udi Manber said that a knol was "meant to be the first thing someone who searches for this topic for the first time will want to read." This was precisely how many Wikipedia users viewed Wikipedia articles. Google hoped to lure authors with two inducements that Wikipedia did not offer: sole editorial control over the knol and the option, if the author wished, to have Google advertising placed with display of the knol, generating revenue that would be shared with the author. If Google succeeded in attracting contributors, it would be a simple matter for its knols to show up prominently in Google's search results, allowing Google to retain users that would otherwise have been directed to Wikipedia's ad-free site.

Wikipedia's very openness could turn out to be a great help to Google in building out its collection of knols. Charles Matthews, who identified himself as a Wikipedia administrator and arbitrator, pointed out that anyone could legally copy the content of a Wikipedia page, which was not protected by copyright, paste it into a new Google knol, add a simple credit, then place ads and "laugh all the way to the bank."

Google's Manber clearly anticipated that Google's knols would likely be perceived negatively by critics as a program that would increase Google's proprietary hold over information. "We do not want to build a walled garden of content," he said with an unmistakably defensive tone. "Google will not ask for any exclusivity on any of this content and will make that content available to any other search engine."

In this one case, yes, Google eschewed exclusivity and could claim a genuinely open policy. But this was not consistently the case, and left the company susceptible to the criticism that it elected to be open only when it had fallen behind a rival in a particular area. Five years earlier, in 2002, Google had begun preparations to digitally scan every book ever printed, a project so daunting that no other company had seriously considered attempting it. By 2007, Yahoo and Microsoft had begun similar projects, but Google held an enormous lead. Danny Sullivan, a veteran observer of the search business, noted in November 2007 that Google was not anything resembling open in its book-scanning project. Others had formed an Open Content Alliance to make the contents of scanned books available as widely as possible, but Google had refused to join the alliance and instead built an insurmountable "walled garden of content," forbidding other search engines from indexing the contents of its book scans. Sullivan challenged Google to show how committed it truly was to the principle of openness by joining the Open Content Alliance.

Google seemingly heard the criticism, and responded with an announcement in March 2008 that made it appear that the long wait was over: the company made available to outside software developers the programming interfaces that would enable everyone to obtain "book info where you need it, when you need it." The Google Book Search team said that it had released the interfaces because "we love books" and the company wanted to "share this love of books (and the tremendous amount of information we've accumulated about them)." The "tremendous amount of information" that Google claimed to be excited to share turned out, however, to be extremely limited. Google offered access to the information on the book's title page, the Library of Congress catalog number, and a thumbnail image of the book. But the company did not permit outside developers to gain access to the actual text of the books that it had extracted from its scans. Dan Cohen, the director of the Center for History and New Media at George Mason University, noted how little Google was providing and expressed his disappointment in a blog post entitled "Still Waiting for a Real Google Book Search [programming interface]."

For book searches, Google still occupied a position of competitive strength. For social networking, it was in a position of competitive weakness. Sullivan also called Google hypocritical for advocating that Facebook, the network with the most valuable social data about its members, open its data to OpenSocial. Sullivan asked, Why didn't Google open up its index of Web pages, which was the largest collection of any search engine, and create an Open Index Alliance, available to competitors, and let the quality of search results be differentiated by the software used to analyze a common base of information? He was not the first to present the proposal—Wikipedia founder Jimmy Wales, among others, had raised it. Sullivan said it was a matter of consistency: "If Google's going to push for those with existing advantages to open up through efforts like OpenSocial and the Open Handset Alliance, an Open Index Alliance just seems like fair play."

It was a poke, not a genuine challenge, and brought out the point that even Google was committed to an open approach only selectively, not across the board. No company was purely open, and no company was purely closed. No independent observer of the industry could dispute, however, that Google was more open than its closest rivals, and the computer industry as a whole was far more open than those it was encroaching upon, such as wireless carriers. Google's story was, in part, formed by its efforts to convince others, within the computer industry and without, that open networks were demonstrably superior to closed networks. Consumers have tended to gravitate to systems that provide more choices, and the evolution of technology was pointed in the direction of open.

Page and Brin had been fortunate to come of age when they did, when it was possible to use a wide open network of information, the Web, and use open source software as the foundation for what they would build. To make full use of the Web, they needed a lot of computing power. On this, they did not stint. They assembled a computing infrastructure that effectively permitted Google to move in many directions simultaneously, without worrying that they would run out of horsepower.

How Google went about creating capacity would turn out to be highly unconventional and strategically important. Instead of treating computer hardware as highly complex works of engineering, delicate mechanisms that, should they fail, would have devastating consequences for Google's operations, and whose manufacture should be left to companies that do nothing but manufacture computers, Google decided to assemble its own machines. This has turned out well. In the course of developing and refining expertise on the hardware side of the business, Google has acquired another competitive advantage over its rivals in Web services, providing the company with the ability to expand the range of its products at lower cost, and without becoming reliant on outside service providers. It's what makes it possible for Google to think big.

CHAPTER 2

Unlimited Capacity

Once upon a time, computers were a novelty that were put on display for their looks. In 1947, when IBM's engineers built a new 120-foot-long machine, the Selective Sequence Electronic Calculator, the company understood that a computer could dazzle the public on the basis of its appearance alone. Part mechanical and part electronic, it cost $1 million to develop and was ornamented with dials, switches, meters, and flashing indicator lights. CEO Thomas J. Watson installed it on the ground floor of IBM's world headquarters in Manhattan, providing passersby on Fifty-seventh Street with a window view. Every day hundreds of people would stop on the sidewalk to gawk at it.

The machine's impressive façade hid the fact that its designers rushed its completion. When a reporter from the *New Yorker* was given a tour with the machine's inventor, Robert R. Seeber Jr., serving as guide, the visitor peered behind a panel and noticed some wires that were not attached to anything. Seeber nodded knowingly. "Yes, it's a funny thing about those wires—nobody knows what they're doing there."

Placing its Selective Sequence Electronic Calculator in a highly visible location was a brilliant marketing stroke on IBM's part. In the popular mind, the machine's massive size and pulsing lights established what a computer was expected to look like. Strictly speaking, IBM's colossus was a single-purpose calculator, but Hollywood copied its looks whenever a movie set required something that could impersonate a computer. Today, machines incomparably more powerful and versatile than the Selective Sequence Electronic Calculator sit on our laps. Hardware no longer dazzles.

If, however, we could see all of Google's computers, arranged in a single place, we could not fail to take interest. Their sheer collective mass would be stunning. Google is a company whose founders suffered privation as graduate students—that is, they did not have enough computers to carry out their research plans. When they started their own company, they seemed determined never to suffer hunger from resource shortages again.

Google would be scalable, designed to expand its ability to search the Web just as fast as the amount of information accumulating on the Web grew. The Google founders were determined not to settle for being selective in search coverage. However large the Web would become, and whatever types of information it would encompass, Google would strive not merely to maintain the quality and speed of its search abilities, but to use expansion as a means to actively improve quality: the more information that was fed into the Google search engine, the smarter it became.

Page and Brin intuitively understood what others failed to fully appreciate: that search technology could be designed in such a way as to positively thrive when asked to organize the immensity of the entire Web. Where other search engines were overwhelmed by the growing volume of available information, unable to distinguish Web pages with the greatest likelihood of being useful, Google's PageRank system was conceived at the outset to squeeze clues about usefulness from the Web with a sophistication that no one else had attained. The more pages its search engine was fed, the more clues PageRank could extract and use in sorting Web pages for likely relevance. In this sense, Google's technology has an appetite of its own.

When Brin and Page set about organizing the world's information, they made two foundational decisions that would turn out to have ramifications not only for their company but for the broader universe of information, including the Web. The first decision was to make Google's ordering of search results entirely a matter of mathematics. Once software formulas produced search results, Google would not permit *any* human editing to refine the results. They believed that a software approach to the problem of searching the Web provided results superior to those that human editors could produce. It was also the approach that was best suited to be scalable. Even if human editors were free of biases, they could not be hired fast enough—and cheaply enough—to keep up with the addition of millions, then billions, of new Web pages.

The commitment to a hands-off, mathematical approach to evaluating the world's information required Page and Brin to make their second fundamental decision: that Google's computers would be able to scale up as fast as the Web was growing. Google would need a computing and storage system with the power and capacity to master questions that would address *all* of the world's information, more completely, and with better results, than anyone else's. Speed was an important consideration—users would not wait around to see search results that failed to appear instantaneously. Speedy delivery required speedy processing, which could be provided only by first investing in massive machine capacity. The Google founders were determined that they would not be forced by practical limits to settle for something less than their vision for *all*. This has required assembling what most likely is the largest cluster of computers in the world.

Google could have elected to rely for its computing power on the most sophisticated hardware available on the market, designed to handle the most demanding processing needs and the highest volume of Web traffic. Its rivals concentrated on the software side and let computer hardware manufacturers handle the hardware side. But scaling its operations is so deeply embedded in Google's conception of its mission, and scaling rapidly is so crucial to Google's differentiating its business from its competitors', that it decided to build its own machines, a path without precedent in the software industry. By using the same standard components that are the heart of a personal computer and building the machines itself from the start, Google has been able to add capacity cheaply, effectively, and limitlessly.

Having sufficient hardware to accommodate an ambitious project was an issue at the outset of the search engine research that Larry Page began as a Stanford graduate student, which was originally designed to "traverse the Web." He added Sergey Brin as a collaborator. The most interesting challenge for the two was indexing the *entire* Web, not just a selective portion of it. As Google's crawler collected ever more Web pages, Page's and Brin's research was hampered by the limited storage capacity of their machines. Google was run on a motley collection of machines in a dorm room. By early 1998, they had gathered 26 million Web pages, which was about half the number that the established search engines, like AltaVista, had attained two years earlier. The Stanford students desperately needed more hardware. For three years, they recalled later, they "snarfed a whole bunch of machines of all different types" by standing at the receiving dock at Stanford where packages arrived at the university. When they saw someone take delivery of twenty machines, they approached the responsible person to wangle use of a "spare" machine for their research.

To increase their search engine's capacity, the two students spent $15,000 of their own funds, spread across three credit cards, for the purchase of hard drives that could store a terabyte of data. They were intent on improving the power of their search technology, but at this point, they had no intention of starting a search engine company themselves. Rather, they wanted to license their technology to other companies, and their site google.stanford.edu served as a demo site for their technology's searching prowess. It was Yahoo cofounder and Stanford alumnus David Filo who advised the pair otherwise; he told them they should go ahead and enter the search engine business, which would serve as the best way for them to continue to develop their technology and improve their chance of being able to license it in the future.

In the meantime, a visitor to their Stanford site had to bring along some patience: the early Google search engine did not respond quickly. In early 1998, Google queries for common search terms took several seconds—sometimes ten seconds—before results were ready for display. Observers of the search engine business at the time regarded Google as a low-traffic curiosity. But even receiving only one query a second, or ten thousand a day, it used fully one-half of Stanford University's entire Internet bandwidth, a fact that brought an end to the university's welcome.

For this reason, in 1998, Brin and Page decided to move their operation off campus and accept the advice to formally found a company. Not only would the move relieve the university of carrying their network traffic, it would separate them from the nonprofit world of academe and enable them to raise money from angel investors for more hardware and additional network bandwidth. Though they were venturing into the commercial world, they struck off on a markedly different course from that taken by other young Silicon Valley entrepreneurs at the time, who were preoccupied with business buzzwords like *eyeballs* and with racing to a quick IPO. Brin and Page showed no interest in eyeballs or taking their company public; they weren't even interested in market share. They approached the business opportunity no differently than they had the research challenge: they were focused on building technology that would scale up as the Web grew, without being limited by hardware or software constraints. Mastering the entire Web interested them not because it offered the greatest likelihood of future profits, which did not seem to be the case at all in 1998, but because it was an absorbing technical challenge.

Computer science, not business, was uppermost in the founders' minds. Having tried as graduate students to pursue their research with limited machine horsepower, the two young men set off to build a company that would invest in computer resources so improvidently that the machines would always be ample for whatever task they could conceive of, no matter how ambitious. The great irony is that their shunning of conventional cost-accounting considerations, then and since, has enabled the rapid emergence of one of the most profitable businesses of the modern era.

Initially, though, their ambition of scaling up Google's search technology quickly ran into serious problems. Expanding the number of pages included in the Google index was easy enough—their crawler had by the end of 1998 brought in about 60 million Web pages. But their systems choked when trying to perform the involuted calculations required by PageRank. The crawl would take seven to ten days to complete, but constructing the index and calculating PageRanks could take weeks after that. Or even longer. A disk error or transient problem in the computer's memory would corrupt the index while it was being built but would be discovered only later. Then it would have to be rebuilt. As the size of the Web page collection grew, the difficulties in creating the index grew exponentially: once a crawl was completed, calculating PageRanks for every page dragged on beyond weeks into months.

Performance issues were also becoming painfully manifest at the Google Web site. Word was spreading that Google's searches produced more useful links than those offered up by other search engines, and Google's traffic increased rapidly from 10,000 queries a day in 1998 to 100,000 a day in 1999. Brin and Page saw, however, that the infrastructure was not scaling up to fulfill their vision. They sought help from more experienced quarters and in early 1999 met Urs Hölzle, a Stanford-trained computer scientist who had received his Ph.D. in 1995 and was on the faculty of the University of California, Santa Barbara. Hölzle spent one day a week at Stanford, where his wife was finishing her graduate program, and Brin and Page invited him to have a look at their systems.

Like most computer companies that ran busy Web sites, Google placed its machines in rented space that was specially designed for computer servers separate from its own offices. The data center provided reliable power with backup systems in case of disruption, as well as cooling systems that could handle, or at least were supposed to handle, the heat generated by the machines. Space was rented by the square foot, so tenants packed as much computing power as possible into their alloted space.

Hölzle was invited to take a look at Google's hardware, which resided in a data center in Santa Clara, about fifteen minutes away, run by Exodus Communications, the leading data center operator. Google's tiny space contained four racks, stuffed with boards using PC components, which sat within two small cages. These were enclosures built with chain-link fencing that extended from floor to ceiling and were equipped with a locked gate. The fencing permitted air to circulate and heat to dissipate and also protected the machines from mischief at the hands of the other tenants, like eBay and Hotmail, whose machines sat nearby in similar enclosures. Google's hardware was exceedingly modest.

When Brin and Page offered Hölzle a job in February 1999, he was attracted to the technical challenge of building systems that could scale. He also liked that Brin and Page were no less interested in the technical issues than he was. He was glad they were not following the herd of dot-com entrepreneurs in pursuit of a quick profit and exit, though he was mystified about how Google was going to make money. Nonetheless, he signed on.

The team agreed that the company's current index of 60 million pages was much too small. The new goal would be considerably larger: the nice round number of 1 billion pages. No one at Google, or anyone else, could measure the size of the Web at the time, and for all anyone knew the correct number of pages they should have aimed for might have been 300 million, 600 million, or 2 billion pages. "We had no idea," Hölzle said later. What they did know for certain was that were Google to succeed in finding and indexing 1 billion pages, it would far surpass the size of the largest search index, AltaVista's, which covered 150 million pages. Aiming so high so early in Google's history also shaped its institutional culture in this formative stage, implanting the expectation within Google that the company should scale its systems well in advance of its competitors.

Google's systems at the time, in 1999, were failing to keep up with 60 million pages, let alone a billion. Search requests came in slowly enough that Hölzle could watch every one scroll by on his monitor. Even processing search queries that came in a relative trickle, the servers were taking three or three and a half seconds to respond to each one. When the requests arrived in a torrent, the system was overwhelmed and the site crashed.

When Marissa Mayer, employee number 20, arrived on June 24, 1999, for her second day of work at Google, the company had about three hundred computers to handle search requests, and that day would be the first in which Google would receive search requests sent to it by its new affiliate, Netscape. Lacking a search engine of its own, Netscape worked with several search engines. Google had wanted to start off with a limited volume of queries from this new source and had directed Netscape to start off gently by sending it only one out of five search requests that came in. But Netscape forgot or ignored Google's wishes and sent Google all of its requests that day. It was too much; Google.com had to close.

That morning, Mayer stopped by the company kitchen and noticed that Larry Page was standing in a corner of the room for no clearly visible purpose. She asked Page what he was doing. "I'm hiding," he replied. "The site is down. It's all gone horribly awry." Mayer said that seeing the CEO of the company in such a state led to her estimate that Google had about a 2 percent chance of succeeding.

The core problem seemed obvious: a system cobbled together with inexpensive PC components was neither reliable enough nor powerful enough to handle the demands of thousands of queries a day. It simply could not scale. All of the major search engines and portals used commercially manufactured servers, machines engineered to serve Web pages efficiently and at high volume. Their components met the most exacting specifications, minimizing the chance of failure. By contrast, Google was using cheap, unreliable hardware.

When Hölzle surveyed Google's systems, however, he deduced that the search engine's problems with response time were not rooted in the hardware. On the contrary, he concluded that Page and Brin had done their homework well, and that using PC components was, without a question, the most cost-effective approach. The problems were in the software, which had been written on the fly in a university environment, and hadn't taken into account the flaws that would be exposed when the volume of queries went up or when a hard drive or other component failed. By rewriting all of the code, Hölzle believed, Google could gain both speed and reliability without having to forego the savings from using PC components.

After the overhaul of Google's software systems had been completed, Hölzle explained in 2003 at a Stanford computer science colloquium: "The great thing about PCs is they're easy to buy, they're cheap, they're relatively fast for how much they cost. But not the world's most reliable machines. So you have to expect them to fail." After gaining more experience, Google's engineers settled on a standard design that packed forty or eighty servers into a rack, each loaded with the equivalent processing power of a midrange desktop PC matched with a large disk drive. For about $278,000 in 2003, it could assemble a rack with 176 microprocessors, 176 gigabytes of memory, and 7 terabytes of disk space. This compared favorably to a $758,000 server sold by the manufacturer of a well-known brand, which had only eight multiprocessors, one-third the memory, and about the same amount of disk space. Google thereby learned how to obtain greater performance for far less money than its competitors were investing.

In spring 2000, Google took a step that put it ahead of many leading Web companies then, and even ahead today: it opened a second data center, on the East Coast, in addition to the original one that it had in California. This center was purposely duplicative in order to provide what engineers refer to as *redundancy,* unneeded capacity that operates in parallel and is always ready in case of system failure elsewhere. At Google, redundancy was spread not only across thousands of machines but also across the two geographically separate data centers that gave Google the ability to suffer major problems at one site or the other while providing continuous service to all of its users.

Adding a second site might seem an essential requirement for any Web company that wishes to provide uninterrupted service. And yet as late as July 2007, Craigslist, Technorati, Second Life, Yelp, LiveJournal, RedEnvelope, TypePad, and other tenants of a $125 million data center in San Francisco, 365 Main, went dark—Craigslist for eleven hours—when a power outage hit part of the city and the data center's diesel generators, which were supposed to provide a backup source of power in just such circumstances, failed.

When Google added a second data center, it not only gained protection against disaster striking the original center, but also shortened the distance that bits had to be moved. As fast as electrons travel, physical distance still affects response speed. Reducing response time by even a fraction of a second mattered to users, as Google discovered when it ran experiments to see if users noticed a difference between 0.9 seconds, on average, to render twenty-five results on a search results page compared to 0.4 seconds needed to render ten results. Users were conspicuously more likely to grow bored and leave the Google site after waiting that interminable 0.9 seconds.

To speed the transport of bits, Google realized that it could open additional data centers all over the map and do so quickly because it did not need to build its own facilities. It could lease the excess capacity available at commercial data center facilities at ridiculously inexpensive rates. In this way, the timing of Google's expansion in the early 2000s was most fortuitous: the wild funding of dot-com start-ups and the companies that provided services to them, like data centers, had come to an abrupt end in 2001, coinciding with a steep plunge in the stock market. Data centers lost their tenants and were desperate to sign new ones. Google was at the right place at the exact right time.

The company began proliferating data centers by renting more cages, then rooms, then floors of data centers, and then entire buildings. Its original landlord, Exodus, went bankrupt. So, too, did other data center owners from whom Google rented amid this artificial abundance. In 2004, in a talk Eric Schmidt gave at the Stanford Business School, he joked about Google's good fortune. While displaying a picture of a rack of servers that had wheels attached, he asked his audience, "Anybody know why the wheels are so important? To roll the racks in? No, to take them out when the data center goes bankrupt. All our data centers have gone bankrupt. Because we use so much power and we negotiate such low rates."

In fact, Google did not usually have to roll its racks out after the data center went bankrupt; instead it was able to negotiate better terms with the landlord for renting the space. All the owners asked of Google was rent sufficient to cover their costs. When it and other tenants filled in the space available for lease in 2003 and 2004, Google began to purchase the data centers at what were, in Schmidt's words, "fire-sale prices." Google also bought up cheap unused fiber capacity that had been laid by others at the most exuberant point in the giddy years of the late 1990s, using it to connect the centers into a network. This made the scattered clusters of machines work effectively as one very powerful, very capable machine. Other computer service companies, like IBM or EDS, operated more data centers than did Google, but no one else had as many machines, in as many centers, running a unified set of software applications.

Google did have to contend, though, with some problems that came with its reliance on facilities that had been built by others in a rush. Cooling was a vital function; when heat was not dissipated adequately, machines failed. Too many machines in too little space for the building's cooling system produced too much heat.

Machine rooms that are unbearably hot for computers and humans alike have been a feature of computing since the earliest days. In 1950, the UNIVAC's five thousand tubes produced enough heat that the engineers that tended it worked in their underwear. Eric Schmidt once recalled how in the 1970s, as a young programmer, he had worked on a mainframe that had to be water cooled and required elaborate plumbing.

The problem of heat dispersal has not been solved with the increase in technical sophistication of the computer industry's semiconductors; in fact, the problem in some ways is getting much worse as machines have become ever more powerful. The faster a machine runs, the more energy it consumes and the more heat it throws off. Energy consumption has increased dramatically also because so many more transistors fit onto a chip. The effect is mitigated by the fact that chips also have shrunk, so power consumption for each chip went up "only" 400 percent when performance improved twentyfold. Still, the net increases in consumption remain enormous. As early as 2005, Luiz André Barroso, a principal engineer at Google, predicted that the cost of supplying power for one of Google's servers could soon exceed the purchase price of the server. He imagined the possibility of "bizarre business models in which a power company will provide you with free hardware if you sign a long-term power contract."

Google explored energy-saving improvements in the design of the computers' power supply, which required using a more expensive component; the expense was quickly recouped with savings in energy costs. The company also looked at reducing its cooling needs and improving energy efficiency by retrofitting the data centers that it had purchased. But as Google's growing needs began to push against the capacity of its data centers, the company began preparations in 2004 for a new approach that would simultaneously ease pressure on its existing facilities and reduce its energy costs; it would build from scratch its own data center facilities for the first time and place them close to where power is generated.

The first data center to be built was at a small town, The Dalles, Oregon, about eighty-five miles east of Portland along the Columbia River and, not incidentally, home to The Dalles Dam, a 1.8 gigawatt hydropower station. The area also offered a fiber optic network that was already in place. This move opened the company up to new scrutiny. Up until February 2005, Google had been able to add data center capacity without drawing notice because its leasing contracts and real estate purchases were with private parties. The company took over existing facilities for which zoning approvals had already been obtained. But the Oregon project involved building a new facility, which required approval from local zoning authorities.

Even so, Google proceeded by stealth. The necessary blessings were obtained, the crucial arrangements with the Bonneville Power Administration were smoothed, a threat by the Bush Administration to privatize Bonneville and raise rates was quietly killed; all of the work to put the deal together was completed while officials were bound by nondisclosure agreements that Google had them sign. The land sale was publicly disclosed only after it was completed, in February 2005. Even while construction was under way, the city attorney and the city manager were bound by confidentiality agreements that they had signed at Google's insistence. Purchases and permissions for additional built-from-scratch data centers were completed in 2007 in Lenoir, North Carolina, and Goose Creek, South Carolina, each center to cost $600 million. Then two more centers were placed in Pryor, Oklahoma, and Council Bluffs, Iowa.

In each case, Google moved ahead with construction out of public view. Its stealth, combined with the tax incentives that the company received, created an image on the editorial pages of local newspapers in these areas of a sinister corporate octopus moving soundlessly, wrapping its tentacles around a small, defenseless community. Negotiations between two parties could never be truly fair if one party seemed to the other to have infinite wealth. Tommy Tomlinson, a newspaper columnist for the *Charlotte Observer,* reasoned that Google was owned by billionaires who could afford the best negotiators in the world. After listing the various tax abatements provided to Google by local and state officials that could cost more than $260 million, he wrote, "It appears our local boys got schooled like a church-leaguer guarding Michael Jordan."

Google attempted to defend its honor and good name in North Carolina in a letter to the editor of the *Charlotte Observer*. Lloyd Taylor, Google's director of global operations, explained that Google had paid county governments millions of dollars to cover expenses and infrastructure improvements related to the project, and the tax reductions that it had been granted merely put North Carolina on par with other states. Without those concessions "to level the playing field, it would have been a better business decision for us to do our expansion elsewhere."

Whenever state and local governments provide incentives to persuade a large corporation to place a new facility in their bailiwicks, the advocates point to the economic benefits that come with new jobs. In the case of Google's data centers, however, local advocates cannot rely on the standard arguments to defend industrial incentives: few new jobs will be generated by a $600 million Google data center. The expansion of Google's physical capacity to hold the entire universe of knowledge requires few humans to tend to the machines. Hardware systems that expected high rates of failure had redundancy built into their designs and actually needed fewer attendants than those systems that lacked redundancy and came to a halt if a component failed. In a public talk in 2005, Urs Hölzle projected on the auditorium's screen a photograph of an interior view of a Google data center—it was so dark that nothing much could be seen. He explained, "We actually do have the lights off more and more because there's nobody [in the room] and we want to save power."

Two hundred jobs was the number that Google said it expected to create when one of its new centers was fully operational. How many of this small number would be hired locally wasn't announced. The *Charlotte Observer*'s Tomlinson pondered the mismatch between the skills that Google needed and those in the possession of the unemployed in Lenoir and concluded: "Google needs computer guys, and Lenoir has laid-off furniture workers. God bless them if they can learn how to run a server farm."

Google was going to be criticized if it failed to hire locally, and criticized if it did hire locally, poaching talent from neighboring businesses, as when Google's center at The Dalles hired an IT expert who had worked at nearby Orchardview Farms. Whether or not Google could offer examples of local talent doing well at Google's facility did not really matter in terms of the execution of the company's strategy. Though Google's local critics did their best to find a damaging argument in favor of blocking the centers, they came up short.

Data centers at dispersed sites constitute the essential postindustrial infrastructure relied upon by the information age economy, just as steam boilers and steel rails were the indispensable infrastructure for the railroad age in the nineteenth century. Google came to understand before its rivals how important centralized computing capacity would be because its founders also appreciated earlier than their rivals that the Internet was evolving into a realm of ever-deepening complexities. When Google was founded, the Web was an online reference desk, but over time, the full Internet, including services that were invisible to users as well as visible, was becoming a complete virtual world, existing in parallel to the physical one. It was becoming incomprehensibly immense, as more of life was lived online. The user's dependence upon a search engine to sort through the universe of possible destinations could only grow. Google intended to remain the one indispensable guide.

In April 2004, Eric Schmidt explained Google's overarching aim of "trying to make Google be a place where people live online." In hastening that process, Google had to make practical preparations in the physical world, in the form of adding more hard-drive platters, mounted on racks that sat securely within a heavily fortified building, and located geographically as close to users as possible to minimize response times. Google's principal competitors, Yahoo and Microsoft, have now also come to the realization that data centers are crucially important to their futures and are following Google's path, building their own centers, but they are well behind.

Google's executives do not see its current building boom as a blip that will soon subside. The company expects that we will move more information that we are accustomed to storing on computers in our offices and homes to servers in centralized locations, like Google's. It also expects us to digitize information that currently resides on paper, and this too will require building more data centers. The popularity of online video also creates demand for more centers; video creates files far larger than those holding text.

With its experience as the leader in building out its own data center infrastructure, Google now looks at the addition of a new data center as a matter of routine. Schmidt has described the process as simple: Fill a large building with servers, then plug in to the overhead power line. Repeat as necessary.

At Google, Page and Brin, the two former students, created a software company that built its own tools. By developing the ability to stamp out data centers cost-effectively in bulk, Google has the means to expand its data collection without limits, to scale its business without pausing. As fast as its business has grown, the company has never run out of capacity and been forced to hold off on the introduction of new services. Nor has the company ever been forced to cancel plans to build a new center or relocate because of local opposition. This permits the company to expand, and expand, and expand. It also provokes a growing nimbus of worry among some users and many privacy advocates as they watch the data centers multiply and wonder how Google intends to make use of all the data, so much of it personal, that it is accumulating in its digital storehouses.

Google could attempt to put the public's anxieties at ease by putting its operations on public display, even if behind a window, as IBM did in the 1940s. But Google's executives have gone to extraordinary lengths to keep the company's hardware hidden from view. The facilities are not open to tours, even to members of the press. (I requested a mere five-second poke-my-head-in-the-door glimpse and was turned down.) A Google spokesperson said that Google executives believe that their hardware expertise provides the company with a competitive advantage that would be eroded were other companies able to get a glimpse inside, even if it was through a journalist's eyes. Secrecy is the norm in any highly competitive business environment, of course, and especially so in the technology industry. But even so, Google stands out for its secrecy.

Guided by its founding mission, to organize all the world's information, Google has created storage capacity that allows it to gain control of what its users are thinking and doing in a comprehensive way that no other company has done, and to preserve those records indefinitely, without the need to clear out old records to make way for new ones. Moreover, Google differentiates its service by refining its own proprietary software formula to mine and massage the data, technology that it zealously protects from the sight of rivals. This sets up a conflict between Google's wish to operate a "black box" (completely opaque to the outside) and its users' wish for transparency.

At the very least, users would like Google to disclose what protections are in place to safeguard their privacy. It is also natural that users would be curious about the machines that hold their personal data, as well as about which employees within Google have access to that data, and about the risks that it might be leaked, stolen, or transferred, for example, to a government agency that requests it. How can users be certain that their personal information won't be put to uses to which an individual would never willingly consent? Privacy concerns extend across all Internet companies, but those concerns are greatest where personal information is gathered in the largest pool. This makes the stewardship of Google's machines a subject of public interest.

Whatever is behind a door that is intentionally kept closed will appear sinister, whether deservedly so or not. For the sake of improving its public image, it's possible that Google may relent and open its doors, at least enough to afford a peek inside. The fact that its data centers run "dark," without attendants, does not itself settle the question of whether a rogue Google employee could snoop on users' activities. But more openness would bring a measure of reassurance to users who are concerned about what happens at Google out of view. Were Google willing to open up more, it would be able to point to the absence of human intervention in the daily operations of the company. The Google model depends on automation to scale. It is software, not humans, that does the work at Google's information factory.

CHAPTER 3

The Algorithm

Anyone can call up the Google home page and summon the full power of Google's search engine without having to sign in or provide any personal information. Gender, race, age, education, occupation—all remain unknown. The search engine has only the search phrase itself to work with, along with an unhelpful Internet address of the machine that sends in the search request.

Google's skill at fielding search requests that are submitted anonymously originates in the founders' focus on extracting as much information as possible from the Web side, rather than from the user's side. An algorithm is a set of rules for solving a particular problem; it's the essential building block used in constructing complex computer software. Google's PageRank algorithm, the formula that analyzes the links that point to a Web page to discern the relative reputation of one page over another, draws on information that sits on Web pages. Google's search engine does not need to know anything about the user other than whatever can be guessed is on the user's mind when the search phrase was typed in.

Developing a core strength in searching anonymously would turn out to help Google greatly in other ways that were never anticipated at the time of its beginnings. As the online world has expanded exponentially and the amount of personal information collected online has grown apace, users have watched with queasiness as one company after another, whether accidentally or intentionally, has released information that users regard as personal and private. With each breach, privacy concerns are heightened, and users look for assurances that their personal information will not be disclosed. Fortunately for Google, its search service does not need to know who its users are in order to perform well.

Google's impersonal, mathematical approach to search also provides it with the ability to serve up advertisements that are tailored to a search, rather than to the person submitting the search request, whose identity would have to be known. In this way, Google is well positioned to compete for online ad dollars with social networking sites like Facebook, which offer advertisers the opportunity to target particular users, but only by selling access to information that users regard as personal and sensitive.

Google's advantage over social networking rivals in not needing its users' personal information to perform Web searches is mitigated, of course, by Google's expanding into many other services beyond search, in which the information that it holds is extremely personal, such as its e-mail service, Gmail. Google is aware that users may worry that its employees could snoop, at will, in the e-mail of the company's users. This problem is not unique to Google. Employees at Microsoft, Yahoo, and AOL can rummage through users' private e-mail messages, too, and these services handle a greater volume of e-mail messages than does Google. So it is a bit unfair for Google to be singled out by users of e-mail who are worried about strangers surreptitiously reading their personal messages. For its part, Google's attempts at reassuring the public have been, at best, only partially persuasive. The company says that only a small number of Google employees are permitted to access e-mail stored by Gmail, which is good. Not so reassuring, however, is the way the company has defined specific categories of users whose e-mail is placed off-limits to a Google employee: "any public figure, any employee at a particular company, or any acquaintance." Does this forbid recreational reading of e-mail messages of strangers? Is the stated punishment for violating this policy—termination—severe enough to be an effective deterrent? Has unapproved snooping ever been detected and a Google employee dismissed? Would the user whose e-mail was rifled be informed?

As much as Google protests that such concerns are unfounded, breaches at other companies create worries that extend to every company that stores users' personal data. Even though it was Facebook's employees, not Google's, who were reported in 2007 to have looked up user profiles (in one case for the purpose supposedly of examining prospective candidates for dates), or faked e-mail messages, or changed users' profile photos, Google's privacy practices have come under increasing suspicion as well.

When Google was founded, Page and Brin did not have to worry about privacy concerns. They were single-mindedly devoted to automating the process of judging Web pages. Their approach was unlike that of Yahoo, the leader in the first generation of Web guides, which relied upon human editors to maintain a hand-culled directory of Web sites. The story of how Google displaced Yahoo and gained the position of preeminence is instructive in the way Google used computer science more adroitly than much larger incumbents.

Google began with nothing more than its search engine, which performed the unglamorous work of indexing and analyzing Web pages. In 2000, the company struck a deal with Yahoo, then the far larger company, to perform Web searches for Yahoo's users. It was not a financial boon for Google, nor did it help it establish its own brand identity—Yahoo's users did not even know that Google was the wholesale supplier of search results, which were presented as if Yahoo had found them. What the deal did provide Google was something that was strategically more important than sales or brand awareness: it gave Google a high volume of search queries, which was the raw material needed to improve its search technology, with its built-in ability to turn quantitative increases in data into qualitatively improved results.

As Page and Brin's technology got "smarter" as it worked with more information, it was only natural that the two sooner or later would give thought to how they might get their hands on as much raw data, about anything and everything, as they could. How the different bodies of information would be interconnected was not regarded as the most pressing problem. Collect first, analyze later. If the information was not already in digital form, then Google would spend whatever was required to digitize it. The company's earliest experience with the Web had shown the wisdom of gathering more information than anyone else, and letting the size of the collection work in one's favor in many ways, producing a more dense collection of cross-references, contributing to the most sophisticated ranking of search results in the world.

Google understood, well before its chief rivals, Yahoo and Microsoft, noticed, that an information collection that attempts to be complete expands on a scale far beyond anything that can be curated by human editors. Just as the human mind depends upon neural connections that develop spontaneously, so, too, digital collections of information will rely on interconnections that are created by software, without human agency. Software algorithms are created by humans, but the complexity of the end products far exceeds anything that human creators could produce manually.

In building a company, Page and Brin used many different algorithms. But in a philosophical sense, the different formulas were not material: all of Google's algorithms could be said to be pieces of the Algorithm, shorthand for the software formulas that the Google founders believed were the best means to solve any given problem. Their confidence in the power of the Algorithm led them to adopt a controversial corollary: that the results produced by the Algorithm should not be edited, adjusted, or touched in any way by human intervention. The only way to scale their systems to handle all of the world's information was by automating all processes. The Algorithm could be manually adjusted and improved, but the tinkering would be with the Algorithm itself, prior to conducting a search. Were they to permit second-guessing the Algorithm and tinkering with search results after the search, such human intervention would slow the system and hobble it. At Google, achieving scale was paramount, and that required relying upon wholly automated processes.

The power of the Algorithm was not widely appreciated in the search business when Google got its start. At the time of the Yahoo-Google deal, Google seemed unlikely to pose a competitive threat to anybody. In its early years, the late 1990s and early 2000s, there was no obvious opening for Google to make its way and find acceptance as the company that would organize the world's information. Yahoo was securely entrenched as the most trusted source for all manner of sundry information and appeared to be fully capable of playing the role well. As a portal, Yahoo was the first place an Internet user would visit online, and the company offered a comprehensive array of services and information that would make its site the last site a user would need to visit. It offered e-mail, classifieds, games, news, sports, weather, stock quotes, and whatever else its curators could think of that would pull visitors in and keep them contentedly in place.

If its users felt a need to explore the Web, Yahoo provided a guide that was widely regarded as the most authoritative because it was hand edited by human editors, who carefully culled wheat from chaff and arranged the listings for Web sites into categories and sub-categories. But the company's executives did not regard the consistently high quality of its Web directory to be a valuable strategic asset. The company accepted the conventional wisdom of the time that a Web search was only a minor component of a popular portal. Two out of three of Yahoo's visitors came to it for other features or services.

At Yahoo, searching the Web could involve two separate stages, though the complexity was hidden. In the first stage, after a search term was submitted, Yahoo looked among the subject categories in the Web directory that its own editors had compiled. If a search term matched any of its directory listings, the relevant directory entries were displayed. If no match turned up, then the search entered the second stage, when Yahoo sent the term out to a search engine with which it had contracted, which looked among copies of all of the pages on the Web that it had collected and indexed. The second stage was considered by almost everyone in the business to be uninteresting, a behind-the-scenes service that could be obtained from any of a number of fungible suppliers, among whom there were no clear distinctions. One seemed just as good as the next, and Yahoo changed its suppliers periodically.

In 2000, Yahoo decided to funnel stage-two searches to a new wholesale supplier: Google. For Yahoo to anoint a two-year-old firm to supply search engine services was a major achievement for then tiny Google. The quality of Google's searches was sufficiently superior that it had succeeded in standing out in a crowded field. Google came out on top among thirteen search sites covered in a 2000 study of user experiences. Still, Google obtained the Yahoo deal not because its search results were superior to incumbent Inktomi's, but because Google was hungry enough for Yahoo's endorsement that it offered Yahoo the lowest price for the service. After Inktomi lost the Yahoo contract, one of its executives sniffed, "We are not in the business of winning search at any cost."

What Yahoo failed to appreciate about Google's potential as a rival was the fact that Google, unlike Inktomi, had a "retail" presence: its own Web site, where it could attract more and more customers itself by serving up better search results. Only two years after Google made its deal to supply search results to Yahoo, Google's market share in the U.S. search business approached that of its patron. Meanwhile, globally, Google had jumped out ahead. By April 2002, Google was responsible for 47 percent of search referrals worldwide, compared to Yahoo's 21 percent. Even so, two more years would pass before Yahoo realized in 2004 that its arrangement with Google was a colossal blunder. Yahoo belatedly replaced Google's search engine on its site with its own engine in an effort to reclaim control over a function it finally understood as vital to its ongoing success. But by that time, Google had consolidated its position as Search Central.

Yahoo has not been able to come even close to catching up with Google. In May 2007, Google's share of online searches in the United States had passed 50 percent according to one survey. Yahoo had a 26 percent share and Microsoft 10 percent. Google's share continued to climb: by January 2008, Google had a 58 percent share and Yahoo had dropped to 22 percent. Rick Skrenta, the CEO of news site Topix.net, made a persuasive case that Google's actual share of searches was much higher than market research surveys showed, and had passed 70 percent even by the end of 2006. In early 2007, Skrenta confessed that his data showed that Google's market share was actually 78–80 percent, and he had rounded down to a conservative 70 percent "so as to be believable."

When Microsoft bid to acquire Yahoo in 2008, company officials offered the argument that if the two companies were to combine their engineering teams, they would be able to better compete against Google. But it was the quality of Google's engineering team, not the quantity of personnel, that best explains why Google's algorithm was able to produce better search results even when Google was a tiny company.

Both Microsoft and Yahoo were slow to appreciate the power of Google's algorithm. In the early years of Google's ascent, Yahoo was held back by its ill-fated decision to rely on human editors. In 1998, Srinija Srinivasan, who oversaw a staff of forty that maintained Yahoo's directory, said that she and her new editors would not be able to keep up with the Web's growth even if they had at their disposal "unlimited resources." Already at that early date, they no longer were attempting to do so—they had decided simply to settle for what they chose to describe as "the best of what's out there." Of course, how they could be sure they were identifying the best of such a rapidly expanding pool of data was a troubling question.

Meanwhile, Google enjoyed the benefits of relying on technology that scaled well. The more data the Algorithm crunched, the better the results. The company does not disclose how many Web pages the Algorithm processes—8 billion pages indexed was the last number it released, in 2004, before it decided not to provide updated numbers. But even by 2000, observers were raving about the apparent superiority of Google's search results compared to others. Danny Sullivan wrote in *Search Engine Report:*

> When I speak about search engines to groups and mention Google, something unusual happens to some members of the audience. They smile and nod, in the way you do when you feel like you've found a secret little getaway that no one else knows about. And each time I speak, I see more and more people smiling and nodding this way, pleased to have discovered Google.

Google also put ever greater distance between itself and its rivals by developing a more sophisticated algorithm for choosing which advertisements should be displayed on its search results page for a given search term. Google used an auction mechanism to let sponsors bid, setting the top amount that they would be willing to pay for every click. This could have been easily duplicated by any of Google's competitors. What Google added, however, was a twist that turned out to make its advertisements far more lucrative than those at any other search site: an algorithm analyzed a sponsor's history to determine the likelihood that a particular advertisement would attract clicks, and it gave the most prominent positions not necessarily to the highest bidder but to the sponsors that statistically had the most likely chance of producing the most revenue for Google, taking into account the expected number of clicks, as well as the amount paid per click. The more searches that Google was asked to perform, the more historical data it collected about the effectiveness of its ad inventory, and the more accurate its prediction model became. Thanks to Google's algorithm, which no one in the industry could duplicate, Google earned far more for each search than everyone else did.

Microsoft, burdened with the belief that no company knew more about writing software than it did, was slow to notice Google's software prowess. The notion that a company like Google, with far less experience, could develop search software that was more sophisticated than Microsoft's was inconceivable. It was embarrassing when a blogger noted in 2004 how superior Google search results were to Microsoft's. A search for "Microsoft blog" on Google led straight to the employee blogs at Microsoft. But the same search on Microsoft's own MSN service led instead to the blogs of reporters at Seattle's daily newspaper, which happened to contain frequent mention of the word "Microsoft" and confused the search engine's algorithm. This was especially embarrassing because the blogger who publicized the superiority of Google's search results was Robert Scoble, a Microsoft employee, writing on a Microsoft blog.

Microsoft's executives did not spike Scoble's remarks, but Google's commanding share of Web search rankled. The defection of Microsoft developers to Google was also upsetting. In 2004, when Mark Lucovsky, one of Microsoft's most highly decorated software developers, met with Steve Ballmer, Microsoft's CEO, to tell him that he was resigning and joining Google, Ballmer did not receive the news of the loss kindly. According to an affidavit filed later in a lawsuit involving another Microsoft employee who left to work for Google, Lucovsky recalled that when he told Ballmer of his resignation and acceptance of an offer with Google, Ballmer threw a chair across the office and vowed to "bury" Google's Eric Schmidt. In Lucovsky's presence, Ballmer also threatened—here the *San Francisco Chronicle* used strategically placed hyphens to avoid having to paraphrase Ballmer's language— "I'm going to f---ing kill Google."

When Microsoft chairman Bill Gates was asked by reporters at the 2004 World Economic Forum at Davos, Switzerland, about what he thought of Google, he was more polite than Ballmer. Gates heaped upon Google some of the highest praise he could think of—the "high level of IQ" that Google had collected reminded him of "Microsoft twenty years ago." In the search competition, he granted that "they kicked our butts," but in his view, Microsoft had done a "good job" on the most common queries that comprised 80 percent of all searches. Its mistake, he explained, was not paying attention to the more obscure topics because "that's where the quality perception is." He smiled broadly, predicting that Microsoft would soon pass Google in innovations and catch up.

Microsoft managers encouraged employees to use MSN's search engine, and also to click on its ads, rather than use Google and send money to its principal competitor. Adam Barr, a software developer at Microsoft who maintained the tartly titled blog *Proudly Serving My Corporate Masters,* wrote in 2005 that, in general, trying to "strong arm" employees to use the company's products does not solve the product's deficiencies, which are all too apparent if employees do not freely choose to use the home team's service.

Barr also did not accept the "don't send money to our competitors" argument:

> Shoot, we own like 3 iPods and an iMac, I use CorelDraw for editing, I buy books by various competitors of Microsoft Press (not to mention publishing with one). Heck, I run Firefox as my browser, although I guess that doesn't involve money. Anyway I probably make dozens of decisions every day that indirectly affect

Microsoft's bottom line in a small way. Does [the airline that I'm making reservations on use] Microsoft for its backend servers? Does that restaurant run Windows on its cash registers? Is all the Microsoft software at my doctor's office properly licensed? Who knows. Yes, I'm an employee and shareholder of Microsoft, but I'm also a consumer and I feel free to exercise my right to dispense my money (or my eyeball impressions) as I want.

Barr was willing to accept the suggestion that employees use MSN's search if it was couched as a nudge to give it another try and see improvements. The first comment posted on his blog, however, was by another Microsoft employee, Adam Herscher, who did not see MSN's search as ready to go head-to-head with Google's. Herscher wrote, "I'd venture to say that Google's end-to-end user experience blows MSN's out of the water," and then followed with a detailed comparison. He concluded, "For what it's worth, I try to use MSN services as much as possible. But until there's parity with Google (i.e., as long as Google provides a better service), I'm going to continue to use Google—and it's probably better for Microsoft if I do."

The next year, in April 2006, Microsoft hired an outsider, Steven Berkowitz, to head its Internet division and lead the improvements that the company hoped would reverse the sliding fortunes of its search service. MSN, as the home of the enormously popular Hotmail e-mail service, had 110 million unique visitors a month and was the second-most-visited family of sites in the United States. Yet the visitors steered clear of MSN's search service. In March 2005, MSN held a paltry 16 percent of the search market, but a year later, when Berkowitz was appointed, it had slipped to 13 percent.

At the end of 2006, Berkowitz, who had been the CEO of another search service, Ask Jeeves (later rechristened Ask), spoke with candor about the quandary he faced. Counting up all users of MSN's various Web properties and services around the world produced an astounding total of 430 million people. Yet "a very small subset of them use our search," he said. "My No. 1 strategy is to keep these people from leaking."

If Google's "high level of IQ" created an algorithm that Microsoft's engineers could not yet match, then Microsoft could try something entirely new: attempt to depict the lack of a powerful algorithm as an advantage, a sign of the company's human touch. Under Berkowitz, Microsoft attempted to turn the tables and promote a new tagline in its advertising: "Algorithm, Meet Humanity." In full-page advertisements that ran in the *Wall Street Journal* and other newspapers in fall 2006, Microsoft tried to spin its deficiency this way: "Let us state the obvious. We're late to the game. We admit it. But instead of shrugging our shoulders and becoming a footnote in search history, we've decided to write a few new chapters." The ad copy depicted the Algorithm in the most negative way, as "a complicated mathematical equation" that produces results that somehow needed additional interpretation so that "we can all understand." To bolster its argument, Microsoft added to its search results some new whizzy features, like bird's-eye views of images and live traffic information, which provided "something more . . . human." The strangest part of this pitch was when Microsoft came close to making the argument that it was better equipped to compete against Google precisely because it was not encumbered with Google's "high level of IQ": the Microsoft ad boasted that its latest features improving the presentation of search results were created by "our people, some of whom didn't even pass calculus. Imagine that."

Microsoft also tried something else: it opened up its checkbook and offered to pay corporations to use its search service. Unlike the "Algorithm, Meet Humanity" advertising campaign, the "Microsoft Service Credits for Web Search" was not publicized by Microsoft. John Battelle's *Searchblog* broke the story, and as the details of how Microsoft had been reduced to paying customers to use its service were extracted, Microsoft came off looking desperately afraid of Google's algorithm. In response to a flurry of criticism in the press, Microsoft put Adam Sohn, director of global sales and marketing for Windows Live, on the line to answer reporters' questions. There was not much he could say, however, to cast Microsoft's attempts to literally buy customers in a positive light. The best thing he had to offer was this wan bromide: "There's always controversy when anyone tries something new."

Microsoft's reputation and pride were hurt, but more important, it failed to slow the steady enlargement of Google's power in many domains. In search, Google continued to expand its market share. In newer areas, such as YouTube's video, Microsoft had nothing comparable. And in Microsoft's own core software business, Google was slowly encroaching with free online services that were direct competitors of Microsoft's Outlook, Word, Excel, and related software. Microsoft did not lack cash—it had more than $21 billion burning a hole in its pocket in September 2007—but the money could not buy it a coherent strategy that could effectively match Google's multifaceted expansion. As for Steve Berkowitz, the outsider who was appointed senior vice president of Microsoft's Online Services group and charged to bring fresh ideas into the organization, his tenure did not last long; he was removed from the position less than two years after arriving.

Not only has Google trounced its rivals by its reliance on the Algorithm, but it has also achieved an extraordinary feat of corporate branding. Its name has become synonymous with searching the Web—*googling* is now a generic term. The company is now so closely associated with superior search that even when Ask, a rival with a better claim to impressive search abilities than either Yahoo or Microsoft, tried to brand itself as a Google-class competitor with its own powerful algorithm, the approach backfired.

Ask attempted to gain market share by offering the purest form of algorithmic search, and in the spring of 2007, the company launched its "The Algorithm Rocks" advertising campaign. Television commercials, billboards, and print advertisements were designed to "educate" the public so that everyone understood that "all search engines are not the same, and the algorithm they use is important." At *thealgorithm.com*, Ask gave long semicomic explanations of the "History of the Algorithm" with irreverent discursions ("It's a Good Thing Robert Frost Never Wrote an Algorithm"). Buried in its midst, all but impossible to see, was an esoteric lecture on how Ask's algorithm was developed at the same time as Google's, but on a wholly separate track, combining technology developed at two other companies, Teoma and Direct Hit.

Alex Bogusky, chief creative officer at Ask's advertising agency, Crispin, Porter + Bogusky, explained at the time of the campaign's launch that *algorithm* is "a funny word that most people do not hear every day, if at all." The advertising that Ask planned for the yearlong campaign would attempt to "inject the word into the consumer arena." Unfortunately for Ask and its agency, the word had already circulated sufficiently prior to the campaign to attach itself with strong adhesion to Google. Three months after the campaign was launched, survey results making the rounds internally at Google showed that most members of the general public who had seen Ask's "We are the algorithm" advertisements assumed that the "we" referred to Google.

The pure algorithmic approach drew a fair amount of criticism from professional observers of the search engine business. *Boing-Boing*'s Cory Doctorow argued that the algorithms that rank pages "embody the biases, hopes, beliefs, and hypotheses of the programmers who write and design them." Tim O'Reilly pointed out in 2008 that humans figure out how the algorithm works and then game the system, designing commercially oriented pages that attain high PageRank and occupy the top spots in search results. He said savvier users learn to deliberately skip to the second page of search results to avoid the spam that is predominant on the first page.

At the company's beginning, Google's founders were adamant that the Algorithm, and only the Algorithm, would determine search results. This approach faced a major challenge in 2004, when users noticed that an anti-Semitic Web site, Jewwatch.com, showed up at the top of Google's results for a search for the word *Jew.* A petition was circulated urging Google to remove the site from its results. Sergey Brin, who, like Larry Page, is himself Jewish, received many e-mail messages from friends who asked him to personally intervene. Brin said he, too, was offended by the site "but the objectivity of our rankings is one of our very important principles. We don't let our personal views—religious, political, ethical, or otherwise—affect our results."

Since then, Google's founders have not relented on sensitive political matters such as manually demoting Jewwatch. The company still maintains that the only way to keep human bias out is to let the Algorithm have the final say. Peter Norvig, Google's director of research, reiterated the point in 2006, saying Google resisted the temptation to make small adjustments when someone complained about the ordering of search results because "we think it's just a slippery slope."

Nevertheless, Google has permitted a wee bit of flexibility when the Algorithm simply fails in a small number of cases without the injection of some human intervention. For example, a search for "O'Reilly" produced results that were related to conservative political commentator Bill O'Reilly, crowding out other possible O'Reillys, such as O'Reilly Auto Parts, a Fortune 500 company. Google acknowledged the problem by creating in such special cases an exception to the Algorithm's rankings. The first page of results for "O'Reilly" is now subdivided into three bands, one for links for miscellaneous O'Reillys, one for O'Reilly Auto Parts, and one for Bill O'Reilly.

Brin and Page understood that manually inserting adjustments was an approach that could never be applied on a mass scale. They did accept, however, that humans could serve as quality-control inspectors. Google hired human evaluators to judge the relative quality of results produced by variations of algorithmic tweaks—in 2007, Google used ten thousand contractors around the world as "quality raters." But their feedback was used for making adjustments to the Algorithm itself and not with search results for a single term. Were Google to permit second-guessing the Algorithm and adjusting results by hand after the search, the system would be slowed unacceptably. At Google, achieving scale was paramount, and that required relying upon almost wholly automated processes (another small exception was its willingness to manually exclude links that users had reported were filled with spam). Yahoo's inability to scale its human-edited directory as the Web expanded showed the limitations of a system that relied upon humans. Google was determined to avoid Yahoo's mistakes and to have the ability to grow as fast as the Web.

Google's algorithms do not transfer smoothly to categories of information other than the Web, such as books and videos. The Web provides an abundance of internal data, in the form of links, that the Algorithm can utilize to make judgments about the quality of the information displayed. Will it be able to master different data that lack similar internal clues? Will Google ultimately need to modify its reliance on formulas and incorporate more human input? Will "social search"—having users' judgments about the relevance and usefulness of a Web page determine its place in the presentation of search results—be able to handle a broader range of information categories than the Algorithm can handle well? The potential of the algorithmic model in new applications, and its limitations, can be better understood by looking closely at how Google has attempted to extend its reach in new projects. In one case, when analyzing current news stories, the results have been decidedly unimpressive. In another, when translating foreign-language text into English, the Algorithm shows surprising promise.

The less promising experiment began in March 2002, when Google decided to try the Algorithm out as a replacement for human editors in sorting, clustering, and prioritizing news stories. When Google's managers prepared to introduce the service, there was some internal discussion about the wisdom of relying wholly on software to make decisions about what stories should be placed in the most visible positions on Google's news site. Jonathan Rosenberg, a Google vice president, suggested, "Throw some editors on that thing—we'll have the best news product on the web." But Larry Page vetoed the suggestion because "manual solutions don't scale."

When Google's news service was formally rolled out in September 2002, it drew upon more than four thousand news sources. In tiny print on the bottom of the news page was a whimsical note: "No humans were harmed or even used in the creation of this page." At the top of a list of frequently asked questions about Google News that the company posed and answered was this one: "Who edits the Google News homepage? One of the headlines is totally out of whack." The answer: "computer algorithms, without human intervention." Google proudly listed the absence of editors, managing editors, and executive editors. No individual decided which stories received top placement, and no political viewpoint or ideology was taken into account. Like the algorithm for Web pages, the company said, the algorithm for news stories "relies heavily on the collective judgment of web publishers to determine which sites offer the most valuable and relevant information." The company knew kinks in the Algorithm remained, so if readers saw "odd results," an e-mail address was provided to let Google engineers know, not to manually adjust results but to help to "fine-tune the algorithm."

The *Washington Post*'s media critic Howard Kurtz paraphrased Google's rationale with sarcastic humor: "Who needs reporters? Why spend money on whiny, self-centered, 401(k)-obsessed human beings when you can produce a nice news Web site with quiet, easy-to-abuse computers?" Strictly speaking, Kurtz's criticism at that time was misplaced—it was editors whose jobs were immediately threatened, not reporters. But a few years later, with the newspaper industry in dire financial straits, Google News could be blamed for contributing indirectly to the disappearance of reporters, too. By directing users to a particular news article online, Google News and similar news-aggregation sites did their part to nudge newspaper subscribers into reading news on a computer screen, not on paper, and to spending their online time browsing Google News rather than browsing the newspaper's own online home page. As print subscribers disappeared, so, too, did the advertisers that had traditionally underwritten the cost of gathering the news. Growth in online advertising on the newspapers' Web sites fell well short of offsetting the disappearance of revenue on the print side of the business, and layoffs in the newspaper business became commonplace.

The Algorithm did need fine-tuning. In one case, a corporate press release somehow reached the top of the featured stories on the business news page. In another, Google's affectless algorithm committed a major gaffe on February 1, 2003, that drew negative attention, when the space shuttle Columbia disintegrated during reentry, killing all seven of its crew members. Failing to detect the magnitude of the event, the Algorithm permitted the story to disappear from the news site's main page several times during that day.

Other anomalies showed up now and then. Google tweaked its formula and filed patents in 2005 for additions to the Algorithm that would take into account many more factors, such as the average story length from the news organization that composed the story, the number of staff members in the news bureau, the volume of visitors to the source's own Web site, the number of countries that accessed the site, and many others. The results improved, and the anomalies disappeared—almost. (A fifteen-year-old New Jersey high school student wrote a fake press release in 2006 that reported he had become Google's youngest employee, and Google News picked up the story without detecting the odor of a prank.)

In the competition for organizing the news, Google's algorithm faced off against Yahoo's human news editors, but in this case, Google did not win. Its algorithm, improvements and all, never was able to catch up with the quality of Yahoo's news site. Google News was not inferior because of the occasional bad day when the Algorithm committed a blunder that a human editor would not. Google News was inferior on its best day, never quite able to match the subtleties that guided the selections over at Yahoo News. Visitor traffic reflected the continuing difference: four years after it had launched, Google News drew only 30 percent of the traffic of Yahoo's news site, which remained the most popular news site on the Web. In this case, algorithm met humanity, and humanity won.

News, by its nature, did not show off the Algorithm's true power to gain sophistication automatically as the size of the data set grows. In the case of Web sites, webmasters endow the Algorithm that examines Web pages with additional smarts whenever they add links on their own pages to those found at other Web sites. The more pages that Google's crawler collects, the more links are gathered by the Algorithm with which to make its judgments more authoritative. When it comes to news, however, while the Algorithm can make judgments about news organizations, it cannot gather the judgments that millions of others have rendered on each news story as they read it. As a consequence, the Algorithm for news does not grow noticeably smarter as the collection of news stories scales up. And news stories are ephemeral, constantly being replenished by new ones, which leaves the Algorithm without a baseline of data to work with in observing the clicks of users, so that it could progressively sharpen its judgment.

Google News cannot serve as a showcase for the Algorithm, but mediocre results in this project have not prompted Google to question the company's founding assumptions. So robust is the Algorithm when searching Web pages that its comparative failure when applied to other tasks goes largely unnoticed by outside Google watchers. Google enjoys the luxury of running experiments like this without suffering a tarnished image if some do not turn out well.

In the case of another project that extended the Algorithm into a new area, the results were superior to expectations. This was language translation, one of the most difficult, intransigent problems ever tackled in the history of computing. In this area, Google hired a small group of researchers in early 2003 and let them have a go at what is referred to as *automatic translation* or *machine translation.* Their efforts have borne fruit. The Algorithm that they have developed is able to accomplish, at least sometimes, translations with idiomatic fluency that is a wonder to behold. It also put to good use the corpus of news stories collected by the more disappointing Google News project.

Machine translation was one of the first applications that computer pioneers envisaged in the mid–twentieth century. In 1953, Howard Aiken, of the Harvard Computation Laboratory, voiced aloud his hope to soon begin word-by-word translation from Russian into English. He thought that conveying meaning accurately would be easy, and literary polish would come as a simple matter of course when the machines became more powerful. The next year, IBM scientists and Georgetown University linguists showed off a machine that produced Russian-to-English translations—and began what would become a long tradition in the field of machine translation, of overpromising and underdelivering on the quality of the results. On the basis of only a 250-word vocabulary, the software supposedly handled politics, law, mathematics, chemistry, metallurgy, communications, and military affairs. The press, however, was asked to take this on faith.

Six years later, an IBM Mark I was translating texts—again, from Russian into English, reflecting the linguistic preoccupation in the midst of the Cold War—at a reported clip of eighteen hundred words a minute, when human translators could translate only twenty-six hundred words in an entire day. The translated text needed more than a little polishing—a passage referring to U-2 pilot Francis Gary Powers began, "It 30 years/flight. By it/its statement, it is older lieutenant air forces United States America." But optimism was in the air, and all that seemed to be missing was "syntactical rules" to supplement the word-for-word matching. The National Bureau of Standards established a "mechanical-translation group" to do research on how to add understanding of semantics and syntax to solve what was called the "water goat" problem (a reference to the phrase that frequently appeared in the English translations produced by machine of Russian engineering papers that used the phrase *hydraulic ram*).

Applied linguistics research improved the quality of machine translations, and one particular firm, Systran, which was founded in 1968 in Paris, would become the leading supplier of machine-translation services to other companies, using linguists to define sophisticated grammars. Language by language, the company added to its offerings of bidirectional translation, extending to forty language pairs by 2005. When Google wanted to provide its users with the ability to view a Web page in a different language than the original, it turned to Systran for the behind-the-scenes machine translation that would be performed dynamically upon a user's request. The quality of the translation was uneven, and at best it could convey only the gist of the meaning of the source document. Idiomatic phrasing remained elusive, but that defect seemed to be inherent to machine translation: no algorithm could replace a human translator.

Systran's rules-based technology was merely one form of machine translation, however. An alternative approach, which researchers at IBM in the 1990s had shown to be promising, was called *statistical machine translation*. Reflecting the movement away from rules-based approaches in artificial intelligence research, it was based not on linguistic rules manually drawn up by humans, but on a translation model that the software develops on its own as it is fed millions of paired documents—an original and a translation done by a human translator, such as a speech delivered in English in the Canadian Parliament and its official French translation. The software looks for patterns, comparing the words and phrases, beginning with the first sentence on the first page in Language A and its corresponding sentence in Language B. Nothing much can be deduced by comparing a single pair of documents. But compare millions of paired documents, and highly predictable patterns can be discerned, with a particular phrase in one language likely, statistically speaking, to be given a particular rendering in the target language. Statistical machine translation was the approach that Google researchers began to explore in early 2003.

Using multilingual documents prepared by the United Nations as the training corpus, Google fed its algorithm 200 billion words and let the software figure out matching patterns between pairs of languages. The results were revelatory. Without being able to read Chinese characters or Arabic script, without knowing anything at all about Chinese or Arabic morphology, semantics, or syntax, Google's English-speaking programmers came up with a self-teaching algorithm that could produce accurate, and sometimes astoundingly fluid, translations. At a briefing in May 2005, Google publicly discussed its work for the first time. To show what could be accomplished with statistical machine translation and a sufficiently large corpus of translated texts, a headline in an Arabic newspaper was displayed, then two translations in English. The first one, provided by rules-based Systran software, rendered the Arabic as "Alpine white new presence tape registered for coffee confirms Laden." The second came from Google's fledgling program, which produced a different translation: "The White House Confirmed the Existence of a New Bin Laden Tape."

Google's translation algorithm, which looked impressive at a controlled demonstration like a press conference, turned out to stand up well to independent testing. In fact, it did exceedingly well. In 2005, Google entered for the first time the annual competition for machine-translation software run by the National Institute of Standards and Technology, which drew researchers from university, corporate, and government laboratories as well as commercial software vendors. Google placed first among eleven international entrants in Arabic-to-English translation (IBM placed third and Systran seventh), and also placed first among sixteen entrants in Chinese-to-English translation (IBM placed sixth and Systran twelfth). Not a shabby showing for the rookie.

The basic statistical measure in these kinds of competitions is derived from a comparison of a translation produced by the machine against a reference translation produced by human translators that serves as the "gold standard." A score from 0 to 1 indicates how closely the machine's translation matches that of the humans— a 1 indicating a perfect match. The scoring is a straightforward counting problem and is done automatically by evaluation software, eliminating subjectivity. The same software has been used outside of competitions, too. Researchers can tweak an algorithm, feed test documents in, and instantly see whether the change results in measurable improvements in the quality of translation.

Google not only built up a translation model using bilingual parallel texts; it also used software to create a monolingual "language model" to help provide fluent rephrasing of whatever the translation model produced. The Algorithm taught itself to recognize what was the natural phrasing in English by looking for patterns in large quantities of professionally written and edited documents. Google happened to have ready access to one such collection on its servers: the stories indexed by Google News. Even though Google News users were directed to the Web sites of news organizations, Google stored copies of the stories to feed its news algorithm. Serendipitously, this repository of professionally polished text—50 billion words that Google had collected by April 2007—was a handy training corpus perfectly suited to teach the machine-translation algorithm how to render English smoothly.

When you are in the business of organizing the world's information, what is learned in one domain often finds practical application in another. If Google's statistical machine translation project benefited by the work of other departments under Google's roof, it returned the favor in various ways. The statistical techniques used to develop a monolingual language model turned out to be a convenient way of developing spell-checking software for any language, including celebrity names that appeared only recently—and all without the need to use human editors or even dictionaries: feed the Algorithm a sufficiently large quantity of published text, and the correct spelling is determined by statistical analysis of frequency of occurrence.

Progress in the research at Google was also greatly helped by the computing infrastructure that was at the disposal of the research group. A data set used by many academic researchers in the field, supplied by the Linguistic Data Consortium, contained 5.2 billion words. Google could handle much larger sets, however, such as the 2 trillion words of monolingual text that it pulled from the Web pages it had indexed. "We don't have better algorithms," Google's Peter Norvig said. "We just have more data."

To find the best translation for a single sentence, Google's algorithm searched a million possible phrase combinations. Hard drives were not a practical medium for keeping the data handy for rapid consultation; only random access memory was suitable. Vast quantities of RAM were needed—and vast quantities were what Google had on hand. Statistical machine translation was well suited for computing that was distributed across thousands of machines, and Google's data centers, though originally built for other purposes, were equipped to handle the computational load.

Having a computing infrastructure on hand that could handle computational problems of any scale gave Google's researchers an enormous advantage over others. The rapidity of their progress was reflected in Google's placing so highly in the National Institute of Standards and Technology's machine-translation competition in 2005, and then, in the 2006 competition, holding its leading position. Google again placed first, among twenty-two entrants, in overall scores for Arabic-to-English translation, and second among twenty-four entrants in Chinese-to-English (edged out by the University of Southern California's famed Information Sciences Institute).

Dimitris Sabatakakis, Systran's chairman and chief executive officer, could not grasp how statistical machine translation could produce results superior to his rules-based technology. After the 2005 competition, he had defended his rules-based approach in a manner that suggested Google, in claiming that it did not use native Chinese speakers, had somehow pulled off a sleight-of-hand trick. At Systran, "if we don't have some Chinese guys, our system may contain some enormous mistakes." He did not understand how Google, without those Chinese speakers double-checking the translation, had beat Systran so soundly in 2005, but he did not sign up for an immediate rematch: Systran disappeared from the competition in 2006. No competition was held in 2007, so whether Systran has decided permanently to avoid direct comparison with statistical machine translation is not yet clear.

Google did not claim to have the most sophisticated translation algorithms, but it did have something that the other machine-translation teams lacked: the largest body of training data. In 2007, Franz Och, the Google engineer who oversaw the company's machine-translation research, said, "There's the famous saying in the natural processing field, 'More data is better data.'" That was why Google was using those 2 trillion words of text that had been pulled from Web pages: the quality of the writing could not be vouched for, but the sheer mass of additional data led to measurable improvements in the translation algorithm.

Google's achievement in machine translation cannot be said to have paid for itself yet. One of the most perplexing aspects of Google's expansion of services is that so many of them contribute nothing, at least not directly, to the company's bottom line. So far, machine translation is a case in point. Google has not rushed to put its machine-translation capabilities into commercial use. Its machine-translation team is a part of Google Labs and is focused primarily on research. On an experimental basis, the group in 2007 supplied users of Google's Web search service with the ability to obtain English translations of text from three source languages: Arabic, Chinese, and Russian.

As far as Google's translation work has progressed, its results are far from polished and idiomatic. When Sarmad Ali, a reporter for *The Wall Street Journal* who is bilingual in English and Arabic, tried out the Arab-English online translation services of Google, Systran, and two rivals in December 2007, he produced a catalog of syntactic and semantic errors for all of them, ranging from "the merely too-literal to the laughably bad."

Speaking about the machine-translation results at a public talk earlier that year, Google's Och presented Google at its best, the organization trying to make information more universally accessible without any visible concern about its own commercial interests. If any in the audience wanted to try their own hand at building a machine-translation algorithm, he said, Google was glad to help. Working with the nonprofit Linguistics Data Consortium hosted by the University of Pennsylvania, Google had begun to supply, for the nominal cost of shipping, a set of DVDs containing the basic training data needed, listing the frequency of various word combinations, from one to five words in length (technically referred to as *pre-counted n-grams*), for a trillion words of English-language documents that Google's crawler had collected from the Web.

Statistical machine translation depends upon parallel texts for feeding the Algorithm—Och said that about 100 million words of parallel data are needed in order to build a system that produces reasonably acceptable results. This dependency upon parallel texts limits the number of language pairings available for machine translation. At present, there are not enough twin texts to create a system to go directly from Greek to Thai, for example, so a bridge language, like English, must be used in the interim. Whether machine translation will ever be able to directly translate texts in any language into any other, or whether a different approach, based on understanding linguistics and building an intermediate meta-language, will be needed, is a question that has not been answered definitively. So far, it appears that with sufficient quantities of data, impossible tasks become possible.

Google's progress, which was startling in its speed, gave reason for optimistic expectations. Its statistical machine translation offerings grew from three source languages, in the spring of 2007, to thirteen, and then to twenty-three, within a single year. The company offered not only non-English–to–English translation but also translation between any pairing of its languages, which by May 2008 were

Arabic, Bulgarian, Chinese in both simplified and traditional characters, Croatian, Czech, Danish, English, Finnish, French, German, Greek, Hindi, Italian, Korean, Japanese, Norwegian, Polish, Romanian, Russian, Spanish, Swedish, and Portuguese.

The machine-translation project illustrates the way Google is driven by the maxim "More data is better data." In the information business, completeness—both within a category of information and across categories—is crucial because ever more data makes the algorithms ever smarter, which in turn serves to increase the distance between Google's leading position and its rivals'.

Google's free phone-based information service, 1-800-GOOG-411, offers a good illustration. The service uses voice recognition software to receive queries about phone numbers for local businesses. The service does not collect a service fee, nor does it carry advertising. Google's Marissa Mayer confessed in an interview in October 2007 that she is skeptical that it will ever become a profitable business. But she is not concerned because Google offered it to collect phonemes, not profits. She said, "We need to build a great speech-to-text model that we can use for all kinds of different things, including video search." Google's speech recognition experts told her, "If you want us to build a really robust speech model, we need a lot of phonemes . . . people talking, saying things so that we can ultimately train off that." More data is better data.

Google knows that the Algorithm does not produce flawless results, but rather than view the Algorithm's inadequacies as the inherent limitations of a fully automatic process, the company views them as the result of insufficient data and still-incomplete tweaking of its inner workings. The company is determined to feed the Algorithm ever more information, which it must look ever further out to obtain. It has reached out to claim as many books as it can get hold of, as many videos as its users would like to submit, as many different kinds of maps as can be overlaid upon the earth and the sky, and as many of the documents that computer users routinely create for home, office, and school.

Some of these additions to Google's information storehouses may appear to be peripheral to its core interests in Web search and associated advertising. Some may appear to be improvident experiments. Some may appear to offer a service that is both highly popular and utterly lacking in revenue production. They may, or may not, turn out to be important to Google's future. Each one has its own story. They all, however, share a common theme: Google's zealous pursuit of new categories of information, which has not slowed or wavered, even when its public image has been damaged by controversy arising from its actions.

When each story of expansion is examined closely, the smooth façade of Google the monolith gives way, and a more complicated picture of on-the-fly decision making emerges. The official corporate culture, which places a premium on the initiative of individuals and small teams, can be seen in these stories. But there is also an unexamined confidence that the interests of Google and those of its customers are in complete alignment, and every new service is seen by Google as an advance for humankind. Some day, when the experiments have run their full course, they may be seen as the masterful fulfillment of Google's mission to organize the world's information, as farsighted vision. Or alternatively, the same stories may one day be read as accounts of misspent resources, evidence of hubris.

CHAPTER 4

Moon Shot

The Web was merely the place to start. During a talk that Larry Page and Sergey Brin jointly gave at the Commonwealth Club in San Francisco in 2001, when Google was three years old, the cofounders explained that as large as Google's index seemed to the layperson, having grown to 1.3 billion pages, the Web itself covered nothing but a fraction of information that should be encompassed. Page explained, "Right now, you can only access the stuff that's on the Internet. You can't access content that's in libraries. You can't access magazines. You can't access newspapers, in general, or old newspaper content. You can't access all the television programs that have ever been broadcast. But all these things will happen."

The digitization of traditional print media had begun long before—while a graduate student, Page himself had worked on projects funded as part of Stanford's Digital Library project—and in 2001 it was not clear whether Google would have to do anything to hurry the process along. Libraries, publishers, and broadcasters could be expected to take care of the chores of digitization and place the files on servers that were publicly accessible, and Google's crawler would index their contents just as it indexed Web pages.

One year later, however, in 2002, Page, Brin, and their Google associates decided not to wait and began to investigate undertaking on their own the digitization of the one category that, more than any other, most fully recorded humankind's understanding of the world: books. The Google algorithm excelled at comparing the presumed authority of one Web page to another, but it could not warn a user when the best information available on the Web was inferior in quality to that found off-line, between bound covers.

Digitizing books was a project that presented challenges wholly different, however, from those entailed in indexing and ranking Web pages. Converting books into digital bits involved computer science less than it did other areas of expertise, such as mechanical engineering (designing imaging equipment), diplomacy (obtaining the cooperation of the largest repositories of books, university libraries), logistics (hauling books to scanning centers and back, without mishap), and legal expertise (ensuring that the effort did not run afoul of copyright law). It also required a financial commitment unlike any the company had made before. Google set out to digitize not merely the books in a single large library, or digitize the most academically valuable books, or the most commonly used books, or the most critically acclaimed books, but instead all books, every single one of the 32 million listed in WorldCat, the union catalog encompassing twenty-five thousand libraries around the world. Every book. Period.

Marissa Mayer would later refer to Google Book Search as "our moon shot." The image is apt, at least in some ways. Digitization of all books had been a dream of many. It was widely considered too ambitious to be attainable in the short term. Similar to President John Kennedy's famous challenge in 1961 to safely land a human on the moon by the end of the decade, Google set a ten-year timetable to achieve its goal. (In September 2007, Google funded another moon shot: the $30 million Google Lunar X Prize.)

Before Google's book project began, however, the company had taken the first step in digitizing content that was not already online when it quietly began the year before to scan catalogs supplied by merchants. The catalogs were placed online and could be searched at a Google site separate from the main search site. No attempt was made to assemble the most comprehensive possible collection; merchant participation was wholly voluntary, and not many elected to participate. Google Catalogs Beta did not give Google experience in high-volume scanning.

In 2002, when Page and Mayer began talking about having

Google scan books, the two ran an experiment to see how much time scanning a book would take. The story that would be retold later on many occasions was that the two turned the pages of a three-hundred-page book, one by one, according to the cadence ticked off by a metronome. The two supposedly extracted a single, but very useful, datum from this exercise: that forty minutes would be needed to scan a three-hundred-page book. From this, they somehow believed that they could estimate the cost of scanning millions of volumes and arrived at a number that fell within the range of the imaginable.

Whether the experiment's results were treated half as seriously as the company legend claims seems dubious, at least from the perspective of the present, when Google will not divulge any details about how it captures the images of book pages. It is possible that the experiment led immediately to the conclusion that scanning bound books, which requires a mechanical arm to move back and forth, was hopelessly slow, and a decision was made to use instead a digital camera to capture a pair of facing page images in a fraction of a second. When Adam Smith, a product management director who oversees the Google Book Search project, was asked in 2007 whether Google used a scanner or a digital camera, he said, "Isn't it the same thing?"

The difference may seem slight but it could mean the difference between a project that would be too slow, and thus too costly to be feasible, and one that would not be. In 2002, when Larry Page visited his alma mater the University of Michigan and met with university officials, he told university president Mary Sue Coleman that Google would be able to scan every one of the university library's 7 million volumes in just six years—at the time, the university estimated that if it used only its own resources, the task would require a thousand years.

Google was a privately held corporation whose stock was not yet trading publicly but whose owners—the founders, the venture capital investors, the early employees—were bound together in a profit-seeking enterprise. Google executives did not view book digitization as an eleemosynary project; they were not contemplating donating funds to nonprofit organizations, like the University of Michigan, that had already begun digitizing books. Instead they were looking at the feasibility of Google performing all of the digitizing itself, and then using the digital copies for its own purposes. Even if Google Book Search did not produce immediate profits, the project would be expected, at some point, to yield a return to Google that was proportionate to the outsized investment that the company would have to make to pursue the project. The prospect of being able to search the contents of books with the ease of navigating the Web was, without doubt, an exciting one. Having a single, profit-seeking company erect the digital doorway to all the world's information that resides in books would, however, when publicly unveiled, not please all onlookers.

Google's "moon shot" differed from NASA's manned lunar landing in another respect: Google had no close competitors willing to match its spending on book search. In the 1960s, space exploration was an extension of the Cold War, and the United States and the Soviet Union were evenly matched in a number of scientific fields. In 2002 and 2003, however, when Google quietly began work on its book search project, no other company was willing to compete with it head-to-head: the investment that the project appeared to require was sufficient to scare off all others initially.

Google had the chance to jump ahead not only because of its own fiscal boldness but also because others who had tried to digitize the world's books had not gotten very far. The first significant project to take on the daunting task was Project Gutenberg, started by Michael Hart in 1971. This was so early that digitization then had nothing to do with scanners and personal computers, which had not yet appeared, but instead relied upon keyboards connected to mainframes, like the one to which Hart had access, which was owned by the Materials Research Lab at the University of Illinois. Hart sought volunteers who also had access to institutionally owned computers and had time on their hands, and would be willing to type in the complete texts of important works of literature that were in the public domain (their typing fingers restoring the old anatomical meaning of *digit* to *digitization*). The appearance of personal computers subsequently made it possible to pitch the call for volunteers broadly.

Project Gutenberg eschewed the notion of "authoritative editions," and welcomed texts that were "99.9% accurate in the eyes of the general reader." It was not well along in covering the world's literature: by 2002, the project had digitized only about 6,300 works, all of which were entirely in plain text, without an image of the original typeset pages. Project Gutenberg's goal of making printed works more widely accessible was a noble one, but one of its inherent limitations was its assumption that a reader neither needed nor wanted anything but plain text, stripped of font variations, running heads, and the subtle design features in a printed book that also inform the reading experience.

The one institution in the traditional book world that had been arguably best suited to take on the massive task of digitization of all books was the Library of Congress. By 1990, advances in scanning technology had brought digitization costs down to the point that the library began a digitization program that experimented with digitization of just about every medium but books: documents, moving images, sound recordings, photographs. The primary focus was limited to building a digital "American Memory" collection of historical materials.

The most ambitious book digitization project was begun in 2001, when Carnegie Mellon University received a $500,000 grant from the National Science Foundation for the "Million Book Project," a digitization effort that attempted to get the most books digitized for the fewest dollars by shipping them to India and China to be scanned. When U.S. libraries were asked to lend their book collections to the project for the greater good, and subject the books to the vagaries of shipment by sea in cargo containers, the libraries balked, for understandable reasons. Brewster Kahle, an Internet entrepreneur who had founded the Internet Archive in 1996, stepped forward to "prime the pump," as he phrased it, with the donation to the project of 150,000 deaccessioned books that he purchased for $50,000 from the Kansas City Public Library.

The Million Book Project raised another $2.5 million from the National Science Foundation and would eventually surpass its original target, digitizing 1.4 million books in China, India, and also

Egypt, before its termination in 2007. Most of the books were in Chinese, Indian, Arabic, French, and other languages than English, and supplied by university libraries outside the United States that were also performing the scanning. It was an experiment whose multinational model failed to pick up self-sustaining momentum.

While Google was quietly sending out fact-finding teams in 2002 to investigate the feasibility of scanning all books, Brewster Kahle was talking up the same goal, imploring the Library of Congress to digitize all 20 million of its volumes. In a talk that Kahle delivered at the library in November 2002, he lyrically described how "the idea of universal access to all human knowledge has been a dream through the ages," arguing that the ancient library of Alexandria had succeeded in gathering human knowledge in one place. Now, he said, the Library of Congress could match and exceed Alexandria, making the contents of all books universally accessible by digitizing them. Kahle was a gadfly, possessed by the idée fixe, so excited that he minimized obstacles that stood in the way of the vision's realization. He casually asserted that the entire Library of Congress's book collection could be digitized for merely $100 million. Kahle did not explain how he arrived at this back-of-the-envelope calculation, but he had to assume that the Library of Congress would happily ship off its entire collection for scanning to Hyderabad, India, the destination of the books Kahle had purchased in bulk in Kansas City.

When Google's team in 2002 looked at the experiences of prior book digitization projects, it learned that costs ranged anywhere from $10 to $100 a book, depending on many factors. If one were to use $50 as an average figure, and aim to digitize the 30 million unique book titles worldwide, the arithmetic yielded a daunting number: $1.5 billion. Google at the time was growing fast, jumping from $15 million in losses on $19 million in revenue in 2000 to profits of about $100 million on $440 million in revenue in 2002. This was heady growth. Given its size then, however, a $1.5 billion price tag on book digitization was simply too large to be financially feasible.

The company decided that it could afford to undertake the book digitization project only because Page and his associates assumed that if they applied their attention to the problem, they would be able to devise a way to obtain images of book pages at far less cost than everyone else. The approach that Carnegie Mellon's Million Book Project was using, shipping books overseas to take advantage of low labor costs, was never seriously considered. Another possible way to eliminate labor costs was to rely on robotic scanners, but what would be saved in labor costs would be dwarfed by the capital investment.

The Google solution to the problem of high costs for digitization was to sort books into two categories—those that were still in print and those that were not—and process them accordingly. If publishers were willing to assist Google, the in-print books could be digitized inexpensively. Publishers could submit the same digital files used to typeset the books electronically, though in many cases these files could not be used because many of the codes used for page elements were not standardized. In such cases, Google could digitize a bound copy of the book quickly and without incurring much expense by taking advantage of off-the-shelf technology that is called within the book trade *destructive scanning:* the book binding is chopped off and the pages shoot through a sheet feeder into a high-speed scanner. This was the easy part. Not so easy would be digitizing—nondestructively—the 90 percent of books that were no longer in print.

Google devised an approach that combined diplomacy to borrow books gratis from the leading research libraries in the West, ingenuity in devising its own speedy work-flow technology for collecting digital images of the printed pages, and low-wage temporary workers to perform the labor-intensive work of turning pages. The human touch was literally visible in some images—fingers can be seen holding the book in place.

Google did not disclose how successful it was in squeezing costs out of digitization. But Daniel Clancy, Google Book Search's project manager, told a Stanford audience in 2006 that a $1.5 billion project "is not a cost that would be acceptable." Other companies that were digitizing books spoke of a cost of ten cents a page. If Google's costs were similar, and a three-hundred-page book cost $30 to digitize, then its stated ambition of digitizing 30 million volumes suggested a total cost of the project in the general vicinity of $900 million, still a staggering sum. The costs were not likely to go down by much because this was a labor-intensive project already using the least expensive labor that the market supplies. Moore's Law, which predicts that the number of transistors that could be placed on a chip would continue to double at regular intervals and enables Google's data centers to halve costs every eighteen months or so, did not apply to the speed of human page turners. Nor did book digitization benefit from scale effects: the time required to photograph or scan each page is unaffected by the volume of books being processed in the warehouse.

Significantly, Google eschewed the easiest way of reducing its costs: by digitizing only a portion of extant books, those that would most likely prove to be of value to its users. By stating from the outset that it would digitize all books, the company neatly avoided the politically fraught task of selecting which books should be included. Misunderstanding Google's radical intention to exclude nothing, French critics suggested that a panel be set up to ensure that the best in Francophone literature was selected. Google's Clancy answered, "We shouldn't have people trying to figure out that *this* book is more valuable than *that* book. So don't spend the resources."

Google's decision to shoot for the moon meant it could not be criticized for making ill-considered selections. But it did make the company vulnerable not just to criticism, but also to lawsuits, over its inclusion of books that were still under copyright and whose copyright holders had not given Google permission to copy the works. This was an issue with which the custodians of the library of Alexandria did not have to concern themselves when organizing the ancient world's information.

Copyright law in the United States required securing from the copyright holder the right to copy, as the name itself explained. But it also provided permission-free copying of small swatches for "fair use" that used the material in a "transformative way" and that did not impinge on the commercial value of the original. Google's digitization project did not seem to fit clearly within fair use or clearly beyond it. The company would make a copy of the entire work, which seemingly would be verboten under fair use rules. Then again, Google was not proposing to make the work available to readers—the copy would be used to prepare an index of the contents. One could try to argue that the index was "transformative" and the copying done in order to prepare the index was a form of "fair use." Google would have difficulty making such an argument, however, if its users found all that they were looking for by using Google's index rather than purchasing the book.

If Google could persuade publishers that indexing their books in copyright would lead to increased sales, and enlist their blessing for the project, it would be able to move forward without worry of lawsuits. By the time it was ready to approach publishers in August 2003, however, reports had surfaced that Amazon was well ahead of Google and already was in negotiations with publishers to make nonfiction books searchable. Without knowing the details of Amazon's plans, Google invited publishers to send it all their books, either in digital or in physical form, for inclusion in its index. If the publisher was skittish, it could send just a few books, and if it was not yet ready to send full texts, then a brief excerpt from the jacket copy, or the book's introduction, or the author's biography would be acceptable. Google offered to place "Buy This Book" links to major online book retailers like Amazon, Barnes & Noble, and Books-A-Million on the book search results pages. Google would provide the links gratis and asked nothing in return if a user used a link to make a purchase.

Amazon broke the trail for Google, soothing publishers who were concerned that hosting digital copies on Amazon's servers increased the risk of piracy. In cases in which book sales were expected to decline if users could browse their pages—cookbooks, travel guides, and any reference works—the books were not considered for digitization. When Amazon publicly unveiled its new service in October 2003, it could boast that it had enlisted 190 publishers, including Simon & Schuster and Random House, and offered the full texts of 120,000 titles, a number roughly equivalent to a large, well-stocked bookstore.

A year after Amazon launched "Search Inside This Book," Google was finally ready to unveil its own foray into book indexing, which it called Google Print. Even with the additional time, Google had failed to sign up as broad a roster of participating publishers as Amazon. Random House was one of the holdouts. To publishers, Amazon was a familiar face, with a proven ability to sell books; Google was known for selling advertising on the Web but nothing else. Adam Smith, who before coming to Google had been a senior executive at Random House, was recruited, along with others with publishing experience, to help Google, as Smith would later say, "talk the talk to publishers."

At the same time that Google was speaking with publishers to secure digital copies of recently published books, it was also talking with major research libraries about digitizing portions of their collections, adding the out-of-print works to the publishers' in-print works to assemble, eventually, copies of every book ever published. As praiseworthy as Google's goal was, however, its ambitions led the company to become impatient and make a major blunder. Instead of keeping its publishers' program entirely separate from its program with libraries, and being patient with the publishers, it decided to rely on the library collections for access to current titles that it had not persuaded publishers to supply with their blessing and permission to copy. The timetable for the moon shot could not accommodate years of pokey negotiations. Google had hoped to complete its moon shot within ten years, but even that seemed unacceptably distant. Daniel Clancy would later say that ten years at Google was equivalent to fifty years at a place like IBM: "The idea that this takes ten years is not something anyone would be happy with at Google."

Google could not contain its impatience. In December 2004, Google Print was expanded—dramatically—with the announcement of agreements that Google had reached to scan books in the collections of the libraries of Harvard, Stanford, and the University of Michigan, Oxford University's Bodleian Library, and the New York Public Library. Nowhere in the announcement did Google point out that a majority of the participating libraries were not as confident as Google's attorneys were that digitizing the entirety of books that were still under copyright, without the copyright holders' permission, was protected by the fair use provision of copyright law. The Bodleian Library was willing to contribute only works published before 1900. The New York Public Library offered only fragile works that were no longer under copyright. Harvard initially limited scans to about forty thousand volumes. Stanford said it would have Google digitize "hundreds of thousands, perhaps millions, of books" from its collection but conspicuously dodged the question of whether any works under copyright would be included. Only Michigan declared that Google would be able to digitize the entire library collection, without limitation. Michigan's 7 million volumes were all Google needed to quickly secure coverage of recently published books for the moon shot.

Authors and publishers alike objected strenuously to Google's abrupt abandonment of the principle that had guided Google Print before this, which was to index works still in copyright only if the publishers granted permission. Google reacted to the criticism with an announcement that created more unfavorable publicity for Google Print: in August 2005, Google said it would suspend scanning of in-copyright books until November, by which time publishers were to have submitted a list of books still in copyright that they did not wish to have Google copy. Google declared it would then resume scanning all books that had not been explicitly excluded by the deadline.

Having a gun placed against their temples was not the best way to calm authors and publishers. Jack Romanos, who was then the CEO of Simon & Schuster, said, "There's sort of this innocent arrogance about [Google]. One minute they're pretending to be all idealistic, talking about how they're only in this to expand the world's knowledge, and the next they're telling you that you're going to do it their way or no way at all." His company and other publishers tried to negotiate a revenue-sharing arrangement with Google as a condition of granting Google permission to index books, and Google showed no interest in discussing the matter. Romanos said, "They had a holier-than-thou attitude that hasn't done them any favors."

Failing to make progress in talks with Google, the Authors Guild filed the first lawsuit in September 2005 against Google for Google

Print Library's "massive copyright infringement." The complaint mentioned in particular the University of Michigan's willingness to supply Google with copyrighted works. The next month, a group of publishers—McGraw-Hill, Pearson Education, Penguin, Simon & Schuster, and John Wiley & Sons—filed a second suit. The plaintiffs vigorously objected to the wholesale copying of entire books that were under copyright by a commercial entity without securing the consent of the copyright holders.

In their suit, the publishers pointed out that Google's publisher program and library program were essentially indistinguishable, except that in the former case, Google sought permission of the copyright holders before proceeding, and in the latter case, it did not, at least in its copying of books under copyright held by the University of Michigan. The inconsistency in Google's approach in the two programs exposed the fact that Google was perfectly capable of abiding by copyright law but had elected for its convenience not to do so. Each of the plaintiffs was, and would remain, participants in Google's Print Program for Publishers.

The publishers argued that their business depended, in part, upon ancillary revenue, such as licensing fees for granting permission for others to publish excerpts of works. In their suit, they pointed out that Google, a commercial entity, was going to display "excerpts" of scanned books in order to "increase user traffic to its site, which then enables it to increase the price it charges its advertisers." Patricia S. Schroeder, the president of the Association of American Publishers, told *New York* magazine that Google was a great search engine, which she personally loved. "But someone has to pay for the content so there's something to search for," she said. "I say to Google, 'Let's make a deal. You won't make quite as much money, but I think you'll do okay. Let's share, boys, come on, let's share! You don't have to be so greedy.'"

The litigation was embarrassing for a company whose informal motto, "Don't Be Evil," had become a well-known component of its public story. "Don't Be Evil" was an unusual corporate value—deliberately so. It originated in 1999, when Google began for the first time to add employees who were not engineers and who were hired for their business acumen. Veteran Googlers were concerned that the newcomers would pressure them to tinker with the order of search results in order to favor the company's advertising clients or build new products that only the MBAs were enthusiastic about. Amit Patel, a Google engineer who had been among the very first employees, conveyed his concern by writing in neat letters in the corner of the whiteboard in the company's only conference room, where it could be seen by Google's salespeople and their clients, "Don't Be Evil."

Several years later, when the number of employees had grown to several hundred and the human resources team was casting about for a set of corporate values, Paul Buchheit, another engineer, suggested that Patel's "Don't Be Evil" be added to the list. Buchheit, who had worked at Intel before coming to Google, was determined to avoid the bland "Strive for Excellence" mission statements typically adopted by large companies. He also wanted "something that, once you put in there, would be hard to take out." After Buchheit succeeded in having the mantra included officially, Patel spread "Don't Be Evil" on every whiteboard at the company he came across, and it became the one Google value that the public knew well, even though it was formally expressed at Google less pithily as "You can make money without doing evil" and was only one of "ten things Google has found to be true." Critics previously had said Google was failing to measure up to its declared "Don't Be Evil" philosophy when it had censored results in 2002 that pointed to an anti-Scientology Web site and when it was nominated for a "U.S. Big Brother Award" by Privacy International in 2003. A Thomas Friedman column in the *New York Times* was headlined "Is Google God?," setting Google up for being humbled. Among the most visible challenges to Google's self-defined credo for ethical business practices, however, were the two lawsuits filed by the representatives of the book world, which pointed its finger at Google and accused it of doing evil. This was a painful affront to Google's self-image.

Shortly after the second lawsuit was filed, Google dropped the tarnished project name of Google Print and adopted a new name, Google Book Search. The company said that "Google Print" had confused users who thought the service was to help users print Web pages. The official company blog post also anticipated that some observers would interpret the name change as a public relations maneuver and denied that this had been a consideration: "No, we don't think that this new name will change what some folks think about this program."

When the lawsuits charging Google with copyright violations mentioned the role played by the University of Michigan, Stanford decided that it would be prudent to permit Google to scan only books published up through 1964. Michael A. Keller, the university librarian, explained, "We're not a public institution. We don't have any state immunity from being sued ourselves." In the University of Michigan, however, Google had a stalwart partner that—with state immunity—did not flinch when the lawsuits arrived. Mary Sue Coleman, the university president, defended Google's book digitization project as "the most revolutionary enterprise I've ever experienced," a project that would provide "a massive, free directory" for publishers that they did not appreciate. She joked that publishers regarded *snippet* as "a four-letter word," but speaking for herself, "I confess I see no difference between an online snippet, a card catalog, or my standing at Borders and thumbing through a book to see if it interests me, if it contains the information I need, or if it doesn't really suit me."

The unobjectionable image of the fusty card catalog would be the one that Google and its defenders would invoke again and again. Lawrence Lessig, a professor of law at Stanford, provided a widely quoted defense of Google's book digitization: The publishers were effectively demanding, he said, "[their] permission to enable a 21st century card catalog. When in the history of man did the law require permission from an author (or publisher) for a work to be included in a card catalog?" The problem with the card catalog defense was that Google search results provided contextual snippets from the actual text, something that had not actually been seen before in the history of man—something less than the complete book, but something more than a card catalog's lean listing of author, title, publisher, and a few subject headings. Google put into place safeguards that were designed to limit a searcher from obtaining more than three snippets for one search term in a copyrighted book for which the copyright holder had not granted Google permission to copy. Still, the snippets would give Google the ability to attract more visitors, and more visitors meant increased advertising revenue and profits. So the twenty-first-century card catalog raised a new question: should Google have to share the profits with publishers and authors?

Or at the very least, should Google share access to its digital books with other search engines? The publishers in their suit pointed out that they had no objection to digitization of books and, in fact, had joined the Open Content Alliance, the digitization consortium that obtains the permission of the copyright holders and then digitizes their works, making the digital copies available to all search engines, whether they were members of the alliance or not. The initiative had begun with Brewster Kahle, of the Internet Archive, and Yahoo, in early 2005, with equipment and software donated by HP and Adobe. It was modestly funded, however. Yahoo did not disclose publicly its financial commitment but it was estimated in the $300,000–$500,000 range in the first year. The alliance was dependent upon handouts from foundations, such as a $1 million grant from the Sloan Foundation in 2006 to scan antislavery material that was held in several libraries.

The initiative was stymied also by Google's head start: Kahle said he was told by librarians at several institutions that they would permit their books to be scanned only once and they could not participate in the OCA because they were already working with Google. "We want a public library system in the digital age," Kahle said, "but what we are getting is a private library system controlled by a single corporation."

Microsoft joined the OCA in fall 2005, with a news report that it would commit to digitizing 150,000 books the next year for its newly announced Live Search Books. It limited the scope of its scanning to works that were out of copyright. Thomas Rubin, Microsoft's associate general counsel for copyright, trademark, and trade secrets, told publishers at the annual meeting of the Association of American Publishers that Google's demand that authors and publishers should notify Google if they did not want their copyrighted works to be scanned assumed that "Google is the only game in town." He noted how impractical such a demand would be if other companies around the world adopted the same policy, placing the onus on copyright owners to track down every company that was engaged in unauthorized copying. Rubin also got off a biting offhand criticism of Google when he referred to "companies that create no content of their own, and make money solely on the backs of other people's contents, [and] are raking in billions through advertising revenue and IPOs."

As a participant in the Open Content Alliance, Microsoft would not only create the two digital copies of every scanned book that Google did—one for the lending library and one for itself—but would also have to provide a third copy to the alliance, which was free to index and display the digitized book on its own Web site. By forgoing an arrangement that would give it the exclusive control that Google secured, Microsoft could only hope that the digitization project would be of sufficient benefit to users of its search service that the investment would be justified. For Microsoft, scanning books by the thousands, rather than millions, was nothing like a moon shot. Danielle Tiedt, Microsoft's general manager of MSN Search, spoke at a trade conference panel in March 2006 about Microsoft's reluctance to take on digitization, given the enormous expense, nonexclusive rights, and uncertain payoff. She said, "I would love nothing better for all of this work to already be digitized, and all I have to do is go call it and index it and make a great user experience." Imagine, she said, if Microsoft had to create every Web page in order to be able to index the page's contents for its search engine. Unfortunately for Microsoft, the contents of books were not already digitized, so Microsoft had to pick one of two choices: "Don't pick that content, or I have to put some skin in the game and actively help in the digitization process to get content in digital format so that I can deliver in what I'm trying to do."

Google's Daniel Clancy sat on the same panel as Tiedt and suggested that one alternative to private companies undertaking the digitization of books would be to have the U.S. government take on the project. "Obviously, we've spent a lot more than $1.5 billion on many things more questionable," he said, but left hanging in the air his concerns about the government "controlling" the images of the book pages.

The panel moderator, Elizabeth Lane Lawley, a professor of information technology at the Rochester Institute of Technology, suggested an entirely different approach, however, avoiding the closed, proprietary project of Google's or a costly one undertaken by the government: a decentralized, bottom-up effort depending upon individuals and libraries of any size contributing to the scanning project in the same way that individual contributors had built Wikipedia. She said, "I think we have started to buy too much into this rhetoric that it's so big that *only* something really big and scary like a corporation or The Government can do it. When in fact, we're starting to learn from these technologies that not everything has to be done in a centralized way."

Whatever might be said about alternative approaches, Google's Book Search showed that a single company, with ample funding and a willingness to defend its copy-first-delete-later policy in court, was going to move far more quickly than a loose confederation of companies like the OCA, which had scanned only 100,000 books by the end of its second year, or a grassroots movement to scan books that had not even been launched. Google signed up more university partners, a total of 28 by December 2007, including Princeton University, Cornell University, the University of Virginia, and the University of Wisconsin–Madison, as well as institutions outside the United States, including Keio University in Japan and the National Library of Catalonia. The University of California, which had first joined the OCA, then signed with Google, committing at least 2.5 million volumes to the project, giving Google sole search-engine rights to their contents. Daniel Greenstein, a University of California librarian who set up the arrangement with Google, said, "I think last month we did 3,500 books [with the OCA] . . . Google is going to do that in a day. So, what do you do?"

The Google juggernaut gained momentum over time, not penalized in the least by Google's decision to hold on to the digital copies for its own exclusive use, without permitting other search engines to index them. Microsoft decided the best course was to emulate its competitor. Just one year after joining the Open Content Alliance and extolling the virtues of sharing digital books with others, Microsoft announced that it would adopt a policy like Google's, blocking other search engines from indexing the books that Microsoft digitized. Microsoft was not willing to match Google's investments, however, and falling ever further behind in the competition to digitize books, became too discouraged to continue. After digitizing only 750,000 books, Microsoft announced in May 2008 that it was shutting down its scanning initiative.

Google's moon shot consumed enormous resources in order to get off the ground, not to mention other costs in legal challenges and unfavorable publicity. The payoff was slow in coming. In February 2006, when Clancy gave a presentation about Google Book Search at a colloquium at Stanford, he was asked, "How has what you've scanned so far changed your own personal behavior, in terms of how you use information?" Clancy was candid: "It hasn't." He had no time to do academic research, he explained, being busy with work and family. Were he working in fields like history or computer science, where material that was in the public domain was abundant, he said he would be able to report that it had made a tremendous difference.

Google's book index was stored in what was commonly referred to in the online world as a *silo,* emphasizing separateness. With the passing of a little more time, Clancy and his Google Book Search colleagues discovered that the book information that they were accumulating could be made immediately useful in new ways that let users pull information out of the silo for their own use or for sharing. In the fall of 2007, Google gave users the chance to set up a "personal collection" of book titles, which could be searched and also shared with others. A new tool gave users the chance to copy the graphic image of a favorite quotation or selected passage from books in the public domain and paste or embed the image in another Web page. And literary references to a geographic location in public domain books could be overlaid on maps provided by another Google service, Google Earth, directly connecting one silo with another.

The most important, and most conspicuous, advance for Google Book Search was its attainment of a critical mass of recently published books. Before 2007, a book search on Google was hit-or-miss, emphasis on miss. Then, suddenly, it seemed to be able to come up with most any title that was in print. The number of books that had been scanned remained small: the company said in September 2007 that it had indexed about 1 million volumes, which left it well short of the WorldCat's 32 million and nowhere near the pace that would be needed to complete the project within the eight years left to meet the original ten-year goal. And yet Google, somewhat miraculously, had achieved excellent coverage of recently published works. How had it done so?

In May 2007, it quietly made the biggest change since it had started the moon shot: it added listings for books whose text had not been indexed, using publicly available bibliographic information drawn from online library catalogs around the world. Overnight, Google Books added all books in print without waiting to scan and index them.

These books were displayed on Google's search results page with "no preview available," a new category distinguishing it from "full preview" (books in the public domain), "limited preview" (books under copyright for which Google has secured permission to show a limited number of pages in its Book Partners Program), and "snippet view" (books under copyright for which Google had not secured permission to display pages).

The entries for the "no preview" books were placeholders, but they provided far more than barebones card-catalog information: lists of references from Web pages; reviews of the book that were available online; references to the books that had been found in other books that were already indexed; and references from scholarly works indexed in Google Scholar. After it arrived at the realization that it had enormous amounts of useful information about books in other silos, including the largest one—the Web—Google could offer users a rich array of supplementary information about any given title, and it could do so without infringing on the rights of the book's copyright holders.

One has to admire the ingenuity of Google's staff, using Google's vast information assets to augment what could be known about a book beyond a bibliographic card. At the same time, one also has to wonder how foolish it had been for Google to be so impatient to build up its book collection that it had asserted a right to make digital copies of books in print without the permission of copyright holders. The two lawsuits filed against it by publishers and by the Authors Guild continued to grind on. In early 2008, the presiding U.S. District Court judge, John E. Sprizzo, set a deadline of April 2009 for submission of motions for summary judgment; trials will come still later.

Everything that Google used to create a customized Web site in 2007 for any book had also been available to it in 2004. Google's Book Search managers may have been blind to the opportunities to cross-link across different silos of information that was in the public domain because such incremental improvements lacked the stirring scale of the near impossible, the transfixing imagery of a moon shot.

With twenty-eight participating libraries, Google's Book Search collections continued to grow as the scanning proceeded, still entirely out of public view. In February 2008, the University of Michigan was the first library to reach the mark of one million books online (361, 441,145 total pages and counting). The progress was not as fast as the original moon shot's—6.5 million books in the university's collections remained to be scanned—but an end was within sight. The university expected to complete the project "early in the next decade."

The legal issues remained outstanding, but the logistical issues seemed to have been tamed. Google was well along in its endeavor to bring the entire world of published text into its digital storehouse.

CHAPTER 5

GooTube

Google's success was based on mastery of words. It was words that its crawlers pulled from Web pages, then indexed and analyzed, determining which pages were deemed the most relevant to a search. It was words between covers that its Book Search project extracted and fed into Google's hungry maw. Wherever words could be found—and digitized—the Algorithm could go to work.

Google could search, however, only words that took written form. In 2004, when Yahoo began including videos in its search results, Google could not. Its crawler completely ignored video files. Yahoo never boasted about its superiority over Google in this regard—because Yahoo itself could find only a small percentage of all the video files rapidly being loaded onto the Web by then. The problem was that most videos were invisible to Web crawlers. Even if they could be found, crawlers could not categorize their subject material because digital video files provided no exterior clues about their contents. Videos proved to be a formidable challenge for search.

How Google responded to this challenge suggests a willingness on the company's part to depart from the approaches that had served it well in developing its core strengths in searching Web pages and serving up relevant advertising. Video presented Google with an opportunity to expand from information embodied in text, which was easy to search, to forms of information that required advances in computer science in order to be understood by the Algorithm. And it also was presented with the opportunity to notice that innovation within its walls did not always keep up with innovation taking place outside. The company could have decided to stick with the tried and true, the Algorithm, and with its own talent to enter new fields, or it could have decided to scale back its ambition to organize all the world's information, deliberately excluding some categories. Instead, it decided that its mission would remain paramount, and Google would take different paths, if necessary, toward its realization. The story of how Google moved into video shows a company that was adaptable, letting go of the Algorithm and embracing, ultimately, the notion that it would have to make its first major acquisition in order to secure a significant position in the competition to organize the world's information in the form of video.

At the start, Google's executives gave no thought to the possibility that video files would require special treatment. Their attachment to automation led them to be content with whatever the Google crawler found in its travels. Video files, lacking descriptive names, were of no interest to the crawler and were ignored. Yahoo realized before Google that standard Web crawls simply would not work well for videos and came up with an innovative idea: inviting the hosts of Web sites to supply some descriptive information about videos they had posted on their sites so that a crawler could collect and use it to expand an index of online videos. In December 2004, Yahoo launched "Yahoo! Video Search Beta" to enlist the assistance of Web site hosts. "Web pages are self-describing," explained Bradley Horowitz, Yahoo's director of media search at the time of the announcement, while "a video link [is] opaque, and you don't know what's inside the video." Web hosts were invited to add a tag to video files that would provide basic information—such as title, actors, and file format—and that would be visible to all crawlers.

Some media companies did take steps to make their video offerings searchable. If one wanted to search online the contents of a particular television series, such as *Washington Week in Review,* or PBS's *NewsHour,* or *Julia Child: Lessons with the Master Chef,* one could often do so on sponsoring producers' Web sites. The sites' search technology made use of the closed-captioning transcripts prepared for the shows. One could search for the occurrence of a name or phrase mentioned in a broadcast, but that didn't do viewers much good because the sites generally didn't offer playback of the segments that were found. The search offered by ShadowTV, a fee-based service that let subscribers search many television news broadcasts, and then view selected snippets, was also based on the closed-captioning texts.

Several companies claimed to have developed voice-recognition technology for searching video, which could identify words from the audio portion of the video file, and did not have to rely on closed captioning. This promised a substantial advance in search. One of those making this claim was an intrepid start-up called Blinkx.

In December 2004, the day after Yahoo announced its Video Search Beta offering, Blinkx made a splash with its announcement of its own video search service, which included forty-two thousand hours of video clips from fifteen television channels. Visitors were promised the ability to search for a term and then be able to watch a brief video clip matched to the term.

With the back-to-back Yahoo and Blinkx announcements, video search became the topic de jour on the Web. Google was not ready. It was still preparing for the launch of its own video service, and would join the others late. Google chose not to follow Blinkx in attempting to rely on voice recognition for its video search. The voice-recognition technology turned out to be far from ready for prime time, as those who tried searches at Blinkx would soon discover. Interestingly, given Google's approach to its book search program, the company also chose not to follow Blinkx's lead regarding the posting of clips without the permission of the copyright holders. Blinkx had not made any arrangements with the media companies whose video it was making viewable, and before long, one of those companies raised concerns. When CNN was told that its clips would be available for free, the company publicly announced that it had not authorized Blinkx to use its video. Blinkx counterclaimed that under the doctrine of copyright's fair use, it could show a clip of up to thirty seconds without needing to secure permission. The likelihood of lawsuits over the impasse was noted in the press coverage.

Google did not follow Blinkx into legal difficulties over fair use, at least initially. The company blundered down a different path. Acting on the assumption that spoken words were no less useful than written ones, Google's video team investigated ways of turning video into text. It seized upon closed-captioning text for convenient searching. Closed captioning, in turn, led Google to focus on video from the major media companies, as they were the only ones that could afford the expense of preparing captioning for their programs. A television industry executive who was briefed on Google's plans said at that time, "Google's trying to bring TV to the Web the same way they're bringing books to the Web." This path would lead Google into obscurity. Videos that were accompanied by closed captioning would turn out to be an inconsequential sliver of the videos that people would want to watch online.

In December 2004, Google engineers at the Mountain View Googleplex installed racks of TV tuners in order to record television broadcasts—and the closed captioning—from ten San Francisco Bay Area stations, C-SPAN, and some other cable channels. The long-term plan for video was to set up an online video store and have users purchase rights to view videos on their PCs. When the company formally launched Google Video in late January 2005, more than a month after Yahoo Video's announcement, it had stored about two terabytes of digital videos. Google thought that was a good start.

What Google unveiled, however, was a service that was woefully behind the competition. To begin with, it did not include any videos on the Web. Google had not focused on programming its Web crawlers to spot video files that were available online, so its index of videos was restricted effectively to only those television broadcasts it had recorded. A Google video search sorted through the closed-captioning transcripts of those programs, and then listed videos that matched the search phrase. There was no link, however, that would begin playing the relevant video. Google's users had to content themselves with a still photograph taken from the matching video episode, passages in the transcript in which the search phrase appeared, and a cheerful announcement of when the next episode of that series would be aired. But as long as the episode found in the search couldn't actually be viewed, why bother searching?

Google Video could not, in short, have started with a more modest and less satisfying offering. Even so, Google's service provoked a hail of criticism from media companies. Executives at CBS and Time Warner's television unit ordered Google to back off. Larry Kramer, the head of digital media at CBS, said that Google "didn't show proper respect for us as potential partners."

The essential mistake that Google had made was assuming that videos were just another source of authoritative information, like all the text-based media that the Algorithm had learned to search through so well. What no one at Google noticed, however, was that video would be more appealing as a medium for pure, unedifying entertainment, and could be produced by anyone who owned a camcorder. The quest for professionally produced documentary or news videos, with closed-captioning transcripts, had led Google badly astray.

In the meantime, a new model for video on the Web was being born. At the same time that Google was taping television broadcasts, Jawed Karim, a twenty-five-year-old software engineer working at PayPal, was giving a good deal of thought to video and the Web. None of his thinking coincided with Google's. Karim had been a computer science major, but he had left the University of Illinois, Urbana-Champaign, before graduating to accept an offer to work in Silicon Valley, at PayPal. His résumé, which included student internships at the University of Minnesota Supercomputing Institute, the National Center for Supercomputing Applications (in Champaign), and Silicon Graphics, reflected immersion in deep computer science problems. The idea that he came up with in his free time, however, addressed a practical problem, not a theoretical one: how to make uploading and playing videos painless. It led to YouTube, the company he would cofound with two friends at PayPal, Chad Hurley and Steve Chen.

The original idea for YouTube is traceable to a moment of serendipitous discovery, in December 2004, when Karim came across a stray statistic that caught his eye. In *Wired* magazine he read an article about BitTorrent, a software technology that allows fast transfer of very large files. The trick is that it uses peer-to-peer networking. BitTorrent, for example, was the technology that enabled the viral spread of a now infamous Jon Stewart television appearance. In the fall of 2004, Stewart appeared on CNN's *Crossfire* and astringently critiqued his hosts, Paul Begala and Tucker Carlson. He called their work "partisan hackery" and singled out Carlson as "a dick." A clip posted online caromed around the Web. In a few weeks it was viewed by 2.3 million people, passed along through BitTorrent. The fact that jumped out at Karim in the *Wired* article was that the Stewart clip had been seen online by at least three times as many people as had originally watched Stewart on CNN.

The Stewart clip was not the first one to enjoy such wide circulation; the emergence of clip culture had actually begun with the sharing of the much-discussed clip of Janet Jackson's "wardrobe malfunction" during the Superbowl earlier that year. But with the clip of Stewart on *Crossfire,* the velocity of viral sharing between PCs had sped up. Soon, the diversity of types of video that people might want to share in large numbers would become clearer. Shortly after the article in *Wired* appeared, the 2004 Indian Ocean tsunami struck. CNN camera crews were not present to capture the tragedy, and it became the first large-scale disaster chronicled primarily by cell phone camcorders.

Karim perceived that viewers who attempted to watch these virally spread videos ran into all sorts of technical difficulties, and he figured that a site that made uploading and watching any video effortless would fill an unmet need.

He regarded sharing videos as the next logical step in the evolution of social networking, or what was then called the "social content space." It could be traced back to the appearance in 1999 of LiveJournal, which offered anyone space to publish personal writings. Each succeeding year brought another innovation. In 2000, HOTorNOT took off: anyone could upload a photo and anyone else could vote on that person's hotness. In 2001, Wikipedia showed the willingness of volunteers to contribute their time to an online project sharing expertise without monetary compensation. In 2002, Friendster established some of the essential elements of a social networking site, such as profile pages and access to the profiles of friends, and friends of friends. In 2003, del.icio.us popularized the sharing of favorite Web pages. Then, in 2004, Flickr combined the uploading of photos to a publicly accessible Web site allowing others to append tags with descriptive labels and comment on them— forms of sharing. Karim thought, why not create a Flickr for videos?

His friends Chen and Hurley agreed that the idea was good, but they wondered, why hasn't someone else already done this? With some investigation, they decided the answer was that they'd happened on the idea with fortuitous timing. Three crucial technological developments had only recently come about: the rapid expansion of broadband connections to the home; a significant drop in the cost of buying bandwidth, which was needed for streaming videos; and the decision by Adobe, the publisher of Flash multimedia software, to include video-playing support. Flash was being installed in most new computers, so this eliminated the problem of incompatible video-encoding formats that users often encountered when they downloaded and then attempted to play a video file.

When the three friends decided to try out their idea on venture capitalists, though, the response was tepid at best. Many didn't even bother to call them back. Others simply shrugged at their presentation. One was willing to grant that the idea seemed "cute." Undettered, Karim, Chen, and Hurley went ahead and founded YouTube in February 2005. They didn't actually need venture capitalists to get started anyway; they had considerable financial assets of their own. All three had joined PayPal in its early days and had become wealthy when eBay acquired the company in 2002.

Karim knew from the beginning that he would not stay at YouTube for long. He had completed his undergraduate degree while working and already had plans to start a full-time graduate program in computer science at Stanford the next fall. The three founders agreed to an arrangement in which Karim would not be a YouTube employee and would receive a smaller stake than the other two, formally holding only the title of adviser. (His presence tends to be omitted entirely in short versions of the company's official history, leaving the impression that Chen and Hurley were the sole founders.)

The three required only two months to develop the code and

launch the site, which they did in April 2005. The only videos they initially had to offer, however, were those that they took of one another to serve as placeholders. The historic first YouTube video was an eighteen-second segment of Karim standing in front of a pen of elephants at a zoo, explaining with a self-mocking wink how elephants have "really, really, really long trunks." This would not do, they knew. So they asked their friends to contribute videos too. Karim's e-mail to his buddies asked, "Can you help us spread the word? Since we just launched, there are no girls in it . . . YET. Can you guys upload your own videos?" They had few takers. Weeks passed, and the site drew only a smattering of submissions. What would become the fastest growing site in the history of the Web came into existence seemingly stillborn.

In May, with the spirits of the cofounders at their nadir, they captured their bleak sentiments on a video shot in the garage that served as YouTube's office. By the end of the previous week, Steve Chen said, he had become "pretty depressed" because "Dude, we have like maybe forty, fifty, sixty videos on the site." It was an appallingly small number. And the quality of what had been posted made him wince—there were few videos he'd want to watch himself.

At this point, they decided to try a desperate measure: they would run an advertisement on Craigslist in the Los Angeles area, inviting "attractive" women to upload videos of themselves. The enticement would be a payment of $100 upon submission of every ten videos. This, too, ended in failure. The advertisement drew not a single response.

YouTube desperately needed content. To attract more amateur contributors, they unveiled in June a dramatically redesigned site. When a user saw a YouTube video that he or she wished to share with friends, a single click would send an e-mail notification to as many friends as desired. This made viewers unpaid marketers, spreading the word about YouTube's offerings. The site also thoughtfully provided a little snippet of identifying code next to each video that could be copied and pasted elsewhere, making it easy to embed a YouTube video on any Web page, including those at MySpace.

Sharing word about a video became painless, and immediately the site began to draw more users. They, in turn, uploaded more videos, which then drew still more users. On a single day, the site drew fifty new videos, then sixty, and then seventy. Once every two weeks, with unfailing regularity, word about one particular video would zip around, making it a widely mentioned sensation. As the number of videos uploaded took off during the summer of 2005, these "viral" hits appeared at ever shorter intervals.

Michael Arrington, whose influential TechCrunch site covered technology start-ups, was the first to take notice of YouTube's jump in traffic and videos. In early August 2005, Arrington praised the service for fast uploads, fast playbacks, and interesting videos. He declared that his absolute favorite was *Matt Dances Around the World*, a much-viewed hit that had been uploaded only four days before. "I suspect YouTube will be quickly acquired and/or duplicated," he wrote. "We love it." That profile in TechCrunch led to coverage on Slashdot, another site widely read among the digerati. Slashdot's coverage ("YouTube—The Flickr of Video?") then brought yet another spike in YouTube's traffic.

In no time, as Arrington had predicted, YouTube's founders faced a field of competitors. Just three months after his YouTube review, when he returned to the subject to cover YouTube's competitors, he listed eight leading contenders: Castpost, ClipShack, Dailymotion, Grouper, OurMedia, Revver, Vimeo, and vSocial. When someone asked in a comment that followed Arrington's post why he had omitted Google Video, Arrington apologized for the omission ("I'm an idiot") and said, "Of course they should have been included." The fact that Google Video had slipped his mind, however, was quite telling. Google Video hardly existed.

Googlers were slow to understand that the most popular video service would not use the same approach that Google had used with Web pages, honing its software formula to determine relative trustworthiness, reputation, and relevance to a search term. YouTube's hypergrowth had nothing to do with algorithms and everything to do with the unpaid contributions of its own users: it was the users who submitted the clips, sorted out the interesting ones from the less interesting, and spread word about the best clips among friends. Viral distribution of hits took care of the marketing end, for free.

Before YouTube appeared, Google Video was slow to relinquish its attachment to professionally produced video. In April 2005, just as YouTube appeared, Google announced that it would accept videos submitted by users, of any length and size, subject to Google's review process. Unlike YouTube, however, Google made clear it was especially interested in submissions from what it referred to as "major producers"—television stations or video production houses with a thousand or more hours of video. Enlisting the owners of large collections of content would not only help seed the site quickly but also speed realization of Google's long-term plan to sell online access to videos.

At the time that Google invited users to submit videos, it was not able to make the submissions available for viewing. Jennifer Feikin, director of Google's video program, nonsensically explained the lapse by saying that Google needed to better "understand how people have authored their video" before it could learn how to search them. The Googlers appear to have thought that the company's brand commanded such loyalty that users would be willing to do almost anything to be associated with it, including contributing videos that could not be viewed.

Larry Page referred to Google's addition of video uploads as an "experiment." Indeed, Google was overtly asking video creators to help the company learn how to enter the video business. Page later described what Google did as being admittedly "weird because it was called Google Video but you couldn't actually watch any video."

Two months later, in June 2005, Google finally had a video viewer ready. Unlike YouTube's Flash-based viewer, Google's required its own separate one-time installation. At last, five months after launching its video site, Google could accept and play user-generated video. The company had not moved very far, however, from its original assumption that video would take off online when professionally produced programs were digitized. The company still clung to the idea that a closed-captioning transcript was essential for searching videos. Peter Chane, Google Video's senior product manager, said, "Once people see that if you have a transcript, you'll do better"—that is, show up in Google's search results—"more people will go back and get their stuff transcribed."

In an effort to avoid antagonizing the major media companies, Google reviewed all video uploads for possible copyright violations before they were made available to the public. Chane, however, self-deprecatingly described the company's review process as "very superficial." Videos weren't actually viewed in their entirety, just skimmed for a quick check that the contents weren't pornographic and didn't include "blatant" copyright violations.

By contrast, YouTube was inviting users to upload "any kind of personal video" as long as its running time was short. The only guidelines for contributors in its first four months were to avoid nudity and stay within a limit of 100 megabytes for any one video file. This effectively prevented users from uploading full-length television programs. A short clip of a favorite show, though, was tacitly welcomed as a form of personal expression. YouTube considered such a clip to be a "personal video."

Once YouTube was widely perceived as the one place to go for online video, which happened during the summer of 2005, the site's dominance was self-sustaining; both viewers and video creators congregated where they knew most videos, and the most viewers, were to be found. A similar phenomenon had benefited eBay, which had emerged from an even more crowded field—competing in 1997 against more than 150 online auction sites. Once eBay had edged ahead of the others in 1998, its lead quickly widened and then solidified.

YouTube's growth was vertiginous; it could be represented on a graph only with a line that angled at almost 90 degrees. Its rate of growth surpassed those of eBay, Google's Web search, Wikipedia, MySpace, Facebook, and any other prior Web site. By November, it was serving 8 terabytes of data every day. A month later, it had doubled again, to 16 terabytes, which was 3 million daily video views.

Just as Brin and Page had at first done with Web search, YouTube's founders devoted all of their attention to building a compelling service and didn't consider how it would make money. As traffic multiplied exponentially and its operational costs ballooned, the company's need for capital grew pressing. In seeking venture capital when it was growing exponentially, YouTube occupied an enviable position in which the traditional roles were reversed: venture capital firms did the pitching, and YouTube did the selecting.

YouTube's entrepreneurs Chen and Hurley (Karim had started graduate school) ended up accepting $3.5 million from Sequoia Capital, the same firm that had financed both Yahoo and Google. In landing YouTube, Sequoia would solidify its reputation as the world's shrewdest investor in Web start-ups. Sequoia did everything right. Perhaps most impressive to the YouTube founders, Sequoia was the only firm they visited that demonstrated interest in actually using the service. The day after Chen and Hurley visited at Sequoia, the partners, their assistants, and everyone in the office, it seemed, had dropped whatever else they were doing to upload and share videos.

Even drawing 3 million views a day, and growing at an unprecedented rate, YouTube was still vulnerable to being overtaken by a far more powerful competitor, such as Google. But Google missed the opportunity to exploit its size to catch up, for at least two reasons. First, YouTube grew organically out of clip culture, which required a loose interpretation of what constituted fair use of copyrighted material. Google would run into serious trouble persuading book publishers that it was attentive to their copyright concerns if it allowed the uploading of clips of television shows, or amateur videos accompanied by copyrighted sound tracks. Google was also saddled with the burden of proving that the company could move beyond a single skill: its lucrative search-based advertising business. Google Video was an opportunity to show that the company could create a new stream of revenue from a pay-to-view service. This is why Google ignored the success YouTube was having with its free service. It still planned to open an online store.

In January 2006, Google unveiled the Google Video Store at the annual Consumer Electronics Show in Las Vegas. The announcement was awkward, nothing like the kind of show Steve Jobs pulls off. One of the partners Google had brought onboard was the NBA, and former NBA star Kenny Smith was on hand. Larry Page seemed all too sincere when the script called for him to pretend not to recognize Smith. CBS's Leslie Moonves, eager to trumpet the availability of CBS programs for sale at Google's new store, said "Google not only is, but will remain, a Very Brady place."

Google remained a Very Brady place for only eighteen months, when it ignominiously closed the video store. In retrospect, it had no chance of succeeding. The pact with the NBA assumed a market demand for stale content—games were sold twenty-four hours after broadcast, as if each one were an instant classic (and the buyer lacked a recording device at home). As for the CBS programs, Google had not fared well in negotiations there, either: the Google Video Store was permitted to offer only one episode of a CBS series at a time. Apple, by contrast, had secured the right from ABC to offer an entire season of shows, such as thirty-five episodes of *Desperate Housewives* for iTunes. Google customers were further restricted to viewing the videos on a networked PC; viewing on a portable device was not an option. Unlike a purchase downloaded from iTunes, a video bought and downloaded from the Google store could be played only if the PC could obtain permission from Google's server, and the permission had to be obtained anew before each viewing. The Google Video Store was a latecomer that never came close to matching iTunes.

Meanwhile, in the spring of 2006, YouTube's growth picked up even greater speed. The 3 million daily page views in November 2005 had grown by April 2006 to an incomprehensible 100 million, a self-propelling cultural phenomenon. Growth required of YouTube's management little but attention to two matters: keeping its site operational and remembering to pay the specialized behind-the-scenes companies—content delivery networks—that maintained copies of the videos on their servers and took care of the distribution of the video streams. Sequoia and a second firm invested an additional $8 million to make sure that YouTube's bills were paid in a timely fashion.

By May, the YouTube phenomenon was affecting the strategy and thinking of every competitor. Google, too, had taken notice.

When Google's Peter Chane was interviewed by *Wired* and asked if "professionalism" in videos mattered, Chane said, "I dunno, but if you watch a video on the Web and you don't get it within a few seconds, you go to something else because it's so easy." This was an answer quite unlike what he would have given six months previously. When a reporter from the *Chicago Tribune* sat in on a meeting with Chane and his Google Video team at the Googleplex, the Googlers' frustration was evident. How could Google fail to offer a service superior to that of a tiny upstart with only sixty-some employees? "We look just like YouTube," Chane said. "We're a cleaner, more thoughtful YouTube—with less features."

YouTube had won the race against Google for content and viewers, but it had not figured out a feasible way to make money. Beginning in December 2005, YouTube began to run a few advertisements. They were displayed on its Web pages, not embedded in videos, and they were too few in number to bring in revenue of any real significance. But their presence on the site created a legal tempest. In July 2006, Robert Tur, a journalist and helicopter pilot, filed the first lawsuit against YouTube, accusing the company of profiting by the theft of copyrighted materials. A clause in the Digital Millennium Copyright Act prohibits a Web site from profiting from the display of copyrighted material, and YouTube's video collection was filled with clips that drew on copyrighted material. What had saved YouTube from legal action up until then was the absence of revenue. If YouTube was now going to advertise, that dodge would no longer work.

Tur had shot a video of the 1992 Los Angeles riots, and the footage ended up on YouTube without his authorization. YouTube's competitors, however, used this case as an opportunity to contrast YouTube's passive acceptance of infringing material with their own strict scrutiny. In August 2006, at the industry trade show Digital Hollywood, Revver's Oliver Luckett touted his company's policy of having a human editor screen every video before it was posted, which resulted in rejection of 10 to 50 percent of submissions due to the use of infringing material. He said that the copyright holders who were the victims of infringement by other sites—clearly a jab at

YouTube—were most often "the little guys," who were ignored by "the new kind of upstarts that don't respect their rights."

One of the "little guys," a woman filmmaker named Ahree Lee who had produced an experimental film for AtomFilms, was not pleased to see that her film *Me,* which consisted of a compilation of self-portraits that she took daily from 2001 to 2004, had been copied and uploaded on YouTube. AtomFilms provided its video creators a share of advertising revenue. Lee's film, which was drawing hundreds of thousands of views on AtomFilms's Web site, had the potential to produce significant income for Lee—until it was copied and uploaded to YouTube. She knew that if she filled out an online form at YouTube's site to request that the film be removed, YouTube would embark upon a lengthy process to determine whether Lee was, in fact, the copyright holder, which would take days, if not weeks. In the meantime, the brief moment when *Me* would be much discussed and viewed would have come and gone. Clip culture did not give any thought to the video creators; the culture imposed no restrictions on the instant gratification of viewers.

Lee happened to live close by YouTube's office in San Bruno, California, and she decided to present her case in person. She somehow managed to get past security and get the attention of someone who heard her out and offered to replace the full three-minute version on YouTube with an abridged one-minute version that at the end would direct viewers to AtomFilms, where viewers could generate income for Lee. A year later, the results were mixed: *Me* had been viewed about 600,000 times at AtomFilms, and more than 3.8 million times at YouTube. What portion of the YouTube views replaced AtomFilms's, and what portion of AtomFilms's visitors had been redirected from YouTube, was impossible to say. In any case, the episode offered little comfort to filmmakers who did not happen to live next door to YouTube.

One might have expected Google to join the other critics of YouTube and condemn the cavalier disregard for intellectual property rights that was found in clip culture. But Google elected to hold back, sensing an opportunity to benefit by adopting YouTube's model of hosting clips without the permission of the creators. Peter Chane was asked at a panel at Digital Hollywood what he thought about a hypothetical fan of *The Daily Show with Jon Stewart*, a regular viewer of the broadcast, who one night happened to miss the show and searched it out on an online video site. Chane said content creators were coming to the realization that posting segments of shows online was "a positive, not a negative." He reported that Google was finding more creators coming to it saying, "We *want* our clips to be online." Revver's Luckett shot back: "I don't see how Hollywood or TV Land . . . is real excited about content that they paid an exorbitant amount of money to produce and create and pay for the stars and do all that" being placed on YouTube for viewing for free. Yes, the actors on *The Daily Show* may be thrilled, because their own popularity is enhanced, but "the people that are monetizing it are probably not thrilled that the ads are stripped out and that it's floating around the Internet."

For YouTube, what the owners of *The Daily Show* thought about clips being uploaded without permission was in fact a vital unanswered question. They weren't a small independent filmmaker like Ahree Lee; *The Daily Show* was owned by media giant Viacom. Were YouTube to find itself in a legal battle with Viacom, it would not even be able to afford the legal equivalent of a slingshot. One hundred million downloads a day did not change the fact that YouTube was still a tiny start-up, just a little over a year old, with only seventy-eight employees and revenue of only about $10.6 million for the year, versus Viacom's $1.6 billion. YouTube also had yet to earn a profit.

Chen and Hurley also knew enough to admit to themselves that their legal arguments weren't likely to go very far in court. As Chen said, "I was really confident on the engineering side, the scalability side, that we could continue to grow out and be able to service the needs for the growth. But it was really more of the legal side . . . that there was just no way we could leverage or hire the resources alone." The two young men decided to approach Google and Yahoo to gauge their interest in acquiring their company.

The timing was perfect. At the very moment YouTube realized that it had made big-company enemies that it could not afford to defend itself against in court, Google realized that its homegrown

Google Video service would never be able to approach the popularity of YouTube. As soon as YouTube made itself available for acquisition, Google pounced. With a $1.65 billion bid that drew wide notice for the generosity of the valuation, Google wrapped up the acquisition quickly.

Before the deal closed, Sequoia's Roelof Botha was asked to explain why YouTube had become so much more popular than Google Video and all other competitors. Botha, whose firm had backed Google as well as YouTube, put his finger on the salient factor: YouTube, unlike Google Video, had become one of the handful of sites that many people visited daily. "At the end of the day, they take a break, have a laugh, want to be entertained." The network effect—the more videos uploaded, the more viewers and creators attracted, and then again the more videos uploaded—was critically important, creating what he described with dry understatement as "a bit of a snowball effect."

Google had recognized that the YouTube model, building a video site around entertainment and social networking, had bested its own dull model, which conceived of video as a professionally prepared information resource. But Google executives could not bear to state the obvious. When asked to comment on the YouTube acquisition, Sergey Brin said, "When I perform a search, I often find that the best answer is not necessarily a Web page. I know that sounds like heresy from Google, but in fact, if you are learning a sport, if you want to build a house, if you want to study a science, often videos are the best medium to learn about those things, to learn how to do those things." There it still was, the Google orthodoxy that it was doing nothing other than what it had always been doing, building out the world's largest reference room, and YouTube was a natural extension, purchased so that Google users could "study a science."

When the transaction was completed in October 2006, Google dropped the high-minded rationalizations and allowed YouTube to grow unimpeded, without imposing a Google master plan upon it. YouTube offices remained where they had been, in San Bruno, about twenty-five miles north of Google's Mountain View headquarters. Google's high command encouraged YouTube to carry on in the same raucous way it had, permitting users to upload almost anything they wished. A couple of initiatives to add some edifying content—such as debates among presidential candidates in the 2008 election campaigns and lectures taped from classes at the University of California, Berkeley, and other universities—did not change YouTube's essential character as the richest repository of popular culture to be found anywhere on the Internet.

Amusingly, its overwhelming lead in online video has not brought Google a new profitable way to "organize the world's information." For all its smarts and size, Google has not made much progress in answering the same vexing question that flummoxed YouTube two years earlier, when it was still a very small, very new, and very inexperienced company, which was, how does one make money from online video? Everything that Google has learned about matching relevant advertisements to users who are searching for something specific on the Web is all but useless in the different world of short video entertainment. And prospective advertisers are skittish about placing advertisements into an automated system that could match their brand with user-submitted videos that are tasteless, profane, or worse. Google is trying to gain users' acceptance of commercials that run as an overlay on top of selected videos, but the efforts have yet to produce revenue that is significant enough to warrant disclosure. An analyst with the Yankee Group said in March 2008 that he would be surprised if YouTube managed to take in $20 million in all of 2007. Yet it was spending about $1 million a day to pay for bandwidth. In April 2008, when Eric Schmidt was asked how Google planned to earn a profit from YouTube, he said that the answer continued to elude the company but it was now deemed "our highest priority this year."

As YouTube's traffic continues to expand, and Google adds still more features—introducing higher-resolution video in March 2008 and new software tools that will make it easier for Web site editors to utilize YouTube videos on their own sites, a program that Google calls YouTube Everywhere—its costs seem likely to increase faster than advertising revenue, at least in the short term.

No other Google venture has entailed an investment as large as this; no other venture brings in so much traffic for so little revenue.

It may well turn out to have been a shrewd bet. But its video assets have brought Google rather far away from its roots as a disinterested party that sent users elsewhere on the Web as speedily as possible, and have pulled it into the entertainment business, where it seeks to keep users happily engrossed with the video diversions that it stores on its own servers. If YouTube really holds an essential part of "the world's information," then so, too, does any media company. As long as Google keeps YouTube, there is no reason why it could not also acquire the *New York Times* or other media properties.

YouTube's motley collection of diversions stands so far outside of Google's original conception of information that what seems least likely is its present status as the company's sole major entertainment division, and one that continues to be a costly work in progress. Either Google will make additional investments in media properties, and deal with criticism that in doing so it is creating conflicts of interest with its core business in Web search, where it is ostensibly a neutral adjudicator of quality, or it will decide that it does not want to be in the entertainment business after all and shed YouTube. The course it adopts will probably be decided not by internal etymological discussions about the meaning of *information* but by scrutinizing the profit/loss statements for the YouTube division—and by estimating the enhanced value to the Google brand from YouTube's astonishing volume of traffic.

YouTube is an anomaly, a venture that raises questions about Google's commitment to the original interpretation of its charter. Other experiments have served to expand dramatically the range of Google's information offerings, too, but have done so in a way that reinforces Google's role as the neutral reference librarian. These have been smooth, natural extensions of Google's strength in organizing disorderly masses of data. Perhaps the one service that shows Google's innovative work in information organization at its best is the one that has added a spatial dimension to everyday information seeking. By integrating geographic information with nongeographic information, conveniently, ingeniously, even entertainingly, Google allows users to see the world in ways never possible before.

CHAPTER 6

Small World, After All

In 2004, Sergey Brin came across a very small company whose online service accomplished very big things: one could use it to travel, virtually speaking, anywhere on earth, with satellite imagery used to provide a visually riveting experience. He was eager to share his discovery of this technical marvel with fellow members of Google's executive team. He interrupted a routine meeting with a demonstration that got everyone's attention. With his laptop computer, he "flew" from a high altitude down to the house of every executive in the room.

It was a feat that required the manipulation of enormous quantities of digital data. Some forms of information can be stored compactly, some not. Web pages composed of text take little space. In 1998, the year of Google's founding, the entire World Wide Web could be stored on hard drives that fit within a dorm room. Such compact storage was possible only because most of the Web's information consisted of text. But were one to think about information about the real world, the information that covers the earth's 57,300,000 square miles of land, considerably more disk space and computing power would be required. Collections of satellite images of the earth constitute one of the bulkiest collections in the entire digital universe—these are measured not in gigabytes or in terabytes, but in petabytes, or millions of gigabytes.

With Brin's demonstration of effortless virtual flight anywhere— using just a laptop—he showed his Google colleagues that technology had evolved sufficiently to make it possible for the general public, using ordinary hardware, to enjoy access to the database of photographs that had only recently been limited to the defense establishment. Still, it was a novelty, a little bit of science and a little bit of entertainment, and nothing more. Brin would convince the others that the imagery of the earth, when integrated with other information in Google's storehouses, could be used for a more ambitious purpose that would reorient the starting point for information searches, literally and figuratively. Instead of beginning with a text phrase, a user could begin with a place. The globe itself could become the organizing structure for information—the idea that would lead to the release of a new product, Google Earth.

The possibility of using geography to organize the world's information was contemplated only because photographic images enlivened maps in new ways, making them nigh irresistible. Satellites equipped to take photographs of the earth were first launched by the U.S. government in the 1950s, and civilian access to the images was limited. But in the 1990s, the U.S. government relaxed its controls and began to permit private companies to launch satellites designed expressly to gather high-resolution digital images of the earth for commercial purposes.

Technically, it seemed easier to send satellites aloft than it was to work with the massive digital files that they sent back down to earth. The images could be used most conveniently if they could be stitched together in a seamless way, creating on a computer screen a virtual globe that a user could navigate by pointing a mouse in any direction. In the late 1990s, there was only one place in the world with the computing resources that were necessary: the basement of the Pentagon, with a machine room outfitted with the biggest beasts in graphics supercomputing, made by Silicon Graphics, the company that had made a name as supplier of the machines used in Hollywood for digital special effects in *The Terminator* and *Jurassic Park*.

In just a few years, however, a virtual globe constructed with satellite images could be displayed not just at the Pentagon, but on any PC connected to the Internet. In Google's hands, the satellite images of the earth would be integrated with overlays of city streets, geotagged photographs and videos, local business listings, and hundreds of other categories of information, many of which were formerly not thought of as geographic in nature but that could be tied in some way to place. Literary biography, for example, can be expressed in a geographic dimension. A "Jane Austen layer" can be superimposed on the earth, showing the places Austen lived or visited, the actual places that appear in her writing, and the places used in the film adaptations of her books.

The geographic possibilities were not limited to just one planet. Images of the moon, Mars, and constellations filled in a panoramic view of the entire cosmos. Google could provide its users with ready access to the remotest corner of the universe because of the founders' original fixation on building unlimited computing capacity. All of its geographic services were handled by the same ever-growing supercomputer designed originally for storing copies of Web pages.

Google has made the earth seem like a single cozy place. But in so doing, it has also made our own presence more visible, whether we wish that or not. We have begun to realize, belatedly, that distance serves to protect our anonymity and privacy. Within the small virtual world, where anyone can see every place and, as photographs are melded with maps, every earthbound resident becomes increasingly visible to more and more people, an individual's sense of privacy dissolves as fast as the earth seems to shrink.

The technology that Google used to shrink the globe was not produced originally by Google's own engineers. As was the case with YouTube, here, too, a tiny start-up jumped far ahead of the much bulkier, slower-moving Google. The service that the general public would later come to know as Google Earth was pioneered by Keyhole, a small start-up company located in Google's backyard.

Keyhole's founders foresaw that finding ways to give the public convenient access to satellite images of the earth would lead to a myriad of uses of the images. In this regard, they were extremely prescient. They were not at all sure about how to go about making a business out of such possibilities, however. What Keyhole planned was a subscription-based online service that would provide consumers with the ability to use a PC to fly around a three-dimensional virtual earth, using actual satellite images instead of the machine-generated geometric shapes of computer games. But when Keyhole was founded in 2000, the world was not yet prepared to look at itself as it actually appears in real images.

Viewing a single detailed image of the earth was one thing; viewing a seamless mosaic of images was quite another, and still required the processing power of a supercomputer. Keyhole's engineers came from companies in business lines that were serious (scientific visual simulation) and fun (computer gaming). They sensed that an opportunity would eventually open up for companies that offered the general public online access to a globe composed of satellite images. Customers' own personal computers, outfitted with 3D graphics cards and speedier Internet connections, would be able to handle the massive amounts of geo-spatial data entailed.

Preparations for greeting the future opportunity had to be timed well, though. If you start early enough, as Keyhole did, you do not have competition. Start too early, however, and you risk exhausting your start-up capital before the conditions for the new market are in place. Keyhole came very close to going under. Google's (and YouTube's) history excepted, most Silicon Valley start-ups do not execute perfect timing—and perish. Keyhole was fortunate to squeak by.

In 2000, most home Internet users relied on dial-up modems that were only about ⅙₀ the speed of a cable modem connection today. Moving the satellite images, which were stored as large files, from the centralized server to a user's PC posed a seemingly insurmountable obstacle. Keyhole's founding goal was to find ways to give the user the sensation of being able to fly anywhere on earth, without periodically encountering a frozen image on the computer screen while new data needed for display was downloaded.

By January 2001, Keyhole had put into place the necessary pieces for realizing its grand vision. It designed software that displayed one image while simultaneously fetching adjacent images that could be displayed next, allowing the user to move smoothly in any direction. The company struck a deal to have its software distributed by Excite@Home, a new company funded by Kleiner Perkins that was going to provide fast broadband connections to everyone. And it secured $4.6 million in first-round financing from Sony Broadband Entertainment. With the funds, it expanded its staff to twenty-five and readied its product for the mass market, spending to be in a position to hit the milestones it needed to reach in order to receive the second round of financing.

By the spring of 2001, however, the dot-com boom had gone bust and the Valley became a very inhospitable place for fledgling companies. Keyhole's CEO, John Hanke, would later describe the time as "our generational equivalent of the stock market crash of the 1920s." Excite@Home went out of business, and Sony shut down its venture capital arm. Keyhole lost both the mass distribution and the follow-on financing it had been counting on. No replacements were to be had. The plan to offer Keyhole's service to the consumer market had to be shelved.

Desperate for revenue, Keyhole rented some booth space at a trade show for commercial real estate brokers in June 2001 in Dallas. Visitors to the booth were able to fly wherever they wanted—from Dallas to Los Angeles, to Phoenix, to Miami, *click click click*—and were probably the first civilians outside of the Pentagon and Keyhole's offices to experience seamless virtual flying with real satellite images. Jim Young, the executive in charge of the show, was immediately smitten and told the attendees that Keyhole's software would transform the industry. Sales to the commercial real estate business saved Keyhole from extinction. With brokers willing to pay $1,000 a year for a subscription, and invest in a brawny $3,000 PC that could handle the graphics processing, Keyhole was able to eke out an existence and continue looking for ways to find a bigger market.

The news business offered one promising opportunity. CNN was keen to use Keyhole's software, called EarthViewer, for zooming down to wherever the moment's news stories were breaking. On the verge of CNN's signing a high nine-digit deal with Keyhole, however, budget cuts were ordered. CNN revoked the offer and instead offered Keyhole a take-it-or-leave-it arrangement in which CNN would receive permission to use Keyhole's software, and in exchange

CNN would pay a token fee and display "earthviewer.com" in a corner of the screen. Hanke was not inclined to agree—he was staring at a $300,000 revenue shortfall and an upcoming payroll that could not be met—but in the end he accepted.

In March 2003 in the opening "shock and awe" of the Iraq war, CNN's EarthViewer simulation of bombing missions over Baghdad, including dramatic swoops down to street level, brought Keyhole's software to the attention of millions of CNN viewers. Keyhole had a tiny customer base at the time, and when the exposure on CNN brought many curious visitors to its Web site, the servers could not handle the load and the site went down. The promotional plug on CNN brought not only the curious but also paying customers, enabling the company to drop the price of a Keyhole Pro subscription to $400 annually.

Keyhole benefited from the hard times prevailing in Silicon Valley in two respects. It didn't have to worry about competing start-ups, the bane of any new company in the Valley. After the crash, new companies that would have crowded into Keyhole's niche could not obtain financing. Keyhole also did not have to worry that it would lose its top engineers to other companies in the Valley dangling tempting packages of stock options. Few companies could go public between 2001 and 2003, so its engineers were not tempted to quit their jobs and chase after seemingly better opportunities that would come with an imminent IPO.

By 2004, however, venture capital firms had cleaned up their portfolios and were starting to look at deals again. Keyhole had made it through the bleak years by relying primarily on sales to real estate professionals, government agencies, and engineering firms. The time had arrived for it to dust off its original plans and try to sell its service to consumers, providing anyone with the ability to circumnavigate a virtual globe.

Hanke visited venture capital firms, found interest, and quickly received an offer for a sizable investment. It was just then, in May 2004, in the midst of finalizing the details of the deal, that Keyhole was invited by Google, its neighbor just six blocks away, to pay a friendly visit and make a presentation. Keyhole did not see why

Google was interested, and its first question was, what do satellite images have to do with Web search? The answer was: Think big. Think of geography as more than road maps and driving directions, like MapQuest. Think of geography as a window upon all information. Think of the earth itself as an organizing device for all categories of information, and satellite images as the way to pull users into a geographic framework. Think of how a user interested in, say, the history of Iraq could virtually fly down into Baghdad, where street-level images would lead to historical documents. The way the Googlers saw the possibilities, satellite images could have everything to do with Web search and any other kind of information search as well.

Google hadn't gone public yet and little was known on the outside about whether the company was doing well or was improvidently spending a dwindling pile of cash on its gourmet cafeterias and other frivolities, reminiscent of Valley spending at its most reckless, circa 1999. Hanke and his colleagues had heard rumors about Google but friends who were working there were secretive. He later recalled, "It was like peeking over the fence of your rich neighbor's house: what's really going on over there?" Now the Keyhole team found themselves on the other side of the fence, in a Google conference room. They faced six Googlers, a mix of business-development people and long-haired male engineers, and were surprised that the Googlers knew all about Keyhole and its software. Was this good, an indication that Google might be interested in acquiring the company? Or did it mean that Google was planning to offer a similar service of its own, which for Keyhole would be catastrophic? The Keyhole team could not read the faces of the Google representatives.

The next day Google called to say it was interested in acquiring the company.

Keyhole had previously tried to sell its technology to Web portals, like Yahoo, that were already using MapQuest and seemed most likely to be receptive to Keyhole's proposal to offer satellite imagery as complementary to road maps. Google did not disclose that it had formed a small group, what would eventually be called Google Maps, to develop its own maps and directions service that would be similar to MapQuest. But in Google's grand conception, maps would serve a larger purpose as one of several related components, along with satellite images and geographic information, to "organize the world's information."

On its own, Keyhole had never even conceived of anything so ambitious. Nor had any of the other companies Keyhole had approached spoken of geography as a universal information tool in such a radically unorthodox way. Hanke recalled, "This was not just a breath of fresh air—it was a *blast*! We thought, they are either delusional or they're visionary."

Another consideration in weighing Google's offer was the likelihood that Google would be able to popularize Keyhole's service much faster than Keyhole itself could. This alone was a powerful inducement to strike a deal. In Silicon Valley, most engineers work on projects that will never be completed—this holds true at large companies as well as small. If engineers are lucky enough to witness the rare day when the product is completed and launched, they will, in the overwhelming majority of cases, witness the product's failure in the marketplace. Hanke said, "Engineers live in fear of pouring their heart and soul into a project for two years, and then having it basically go on a hard drive and never see the light of day, certainly never see satisfied users, and never hear anyone say, 'Hey, that's an amazing program that you've written.'" Having Google express an interest in their work brought everyone at Keyhole closer to realization of the dream that not just thousands of people, but possibly, maybe, if the possibility could be imagined without jinxing it, *millions* of people would use it someday.

The Google offer was a mix of cash and stock. Whether the stock would really be worth much at any point was an open question. But when Google disclosed to Keyhole its current income statement, worries on that score were removed. What the public could not yet see was that Google's Web search advertising was making a nice profit. Keyhole agreed to be acquired, and over a weekend, the company moved into an empty Google building. Also installed on the floor was the Google team that was working on Google Maps, whose core had come from another recent acquisition, Where2 LLC. No formal organization chart brought the Google Maps and Keyhole teams together. The plan was simple: put engineers with similar interests in the vicinity of one another and let them figure out who would like to work with whom. This reflected the preference of the senior triumvirate to use a light touch in creating formal hierarchies at the lower levels and permit teams to organize themselves as much as possible.

Google Maps was well along in development when Google's acquisition of Keyhole was completed in October 2004. When Maps was released in February 2005, the Keyhole technology was not yet integrated with Google's. The principal innovation that Google Maps offered in its very first incarnation was providing users the ability to use a mouse to drag the map in any direction, which brought into view adjacent areas without needing to redraw the entire page, creating an illusion that the computer had maps of the entire world at the ready—it accomplished this by downloading only the data needed to extend the map that was being displayed. It showed streets and driving directions, but did not yet offer an option to display a satellite image as an underlying layer beneath the street grid.

Keyhole would provide the satellite imagery for Google Maps. But Maps was designed to display a single square of roads, and was not designed for high-speed travel. Although one could move in any direction, it was not much faster than walking by foot. It did not permit one to fly around the globe the way Keyhole's own software permitted. Technical limitations of Web browsers like Internet Explorer or Firefox made it impossible to provide smooth navigation of high-resolution images. Google wanted to offer users the same breathtaking three-dimensional flight that Keyhole had offered: Keyhole promised in 2004 that "you can fly through 12+ Terabytes of Earth imagery and data—spinning, rotating, tilting and zooming—think magic carpet ride." But users had to first install the specialized Earth-Viewer software that Keyhole had developed, which Google renamed Google Earth. This irksome extra step presented a marketing challenge to Google: its users, who were accustomed to using its other services without being asked to install additional software, had to be persuaded to go to the trouble of downloading the Google Earth software to their computers before they could take a test flight.

To encourage users to give it a try, Google decided to make Google Earth available for free, without a subscription fee, at least for home and personal use. Nor did it rush to collect a payoff immediately by placing advertising for local businesses on the images—advertisements would begin to show up only six months after its release. Google, no less than the Keyhole team, was giddy about bringing to a mass audience this new way of accessing information; as work proceeded prior to the launch, business considerations were not uppermost in their minds.

The Keyhole database that Google acquired was not all that Google hoped for. As a start-up, Keyhole had limited resources and had decided to focus on buying the images most likely to be of interest to its customers, who happened to be in the United States. Its coverage of the rest of the globe's surface was skimpy. This would not do for Google, which took considerable pride in the global reach of its business. Brin, who was born in Moscow and emigrated to the United States with his family at the age of six, was the one who most insistently pushed the Keyhole team to think outside U.S. borders. How could Google release a product called Google Earth that had only scanty coverage of most of the world? The staff set to work acquiring a globe-spanning collection of satellite images.

As the preparations for the release of Google Earth were under way, Google Maps did its part to draw more users to Google. That was accomplished by clever individuals outside of Google who wrote code so that data from outside of Google could automatically be superimposed upon a Google map, creating new uses for maps and giving users new ways to think geographically. Google made this possible when it permitted its users to pull map data from Google's servers to create their own hybrid mixes of maps and data, which were handled by their own Web servers. The new creations were called *mashups.*

The first Google Maps mashup was devised by Paul Rademacher, a software developer at DreamWorks Animation. He perceived that housing ads on Craigslist could be linked to a Google map and wrote code that showed each listing as a push pin in the appropriate place on a map. The Web site he set up, HousingMaps, immediately drew thousands of grateful Craigslist apartment hunters. Google noticed, and added features that made developing mashups easier. Its first step: Google hired Rademacher.

When Google Maps were enhanced by mashups, they were capable of showing much more than streets. Mashups mapped fast food restaurants in San Francisco and other cities; lowest gas prices in New York State and other places; crime reports for Chicago and other cities; and news stories in the day's *New York Times* or other news outlets. These and thousands of other mashup sites served as an introductory version of a geographic interface to other information that had not been originally organized by geographic references.

When Google Earth was released in June 2005, its database of satellite images had been filled out and made truly global. Anyone who took the trouble to install the software could zoom to any destination on the globe, but the one place that most users wanted to see first was their own home. (Brin had anticipated that this would be the case when he had given each of his colleagues a quick visit to their homes, one by one, when he had provided them with a demonstration of Keyhole's software the year before.) Not everyone was impressed by Google Earth. Barry Diller, CEO of IAC/Inter-ActiveCorp, whose holdings included Google competitor Ask Jeeves, scoffed, "After you've seen your house and all those other buildings that look like toothpicks from that height, what do you do?"

To begin with, one could indulge in armchair tourism, and go anywhere—reaching Timbuktu, Mali, took a traveler in North America about three seconds, the same time it took for the computer to zoom up, zip over, and then zoom down to any other spot. Eric Schmidt recounted in public talks how he had fulfilled a lifelong ambition—to visit Everest—from the comfort of his office. Web sites like Virtual Globetrotting, Google Earth Hacks, and Google Sightseeing popped up, displaying the most interesting satellite images that users had stumbled upon (the tagline for the latter site was "Why Bother Seeing the World For Real?"). Virtual tourism was highly diverting, but it didn't fully answer Diller's challenge.

Enthusiasts showed the way, building their own layers of information, annotations, photographs, and mashups on top of Google

Earth. Google would eventually even give users some latitude to correct the locations of houses and businesses and add new places. User contributions gave the service a distinctly noncommercial feel. Yet when users wanted to find goods or services in a particular place, Google Earth was ready to supply local business listings, which gave its users a second reason to rely upon it. Users could see exactly where they needed to go to find whatever it was they sought, and could do so staying within the familiar mini world of Google Earth.

Google sought to minimize irritating its users with requests to fill out many boxes on a screen when they wanted to see local businesses placed on a satellite image. Thanks to its work on algorithms in other parts of Google's business, Google Earth software was able to pull apart a phrase like "cheap hotels NYC" and distinguish which part referred to a place and which part described what was sought, and then place upon an aerial view of New York an overlay of inexpensive hotels.

Finding local businesses this way was as easy as using the yellow pages, but initially the public simply shrugged. Not everyone wanted to take the time to download the Google Earth software onto his or her computer. If one wished to use Google Earth simply to find nearby businesses, one did not get a chance to experience the sensation of flying, and Google Maps served perfectly well for finding a local plumber or nail salon.

Yet Google Earth, with its capacity to incorporate the creative additions of enthusiastic volunteers who were excited about the technical capabilities of the software, grew and grew. Before long, hundreds of thousands of different answers to Diller's question spontaneously bubbled up. Humanitarian uses of Google Earth made front-page headlines. When Hurricane Katrina struck, the service helped the Coast Guard rescue victims by comparing images before and after the flooding, revealing the places where housing had been inundated. Its images elsewhere dramatized the effects of clear-cut logging in the Amazon rain forest in Brazil, and it provided the U.S. Holocaust Memorial Museum the means to visually bring home the ravages of genocide in Darfur.

Google Earth gave users the feeling that physical distance did not matter, that everyone on earth was one's neighbor, close at hand. It vanquished the very distinction between the familiar and the unknown; all places could be known, or at least felt as if they could be known, when they, too, could be visited and brought rapidly into focus as the user experienced the sensation of flying halfway around the globe, descending from a high altitude until reaching a hovering point near the ground, all accomplished in a couple of seconds. In 2007, John Hanke said in an interview:

> The ability of people to connect from the very local to the earth as a whole then back to their own, very local place, is a really powerful way to make these connections that might otherwise be remote and abstract. We're inclined to think of events as happening "out there somewhere"—"somewhere else"—and I think there's something in the experience of flying with this continuous motion from a place that you know and the familiar details of your town or city or community to this remote area, where you can also see recognizable human details, you make that connection. Historically, with *National Geographic,* you have this beautiful map, and then you have this beautiful picture, or this disturbing picture, and it's up to you to make this connection between yourself and a shape on the map. That's a pretty hard thing to do and is very different from starting out and just continuously flying in, and then the details resolve as you're coming down in this continuous zoom. It's not just the dot on a map.

American astronaut Bill Anders's photos of the earth, taken in 1968 during the Apollo 8 mission, had vividly shown earth's inhabitants how small a place the planet seemed when framed against the void. Now, Google Earth made the planet seem even smaller, a place where we are all virtual neighbors, separated by only a few mouse clicks. Robert M. Samborski, executive director of the Geospatial Information and Technology Association, a trade organization, said in 2006, only a year after the release of Google Maps and Google Earth, that "Google's done more to raise the awareness of using maps than the industry's been able to do in the past twenty-five years."

Google Earth also drew attention for its utility in less serious pursuits. Oddities turned up among its images. The Badlands Guardian, for example, a natural geologic formation near Alberta, Canada, was often visited by online aviators. It resembles a human head, wearing Native American headdress—and also appears to be naturally adorned with iPod-like earbuds that hang down—on a scale that makes the figures on Mount Rushmore look like miniatures. One could also pay an overhead visit to the Arizona farmer who carved a giant portrait of Oprah Winfrey across ten acres of cropland, or to the forty year-old barracks complex at a U.S. Navy base near San Diego that, from an aerial view, resembled a swastika.

Sky in Google Earth, introduced in 2007, allows viewers to look upward and travel to individual stars (100 million) and distant galaxies (200 million). Attention could also be redirected back down to earth to a more familiar group of stars, found in Hollywood and its vicinity. Fans with no official connection to Google added home listings for Tom Cruise, Halle Berry, George Clooney, Angelina Jolie, and other film notables. Software that could be used for such breathtakingly disparate purposes, high and low—with the power to send a traveler either to the farthest edge of the known universe or to hover above Jim Carrey's estate—makes anywhere and everywhere appear accessible. The natural corollary, which was not fully appreciated at first, was that soon every nonfamous person in the universe will be accessible to everyone else.

Shortly after John Hanke joined Google, he began to hear the first rumblings of the general public's uneasiness about satellite images breaching the privacy of individuals. Hanke attempted to allay concerns by explaining that the satellite images that Google used were generally six to twelve months old. Users could not swoop down and spy on a neighbor's back yard in real time. Nor was the resolution of the photographs sufficient to permit a Google user to pick out any meaningful details. He added reassuringly: "It's not like you are going to be able to read a license plate on a car or see what an individual was doing when a particular image was taken."

Strictly speaking, Hanke was correct: the resolution of the commercially available satellite imagery at that time was insufficient to portray clearly objects that were smaller than two feet. The resolution was improving rapidly, however. Aerial images—that is, those taken at very high resolution by airplanes at much lower altitudes than satellites—would increasingly be Google's source of images for densely populated places. Only a year later, in 2006, the first sighting of seminude sunbathers visible in images snapped by an aerial camera excited much commentary on blogs around the world. The human figures are just barely discernible atop a house in the Netherlands; they drew attention not because they are distinct enough to be prurient but because the image graphically conveyed just how far aerial imaging technology had advanced. Surely the woman who was basking in the sun topless, facedown on the deck of her own house, did not realize that she was publicly visible—from far, far above.

Aerial photography would not seem to be all that intrusive, not when compared to what soon arrived: cameras mounted at street level. Just as Hanke was trying to reassure the public, a Google competitor launched by Amazon, called A9, dispatched camera crews to drive along the streets of ten major cities and snap photos of the storefronts of every business, with the ambition of eventually including every business in the country. Soon after, Microsoft announced, in December 2005, the availability in beta form of what it called "bird's-eye imagery" for cities covering about 25 percent of the U.S. population. The birdie, which was a low-flying aircraft, took pictures at a 45 degree angle, which made the landscape much easier to recognize and provided far more useful information than images taken from directly above cityscape objects.

These initiatives were logical extensions of the same project that Keyhole had begun and that Google was putting its own considerable weight behind, combining the specificity of a photograph with the abstraction of a map. Satellite images were the easiest way to get started and cover large swatches of the earth quickly. But the project had a logic of its own: the closer to the ground and the more detailed the images, the more useful they would be to users. A year after Google Earth's introduction, Google was well along in upgrading its medium-resolution images, which represented 15 meters per pixel, with high-resolution ones at 70 centimeters per pixel that covered about one-third of the global population and provided sufficient detail to pick out cars and houses. Images with still finer resolution, of 10 centimeters per pixel, would follow. So, too, would a fully featured flight simulator, tucked into a new software release without announcement—Google seemed almost embarrassed by the technical riches that it was able to incorporate into Google Earth.

The problem was that there was no natural way of determining that 15-meters-per-pixel resolution was socially acceptable but 10-centimeters-per-pixel resolution was overly invasive. Nor was there any law or code that decreed shots taken from above were acceptable but street-level views were not. If you were in the mapping business, you would seek out as many images, in as high a resolution as you could, from whatever vantage point provided the most visual information.

Neither Google nor its rivals had any choice: in the information business, an imperative is at work, pressing for more, more, more. Right from the start, with its insistence on indexing all Web sites, not just a good selection, Google had appreciated the need for completeness. In its Book Search program, it showed a willingness to take on the most daunting of logistical challenges. With such new services as Google Earth and Google Maps, Google tried to offer products that were more comprehensive than its competitors, but its rivals were in close pursuit. In the heat of this competition, no company was willing to pause and ask whether it had gone too far, breaching individuals' reasonable expectations of personal privacy.

Google's introduction of Street View to Google Maps in May 2007 was inevitable, not only because of Google's own history and increased competition, but also because the combination of street-level photographs with street maps was so natural a pairing. In fact this combination was so natural that it had been discovered a full century before, in the early days of automobiles. In 1907 Rand McNally published *Photo-Auto Maps,* which used photographs of streets and landmarks, with an overlay of helpful arrows, to show drivers a recommended route.

Inevitable as Google Maps's Street View was, if considered in the long view of events, its introduction was not universally well received. Initially, only streets in San Francisco, New York, Las Vegas, Miami, and Denver were available for viewing, but this was sufficient to produce many complaints about breached privacy. Mary Kalin-Casey, who wrote to the popular tech blog *BoingBoing,* received wide attention as an early "victim"—her complaint was that her cat was plainly visible in the Street View image that included the exterior of her living room window. Kalin-Casey wrote, "I'm all for mapping, but this feature literally gives me the shakes."

Wired magazine's blog invited readers to submit the most interesting "urban street sightings" found among Google Maps's Street View images. Among the entries that readers voted as favorites were several photographs of young women in bathing suits lying on the grass ("Stanford coeds enjoying the sun"); a woman in a car whose door was open as she prepared to step out, and though her face could not be seen, a portion of her underwear could ("I think I see a thong!"); and a man apparently climbing up the front of a locked security gate ("Break-in in progress").

Just as with the reaction to Book Search, Google was taken aback by the negative publicity Street View generated. After all, its cameras saw nothing more than what anyone who was driving down the same streets at the same time would have seen. The company had taken one precaution: it had anticipated the need to protect the identities of anyone in the vicinity of domestic violence shelters and had removed images of the shelters. Other than that, Google had proceeded on the reasonable assumption that it need not treat public space as if it were private.

What neither Google nor its critics realized was that our anonymity while walking about in public space in the predigital age was protected not by law but by the crude state of technology—we felt invisible only because cameras were not in place to capture our images. Similarly, what had once been a paper trail of our unwanted encounters with the legal system remained invisible, practically speaking, because it sat in folders in the courthouse, requiring that a curious citizen expend energy and time in order to examine it. Placing those records online, where they could be easily accessed by anyone, from any PC connected to the Internet, accomplished what street-view images also did: things that were always a part of public space were rendered easy to see for the first time.

As always, Google was preoccupied with its quest to improve the technology for gathering information and serving it up to viewers in useful ways. Its engineers had done exactly what they were supposed to do. They had built software that melded street maps and photographic images and devised ways to improve existing technology. In the case of four of the first five cities covered by Street View, Google had relied on images collected by another company, Immersive Media, which had invented a "geoimmersive" video camera that resembled a ball, with eleven lenses distributed around its surface. When mounted upon the roof of a car or van, it recorded a spherical video, continuously tagged with GPS data, that when played back could provide a 360-degree view from any spot. Not wholly satisfied with Immersive Media's images, however, Google had also tried out its own equipment for San Francisco's streets, which produced similar 360-degree views with the added improvement of extremely high resolution. The difference in quality was striking. When Lance Ulanoff, an editor at *PC Magazine,* attempted to sharpen with the help of Photoshop the somewhat blurry face of a woman that Google Street View had captured on the streets of New York, he found that the resolution was simply too poor. But in San Francisco's Street View images he could easily read license plates—and also see in sharp detail the man who had become infamous on the Internet because he happened to be standing in front of a strip club when the Google camera car happened by.

Legally speaking, Google was absolutely correct to argue, as Peter Fleischer, the company's global privacy counsel, did, that "in the U.S., there's a long and noble tradition of 'public spaces,' where people don't have the same expectations of privacy as they do in their homes. This tradition helps protect journalists, for example." Practically speaking, however, Google had to back down in the face of heated criticism. About ten days after the product was launched, the company began to remove images when an individual discovered his or her face in the Street View image and asked Google to remove it.

Tellingly, Google accommodated these requests without publicly announcing that it was doing so. Schmidt, Page, and Brin still hoped to preserve the general principle that individuals did not enjoy a right to privacy when standing in public space. A few months later, however, Google retreated further, acknowledging that it would remove any image that contained a person's face or license number, regardless of who submitted the request. Having conceded the point that the faces that incidentally appear in the images have no bearing on the usefulness of its street views, it was just a matter of time before Google attempted to automate the process of removing facial detail. In May 2008, the company began to test software that automatically blurred faces on its New York images.

Google did not rush to introduce Street View for Google Maps outside of the United States. Without precedents established elsewhere by other companies for street views, Google anticipated an international outcry about invasions of privacy. Satellite photos had already led to much grief for Google. When Google Earth was introduced, the governments of South Korea, Thailand, and Russia complained about images in which military facilities and government buildings were clearly in view. A Russian security analyst acidly said, "Terrorists don't need to reconnoiter their target. Now an American company is working for them." Google retorted that whether it displayed the images or not, it could not stop their circulation online because they originated from other sources, but this line of argument did not appease the governments that were upset.

When the RAND Corporation looked in 2004 at the availability of geo-spatial information, including satellite images, that would "help terrorists and other hostile forces mount attacks in the U.S.," it concluded that less than 1 percent of geo-spatial information that was made publicly available on federal Web sites and databases was not readily available elsewhere. Federal, state, and local government officials, apparently unaware of the fact that satellite images that Google Earth used were supplied to Google by other companies and widely distributed, did not hesitate in ordering Google to remove from Google Earth whatever images they deemed compromising to national security. Vice President Dick Cheney's residence at the U.S. Naval Observatory in Washington, the U.S. Capitol, and the

U.S. Military Academy at West Point were declared off-limits. The zeal of some officials extended also to protecting prying eyes from seeing overhead views of an amusement park in Rye, New York, a sewage treatment plant in Yonkers, and the site of dearest importance to our national security, the headquarters of PepsiCo, in Purchase. The futility of these measures was revealed in many instances when the images that were removed from Google were discovered on other sites. For example, a nuclear power plant in Ohio that was blacked out on Google Maps was available in clear detail on Microsoft's maps. Massachusetts officials, who tried to obscure the locations of state facilities in images they supplied to Google, were left looking foolish when Microsoft and Yahoo obtained undoctored images of the same state facilities from commercial sources.

Nonetheless, it was Google that was depicted as acting irresponsibly. One cartoon showed a barber offering a customer not just a mirror but also a PDA to use to examine the just-completed haircut: "Would you like to see the top on Google Earth?" This was harmless fun, but more serious criticisms were leveled. In June 2007, in the wake of arrests related to a plot to blow up fuel tanks at Kennedy International Airport, Thomas P. DiNapoli, New York's state comptroller, held a press conference and criticized online mapping services, naming Google Earth in particular, for providing "too much information" that "might compromise counterterrorism efforts." The suspects had used Google Earth to obtain an aerial view of the airport, but how this provided "too much information" was not clear—the New York Times accompanied its news story of the plot with an aerial photograph showing in crystalline detail the same fuel tanks at JFK. Still, the temptation to demonize Google was irresistible. Assemblyman Michael N. Gianaris chimed in: "In light of the use of Google Earth in the JFK plot, we must ensure these programs are not used as blueprints for an attack on our country."

Hearing such alarms, Americans naturally would feel a tug of worry about national security vulnerabilities. In such circumstances, we all too readily forget the bedrock democratic principle that American librarians have always understood and protected: access to information must never be subject to government control. Classified military secrets are the only permissible exception. Censoring images shown by Google Earth is no more effective than censoring book acquisitions at the local public library: the information originates elsewhere and will circulate no matter what symbolic action may be taken at one particular place to block its distribution.

The abundance of information that is now available online was brought home to Google's own Eric Schmidt in 2005, a few months after Google Maps was released. When Elinor Mills, a reporter for CNET News, decided to explore a story about Google and threats to personal privacy, she devised an interesting exercise: she gave herself thirty minutes to see what personal information could be discovered about Eric Schmidt using Google.

Schmidt's net worth, his political fund-raising activities, and his hobbies were readily found. Mills wrote, "That such detailed personal information is so readily available on public Web sites makes most people uncomfortable." Schmidt lashed out wildly, not at the public Web sites on which his personal information resided, but at the messenger that delivered the news. CNET was informed that Google was unhappy with the use of Schmidt's "private information" in its story and as punishment Google as a matter of company policy would not respond to any questions or requests submitted by CNET reporters for one year.

Ridicule was heaped upon Schmidt from various quarters. The *Register* derided his "hissy fit"; hadn't Schmidt promised publicly to build "a Google that knows more about you"? A *New York Times* headline sardonically read, "Google Anything So Long As It's Not Google."

Schmidt, of all people, should have understood that CNET, like Google, cannot control what information is placed on the Web sites of other organizations. His bizarre reaction overshadowed Mills's original story, which had been quite discreet, in fact, in not putting in the story Schmidt's home address, which she also found online. If she had wanted to, she could have used Google Maps to give her readers handy directions to Schmidt's home doorstep.

In speeding the democratization of technology and information, Google had made the world a smaller, more intimate place. But in a small world, its wealthiest residents feel more vulnerable to unseen threats. This had not been anticipated by Schmidt or anyone in the Google conference room when Brin had used Keyhole's software to "fly" to the houses of the others.

After two months passed and Schmidt had regained his composure, Google quietly restored a normal working relationship with CNET. Schmidt never released a public mea culpa. But by dropping the sanctions against the news organization, he belatedly showed his understanding that he had undermined Google's most basic message, which is that users will find online, with Google's assistance, whatever information they need. The company has helped to bring a high-resolution view of the entire globe within reach of our itchy fingertips, but if anyone believes the drawbacks outweigh the benefits, blame cannot be assigned to any one company. The world is experienced as smaller because computer technology now makes it possible for it to seem so, and that technology does not come with an "undo" button.

Google Maps's Street View created unease not just because images of identifiable people were being collected but because it was Google that was doing the collecting, the company that seemed to be collecting more and more information about everything. Had another company, say MapQuest, introduced Street View, a company that wasn't attempting to "organize the world's information" and didn't possess information other than road maps, directions, and traffic conditions, it seems unlikely that Street View would have excited the same reaction.

Before long, we are likely to look back upon Street View or the first-generation mashup as crude experiments. We will come to rely upon mashups that combine not two but many disparate sources of information—restaurants, menus, professional reviews, customer reviews, health department inspection reports, the presence of friends in the vicinity, one-click reservations—overlaid onto a single map, updated continuously. And we will become accustomed to having access to all of this information, seamlessly integrated together, anywhere we happen to be, on any Internet-connected device, on any screen, tiny as well as large.

The Google vision is of a multidimensional mashing together of all information, integrated in novel ways yet instantly accessible from a centralized computing "cloud." The geo-spatial dimension is one addition, and the personal dimension is another, including the very personal. Beginning with its users' e-mail, Google has taken steps to incorporate into its storehouses the digital documents that users regard as the most sensitive ones they possess. One by one, it has added new categories of information that it offers to store on its servers: word processing documents, spreadsheets, calendars, and other personal and office documents. Central storage provides convenience, to be sure, but it also creates a tension between greater convenience and diminished privacy, or at least worries about diminished privacy. When a single company is determined to organize the world's information, including one's very own personal information, will the service be welcomed more than feared?

Just as Google discovered when it introduced Google Maps and Google Earth, making our world seem smaller also serves to make us feel more vulnerable to unwanted attention from others. Putting our most personal information on the same servers that hold publicly accessible information triggers anxieties that Google's reassurances about privacy protections can never completely quell. The anxieties are less about measurable risks than about inchoate concerns. We are only too happy to avail ourselves of greatly improved access to information about others, but then, oblivious to our inconsistency, we object to others having greater access to information about ourselves. The more control we gain of information, thanks to Google, the more we also experience a nagging worry about loss of control of information most dear to us.

CHAPTER 7

A Personal Matter

Google began in the information business, but the hardware and software it developed to handle the world's information turned out to be able to do more, much more. Without planning to do so, Google has embarked on its most audacious initiative to date, offering to replace the basic software that runs on individual computers with software services that run on its own machines. Customers will send the data or documents to the "cloud," and Google will take care of everything else. Software as a Service, as it is called, promises to perform just as ably on a centralized server as the software that we place on our own machines. Eventually.

Software as a Service offers other tantalizing collateral benefits: much lower costs; elimination of upgrade hassles and virus-infection headaches; and the ability to leave laptop computers at home and rely instead on much simpler devices for portable computing, like Internet-connected cell phones, which do not need much processing power because software performs the necessary work on the centralized server.

A shift from local computing, using software that is installed on the PC, to cloud-based Software as a Service, using software that runs on a centralized server, represents a threat to two of Microsoft's core businesses: its Windows operating system franchise and its Office applications suite. Software as a Service renders the kind of operating system used on a customer's end irrelevant: it could be a Mac system, Linux, or something other than a PC entirely, such as new kinds of ultracompact tablet computers that will be Internet connected, what chip manufacturer Qualcomm calls "pocketable computing." Nor will customers have reason to purchase new copies of Office if they can create Office-like documents using software that runs on someone else's computer and is available for much less cost. In 2008, Google further encroached upon Microsoft when it began providing Google Docs users the ability to work on documents even when they lack an Internet connection, such as on a plane. Google engineer Philip Tucker described it as "bringing the cloud with you." When the connection is restored, the work that was done off-line is automatically sent back up to the cloud.

Google's interest in expanding beyond a role of merely providing information to one of providing software services for a wide gamut of purposes has become visible not as a clearly announced vision but in bits and pieces. Google has not declared itself to be a strategic competitor with Microsoft and it seems to have taken pains to downplay the competitive threat that its Software as a Service poses to Microsoft's businesses. When Eric Schmidt was chief executive at Novell, he repeatedly warned that it would be foolish for any company that challenged Microsoft to "moon the giant." Google was reluctant to develop a Web-based e-mail program partly because many Googlers believed that doing so would, in the words of one Google engineer, "incite Microsoft to destroy Google."

Google's Software as a Service offerings have been introduced without the benefit of decent marketing—beginning with Google Apps for Your Domain and evolving into today's simpler Google Apps. Among the applications are an online word processor that it acquired in 2006, originally called Writely, and an online spreadsheet that Google developed internally. In October 2006, the company rechristened the two as Google Docs & Spreadsheets. Determined not to be copying its rival, Google stubbornly refuses to use the name that would be most natural: Google Office.

One by one, Google has added online versions of Microsoft software that users were accustomed to using on their desktop. Google Calendar was released in beta mode in 2006. A PowerPoint-like presentations module for Google Apps arrived in 2007. As Google expands its portfolio of services, its servers host categories of personal information that extend well beyond the functions of Microsoft Office: online purchase histories (Google Checkout), instant messaging (Google Talk), blogging (Blogger), social networking (Orkut), and recordings of phone conversations (GrandCentral). Eric Schmidt predicted that only a few, specialized applications, like high-end graphics processing, would stay on desktop computers, while 90 percent of the computing for which we use desktop PCs today would be handled in the cloud, on remote servers like Google's.

The first step that Google took in the direction of building Software as a Service was to offer its own e-mail service, Gmail. Adding e-mail marked a significant departure from its original single-minded focus on Web search. When Sergey Brin was interviewed by the Stanford student newspaper in April 2000, he said that Google was deliberately following a different path from Yahoo, which offered a complete set of information services that were intended to keep users from having any reason to go to another Web site: "All we do is search," he said proudly. The year before, Larry Page had said, "I won't say we won't add services, but we wouldn't put free email on our site unless we thought we could do a much better job." In those earliest years, Google was supplying search services on a wholesale basis to Yahoo, and it hoped to supply search to other portals, all of which had their own e-mail services. By deliberately sticking to search only, he said, Google minimized "the competition we have with people we might work with."

Google's focus on search led it inexorably to e-mail, however. Internet users spent far more time working with e-mail every day than they did carrying out Web searches, and e-mail messages were as difficult to search as the Web had been before the arrival of search engines. Important messages were mixed with unimportant, and when the accumulation of messages grew beyond a certain point, it was difficult to find a particular message easily. Sorting messages into folders was helpful but required a maddening investment of time. Many users did not bother, with the result that many messages a user would have liked to save fell victim to mass purging when the in-box became full. It's not surprising that Google, the company with the all-encompassing mission of organizing the world's information, would feel compelled, sooner or later, to have a go at organizing e-mail, too.

Google's e-mail project began in modest fashion. Paul Buchheit, Google employee number 23 who had coined "Don't Be Evil," was asked in 2002 if he would be interested in starting work on an e-mail product. He had experience working on another e-mail project before joining Google and was delighted to be asked: he was the much-vexed recipient of five hundred messages a day and wanted to have a better way to search his messages. A colleague, Sanjeev Singh, joined him on a part-time basis, but it took a while before the rest of a small team was assembled. When Brian Rakowski, an engineer freshly graduated from Stanford, was told he would be assigned as associate product manager to Google's e-mail project, he was taken aback. E-mail? What did e-mail have to do with working on search algorithms?

The answer was simple: Brin and Page had come to view e-mail as an unsolved search problem. A move into e-mail now seemed natural to them, but they did have to persuade other Googlers. "Look," they said to skeptics, "the information in e-mail is at least as important as some random Web page. The fact that you can't find an e-mail that you want is ridiculous."

Once the newly hired Rakowski adjusted to the idea that Google was planning to provide an e-mail service, he plunged in happily. He had spent his share of fruitless hours attempting to retrieve particular messages that refused to appear, and he realized a user could find any message in a trice if Google's search engine could be applied to the problem. Most veteran Google engineers were more resistant to the idea. Their main concerns were that e-mail would be a distraction, diluting the company's focus on its core strength, Web search, and that it would be costly, requiring more hard drives to store messages and attachments. Who would be willing to pay for it?

The e-mail service that would become Gmail would indeed be costly. Rakowski was asked to prepare financial projections that showed scenarios of all kinds, but Gmail promised to be a money loser under even the sunniest assumptions. Page's and Brin's support of the project wasn't unconditional. The team had to pass periodic executive reviews. It would have to figure out how to make a profit from the service, and it would have to demonstrate that the payoff was large enough to risk alienating Google's two largest partners at the time, Yahoo and AOL, both of whom had enormously popular e-mail services. The Gmail team got by with candor: we admit we don't know at this point how we're going to make money, but as we learned from our experience with Web search, if we provide the public with something useful, we'll eventually figure out a way to make the service profitable.

Buchheit and Marissa Mayer shared an office and often discussed business models. Later, Mayer recalled telling Buchheit, "Look, this is easy. We're going to give them small mailboxes for free, and up-sell them into larger mailboxes. That's what everybody does." Buchheit counterproposed placing advertisements on Gmail. "Paul, Paul, Paul," Mayer replied.

> Ads are never going to work! Either we run banner ads, and they're not going to be targeted, and people will develop blind spots, and they'll fail in terms of effectiveness, and, we're not going to get money, and annoy our users. Or, we're going to target the ads at their email, which is just going to be creepy and weird. People are going to think there's people here reading their emails and picking out the ads—it's going to be terrible.

The two went back and forth, with Mayer returning again and again to her prediction that the ads would be either "irrelevant" or "cause a lot of privacy concerns." The highest priority, she felt, was to fix the problems that afflicted their prototype so that it could perform the basic functions of sending and receiving messages. About 3 A.M., the time the two customarily brought their work days to a close, Mayer prepared to go home but Buchheit stayed behind. Her parting words to him were, "So, Paul, we agreed, we're not exploring the whole ad thing right now?" He said he agreed.

But in an empty building in the wee hours of the morning, no one was around who could deny his having a little fun with the e-mail prototype, which was sufficiently functional that he, Mayer, and four other Google employees were relying upon it, including Brin and Page. Buchheit downloaded semantic analysis software from the Internet that could analyze any block of text, identifying the grammatical function of every word in every sentence, and then figure out the sentence's meaning and distill the meaning into a few keywords. He hooked it up to the ad database that Google used for Web search results, which was designed to match a given keyword with particular advertisements. Then he connected the advertising code to the e-mail program so that it automatically served up ads based on the content of each individual e-mail message. By 7 A.M. he had the satisfaction of seeing a functioning ad system running, and he went home.

When Mayer came into the office around 9 A.M. and logged into her e-mail, she saw the ads and was irked. She weighed calling Buchheit immediately to have him restore the system before Brin and Page saw the ads, as she knew they "sometimes have weird views about privacy and what's creepy, and what's not." Brin, in particular, had been outspoken about his belief that attempting to target ads based on what users were reading, rather than what they were actively searching for, would never work effectively, and the ads would be perceived as an aggravating distraction. She decided to let Buchheit sleep for another hour before ordering him to return to the office and take the ad function out. But before long, she noticed that a few ads that accompanied her e-mail seemed reasonably useful. In one message, in which a friend had invited her to go hiking, an ad for hiking boots appeared. In another, mention was made of Al Gore's upcoming visit to the company, and the ad server displayed ads for books related to Gore. She decided to let the experiment run a bit longer, and was glad she did. When Brin and Page rolled in and saw the ads, they were delighted. Seeing how well even a rudimentary prototype of an ad-matching service worked convinced Brin that he had been wrong to dismiss it.

Buchheit's improvised use of semantic analysis demonstrated that algorithms could do a satisfactory job of selecting advertisements to accompany any given text that was displayed online. This late-night experiment became the basis of Google's second-most-important advertising program, AdSense. Google offers Web site owners the opportunity to run advertisements on their Web sites that are supplied by Google's network of advertisers. For participating Web sites, Google's software crawls the site, performs semantic analysis on the text on each page, and then automatically selects ads that are displayed on the right hand side of the page, matched to the meaning of the text. It calls this "contextual advertising." Site owners and Google split the proceeds when visitors click on the ads.

When the Gmail team stumbled across the opportunity to use semantic analysis software to serve ads matched to any text, even text on other Web sites, Google moved quickly to introduce the service. AdSense was launched in March 2003, a year before Gmail was ready.

Mayer had been concerned that users would perceive advertising that was closely matched to the contents of their e-mail as "creepy," and that was an issue that would surface as soon as the product was publicly released. But in the near term, the team became preoccupied with other, more technical issues in getting the service up and running. The hardware and software infrastructure that Google had built for Web search was not well suited for hosting e-mail. File systems that had been designed to be updated occasionally, when Google's Web crawler noticed a change at a Web site, had to be redesigned so that they could be updated continuously. This necessitated significant changes in Google's back-end software systems.

Google also had to learn to treat data that it was collecting with greater care. The inexpensive hardware it relied upon was expected to fail, and the company expected that some of the information its crawlers had captured would occasionally be lost before the system had made backup copies. Those data losses were inconsequential as long as the service being offered was merely Web search because the lost information, before long, would be captured by the crawlers again. A lost e-mail message, however, was not replaceable. Google's e-mail system would receive only one copy, and it would land on a machine whose components could not be relied upon. Google had to redesign its system to be truly fail-safe.

Google could have resorted to buying the special hardware used by the leading Web e-mail providers for solving this problem. Google's engineers did consider this option, but the company's grand vision for its e-mail service made that impractical for economic reasons. At the time, Yahoo provided its e-mail users with 4 megabytes of storage. Google, however, was preparing to offer 250 times more—1 gigabyte—to each user for free, providing what was seen at the time as sufficient space to permanently store all e-mail messages that an individual ever received. It would have been exorbitantly expensive for Google to use the hardware that others were using, which had the most reliable—and most expensive—components available. The only way Google could execute its plan would be to work with the same inexpensive hardware it used for Web search and develop new software systems that would ensure e-mails would not be lost.

By early spring 2004, work had progressed sufficiently that a date for launching the service could be penciled in. Brin weighed in with the suggestion that it be introduced on April 1. After all, April Fool's pranks were a treasured tradition at Google. What better joke could be arranged for the day, Brin said, than to introduce a real product in such a way that the public would not know whether it was to be taken seriously or laughed off as a prank?

The press announcement of the "preview release" of Gmail mixed the serious and the comical. The headline said that Google had created "search-based Webmail," a transparent attempt to make the expansion of Google's Web search business seem a natural one. It explained that search was the number two online activity and e-mail was number one, and appended a strange comment from Brin and Page: "'Heck, Yeah,' Say Google Founders." The inspiration for the project was attributed to a Google user who "kvetched" about wasting time trying to find messages and having to constantly "delete e-mail like crazy" to stay under the 4-megabyte limit imposed by a Google competitor. With 1 gigabyte of storage, Google offered its users a way "to be able to hold onto their mail forever."

Predictably enough, the announcement was received with puzzlement. Was Google serious? The "Heck, Yeah" suggested not. The promise that users would be able to hold onto e-mail "forever" also seemed like a joke. Who could possibly afford to offer a free service that made promises that extended to "forever"? The fact that Gmail was not available initially to anyone but a tiny group of invitees meant that most of the curious could not sign up and see for themselves, which further stoked skepticism. While some news publishers, such as the Associated Press and Reuters, treated the announcement seriously, others treated it as a publicity stunt. At *Slashdot*, one person chortled that mainstream news organizations had fallen for a joke that would "go down in history as one of the biggest pranks ever pulled." The confusion led the British news site *The Inquirer* to call the announcement "Google's April 1 Cock-Up."

The fuss was a boon in free advertising for Gmail. But the public's initial reaction was wary, just as it tended to be whenever Google announced an expansion of its information collections. Some initial Gmail users were spooked by the feeling that Google was "reading" private e-mail in order to match ads. There was also some grumbling about Gmail's decision not to offer a delete button. By forcing users to work their way through cumbersome menus in order to delete a message, Gmail encouraged users to simply ignore and retain their unwanted e-mail. The two problems, of Google's reading e-mail and retaining e-mail, seemed connected in a sinister way, as if Google was intentionally trying to probe as much of its users' private lives as it could for commercial purposes.

Whether a delete button should be provided was a question that had been debated at length by the Gmail team. Buchheit was a dogged advocate of no delete button and his arguments had prevailed. Users would be best served, he said, by a design that made retention of e-mail the easiest course. He wanted to save users the burden of "cognitive overhead" as they pondered whether to save or delete messages. With Google search available within the Gmail system, users would eventually realize, he believed, that it was best to just archive everything.

To Gmail's first-generation users, however, e-mail was highly personal, the most personal information that an individual processed on her or his computer in a day. They didn't want to be told how they should manage their messages, and they were demonstrative about their feelings. Jen Fitzpatrick, a senior engineer at Google, later said that every member of the Gmail team had stories to tell about "their family, their friends, random strangers they would meet at parties when they would tell them they worked on Gmail—the common refrain was, 'I want a delete button. Don't you get it? I want a delete button.'" In January 2006, almost two years after Gmail's introduction, a delete button was added.

The other problem, the concern that Gmail's ads were encroaching on users' privacy, was not so easily solved. Googlers had convinced themselves that Gmail users would see advertisements as helpful. In their 2004 *Playboy* interview, the two Google founders were grilled about Gmail. Yes, Page admitted, the matching of ads to the content of messages "seems a little spooky at first," but Brin emphasized that the only alternative would be intrusive "big glaring videos" that would appear before a message appeared, so "it's a pretty obvious choice."

The Googlers were flummoxed when Gmail's first users were uncomfortable about Google's deciphering the meaning of their e-mail messages. It did not seem fair that Google was criticized for this—after all, the other Web e-mail services also used software to scan the contents of messages, looking for viruses and spam. All e-mail messages could be said to be scanned, too, whenever a user performed a search. Brin tried to call attention to the fact that scanning was "automated—no one is looking, so I don't think it's a privacy issue." But the fact that Google introduced ads that were linked to the contents of the e-mail messages seemed to make the difference. Yahoo Mail and Microsoft's Hotmail were getting a free pass on their automated scans simply because their systems ran banner ads, as most Web sites did, oblivious to the contents of the rest of the Web page.

The attack on Gmail that most frightened Google was mounted in the California Senate, where Liz Figueroa, a Democratic state senator, sponsored a bill placing limits on the information gleaned from "scanning" of e-mail messages that could be shared with third parties. Figueroa said that her legislation "guarantees that our most private communications will remain just that—private." The California State Senate passed the bill, but it died after being sent to the state Assembly.

One could argue that Google should have anticipated the public's distrust of its plans for Gmail, with its centralized, permanent storage of personal data. Microsoft had tried years before to move users' personal data from scattered places into a centralized repository in the cloud. The spectacularly unsuccessful outcome of Microsoft's efforts should have provided cautionary lessons for all who followed.

In 2001, three years before Gmail was introduced, Microsoft had launched its own centralized data storage service, My Services, which would include, in due time, an address book, personal calendar, word-processing documents, and e-mail. Its users would retain full control over who would have access to their information, which was supposed to make My Services "user-centric." The first offering would be Passport, a service that would permit a user to use a single log-in name and a single password at all Web sites that signed up to participate and work with Passport's master repository of log-in information. Microsoft planned to show how convenient the service was by introducing Passport first to Hotmail.

The company thought its plans for a new family of information services would be heaped with praise. But the project, all too aptly named HailStorm, was instead assailed. The unfortunate name made for an inauspicious beginning. Mark Lucovsky, the senior Microsoft engineer on the project, had been responsible for assigning a temporary name while the project was in development. He chose Hail-Storm for fun, knowing that it would aggravate Microsoft's marketing group, which would come up with the final name. The Microsoft marketers dithered, however, and when the day of introduction arrived, no replacement name had been agreed upon, so, by default, HailStorm it was.

The service drew nothing but derision. Microsoft was a company that had failed to secure the public's confidence that it could handle sensitive personal data. In the previous twelve months, Microsoft had issued twelve security-related software updates for its Internet Explorer, trying to address gaping vulnerabilities. It had also suffered the recent embarrassment of an intruder breaking into its own internal corporate network. In order to address the breach, the company was forced to block all external access for a while, even preventing forty thousand of its off-campus employees from using its own network.

Perhaps the biggest obstacle to Passport's winning acceptance was the public's unease about a system that made all of one's personal data, including credit card information that Microsoft offered to manage as an "electronic wallet," accessible with a single password. Having one's personal information scattered in various places seemed to many people to be a sensible form of protection from identity theft, a problem that had become impossible to ignore. Earlier that year, a Brooklyn restaurant worker had been charged with successful online theft of the identities of Oprah Winfrey, Steven Spielberg, and Martha Stewart.

When HailStorm was introduced, a coalition of privacy groups mobilized and formally complained to the Federal Trade Commission about "Microsoft's ability to track, profile, and monitor" users of its Passport service. Microsoft had no allies in this fight, and HailStorm was dead on arrival. When Microsoft was unable to sign up a single company willing to work with it on the project, the company quietly dropped it.

Google's executive leaders were determined to succeed precisely where Microsoft failed. The introduction of Gmail drew criticism, but nothing like the public outcry about HailStorm, because Google had merely introduced e-mail alone, not a comprehensive plan that would encompass the centralization of all personal documents. The criticism of Gmail soon faded, the bill in the California legislature was never passed, and Google was able to proceed.

Google learned from its Gmail launch. Brian Rakowski enumerated the mistakes that Google had committed: the company had not prebriefed journalists and had not conferred in advance with the leading privacy advocates, like the Electronic Frontier Foundation and the Electronic Privacy Information Center. The proper sequence, he said, was to first "get their opinions and figure out if you're doing something wrong."

In looking back, Rakowski marveled at the public's focus on the scanning for matching ads, while ignoring much more serious privacy issues, such as the increased risk that e-mail on centralized servers could easily be subpoenaed or personal information in e-mail messages could be shared with advertisers. "Nobody was talking about those privacy issues and the few things we were doing to protect users' privacy," he said. Rather than talking about the inherent "downside" to storing your e-mail on a server "that you don't control," users were worried about the matching of ads to content by a nonhuman device. How many times would Google have to field the same question from users—"Is Google reading my email?"—and answer with, "Google is NOT reading your email"?

Brad Templeton, the chairman of the Electronic Frontier Foundation and a sometime consultant to Google, agreed that the matched advertisements were not a substantive problem, and called the concern about Gmail "silly and a bit paranoid." But he conceded that the widespread fear of computerized scanning of e-mail, however irrational, could not be dismissed: "It is not only important to have your privacy; it is important that you believe you have your privacy," he pointed out. The mere suspicion of being monitored "changes your behavior and you become less free as an individual."

Templeton might not have found the advertising problematic, but he did have other concerns about Gmail and Google's privacy policies. The Electronic Communications Privacy Act (ECPA), which treated e-mail as a private means of communication, like a phone call, required that police obtain a wiretap warrant in order to read it. Once an e-mail message was stored centrally, however, it would no longer be considered as private communication, but rather as data in a database, and would not be protected by the act. Not only that, but Google's privacy policy allowed the company to look at—or even release to a law enforcement agency—a user's e-mail in circumstances that would never be permitted were the company to gain access, theoretically, to its customers' postal mail. This was true not just of Google, but also of its competitors, like Yahoo and Microsoft, which were also combining Web-hosted e-mail with Web search. Templeton was concerned about a "troubling risk" that e-mail would become a target for government surveillance. He noted, "When our papers are at home, mass surveillance of them simply doesn't scale. It's too expensive. Online, it scales well."

Google stood apart from its rivals in its success in adding many other categories of personal information to its centralized collections. As individuals spent more and more time online, records of what they did and what they thought were created automatically, and Google happily offered to serve as the single home for all of it. If a single user were to fully utilize all of Google's services, the amount of sensitive personal information that would end up residing on Google's servers exceeded what Microsoft had envisioned for Hail-Storm. Yet as Google expanded, it did not face a firestorm of protest about what it was storing after the initial fuss about Gmail passed.

Google's ability to proceed unimpeded, without drawing public ire, is partly explained by the fact that Google's newest personal information services were dwarfed by much more successful offerings from its competitors. Google Checkout, a service that stored a user's credit card number, to be quickly tapped when shopping online, was unable to take much market share away from eBay's PayPal, another online payment system. Google's Orkut was an extremely popular networking site in some places in the world, but not in the United States. Even Gmail, the service that had gained the highest visibility of any of Google's newer offerings, was in a distant fourth place among Web-hosted e-mail providers three years after its introduction.

Google's expansion was also helped by the cultural shift toward much freer public display of personal information on the social networking sites. Intimate disclosure became routine on MySpace and Facebook, and reached its natural apotheosis at newer live video sites, such as Justin.tv, where everyone was invited to "lifecast"—treating one's daily life as entertainment suited for broadcast—to the world via the Internet, unedited, twenty-four hours a day, seven days a week. Even if the number of lifecasters remained small, and their average age skewed young, their mere existence was a leading indicator of the spreading acceptance of private lives being made public.

John Battelle, an entrepreneurial publisher and longtime observer of Google, who in 2005 had written a book about the company, *The Search,* was one of the few who raised concerns that Google users were granting a single organization control over too much data. In

June 2007, Battelle said in a blog post that he had reached what he called his "Google saturation point," and was no longer willing to "let too much of my online life run through any one control point, regardless of who it is." He decided deliberately not to use Google Calendar and Google Spreadsheets for some business planning because he didn't want Google to have access to information about his publishing business. What exactly "Google" would do with the information—he self-mockingly put the company's name within quotation marks, making fun of his own implied notion that the corporation would act as if it were a person—he did not say, and attributed his concern to "some primal lizard brain fear of giving too much control of my data to one source."

Google's Matt Cutts saw Battelle's post and added his own comments, which were supposed to be reassuring: "Given Google's strict privacy policies, I wouldn't worry about something like using Google Calendar or Gmail." Cutts said he would make inquiries within Google and try to get a colleague to talk at length about the policies that the company had in place to protect personal data. But "Don't worry" was not much of a response. Battelle revisited Google's terms of service that its users must accept and found language that was anything but reassuring to a business that was competing in any way against Google: "By submitting, posting or displaying the content you give Google a perpetual, irrevocable, worldwide, royalty-free, and non-exclusive license to reproduce, adapt, modify, translate, publish, publicly perform, publicly display and distribute any Content which you submit, post or display on or through, the Services." Google also reserved the right to "use personal information for auditing, research and analysis to operate and improve Google technologies and services."

Yet the chief concern now expressed by Google's users wasn't that someone at Google might take a peek at their personal data; it was that Google might be sloppy and not take good care of their data. In February 2007, Larry Dignan, a columnist for *ZDNet*, addressed this concern. "Will You Trust Google with Your Data?" he asked, and answered, "No." Speaking as a businessperson, he reasoned that if Google were to lose a company's data, it might not treat the incident with due seriousness because Google disclaimed any liability for damages beyond the subscription fee—this amounted to no liability if the service was offered for free. Dignan said he spoke as someone who had watched hosted data disappear permanently and had learned the importance of selecting a "data keeper" carefully. He suggested that corporate data would be safer in the hands of a software company like Salesforce.com, whose entire business was Software as a Service and whose very existence depended upon maintaining a sterling reputation for reliability.

As large and seemingly successful a company as Google appeared to be, it remained an unknown to those who ran the information technology departments in large companies and government organizations. Its dominance in the world of Web search did not impress technologists, whose concerns centered on Google's ability to have its Google Apps running and available to its customers 99.9 percent of the time, as it promised. They also wanted to see convincing evidence that Google's systems could handle the increased load of Google Apps without accidental data losses.

Google's strategic vision, of moving all computer users to the cloud, would remain unrealized unless it devised a way to gain the trust of customers. It needed lots of customers to show that Google Apps scaled—but until it could demonstrate that the new service scaled, corporate customers would not be willing to sign up. The only way it could win over customers, at least initially, would be by giving the software away for free, and yet do so in a way that did not undermine its ability to charge customers later. Google Apps managers realized that college and university campuses were the ideal place to give Google Apps services away, with student populations that would be large enough to demonstrate that the service scaled well. Google Apps Education Edition would be offered to campuses without charge and free of advertising, which gave it the opportunity to extend the Google brand without being accused of seeking immediate financial gain. A Google Apps Premier Edition would be sold on a subscription basis to corporations, which would be charged $50 annually for each user.

In October 2006, Arizona State University was the first major campus to roll out Google Apps Education Edition for its sixty-five thousand students. In the year that followed, many other universities tested the service, but adoptions by entire institutions came slowly.

In the meantime, Google experienced for the first time the problem that the Gmail team members had lain awake at night worrying about when they had first conceived of putting Gmail on Google's unreliable hardware: permanent loss of all Gmail messages for a handful of its users. The possibility had been anticipated and safeguards were supposed to make sure that it could not ever possibly happen. But in December 2006, some Gmail users began posting an incredible story: they had logged on to their accounts and found that everything—in-box mail, sent messages, contacts—had disappeared.

The story was followed closely at *TechCrunch,* but Google was fortunate that it did not receive wide coverage in the print media. The company sent *TechCrunch* a note that acknowledged that "a small number of our users—around 60" had lost all of their e-mail messages, but it did not explain what had gone awry. It offered only bland corporate-speak—"We know how important Gmail is to our users"—and vague claims about "extensive safeguards" that guaranteed that "this is a small and isolated incident."

The incident did not have major repercussions, but only because prospective customers were not interested enough in Google Apps to bother to notice. Progress selling the Premier Edition to corporate customers came even more slowly than giving away the Education Edition to higher education. In the first quarter of 2007, Google collected only $37 million from sales of software licenses, less than 1 percent of its quarterly revenue, and much less than 1 percent of the $4.8 billion in revenues that Microsoft's business division, which included Microsoft Office, reported for the quarter. Nevertheless, Microsoft treated Google Apps as a potent threat to the core of its existing business, and would not permit Google to use giveaways to higher education uncontested. Significantly, Microsoft decided to battle Google online, and offer Web-based e-mail and chat to colleges and universities for free. It was not fully comparable to Google's package:

Microsoft's lacked online word processing and spreadsheet capabilities and also lacked a calendar. But Microsoft's entry provided campuses with a real choice: free e-mail and a suite of software equivalent to Office from Google, or free e-mail software from Microsoft, in a new program that Microsoft gave the awful name of Windows Live@Edu—not as bad as HailStorm but bad enough to be an embarrassment.

With its long history of working with campuses, Microsoft had an insider's advantage over Google. It also could compete effectively with Google without matching the various Office-like applications that Google provided because campus administrators were interested in e-mail and not much else. Students had always paid for their own software applications like Office; whether they continued to do so, or were spared doing so by adopting Google's online Software as a Service, was not a concern of the administrators. Microsoft quickly signed up campuses in fifteen countries that were willing to try the service.

One notable trophy gained in the spring of 2007 was the University of Pennsylvania, whose School of Arts and Sciences, and also its business school, Wharton, concluded a long evaluation process for adopting a new e-mail system that had begun a year before—and culminated with the selection of Microsoft over Google. One of the criteria that university officials used when looking at the competing offerings was the companies' commitment to protecting the privacy of student information. Both Google and Microsoft scored poorly; both conceded that they might turn over to government officials information such as users' search histories or browsing patterns, if the government requested. A student advisory board recommended that Penn adopt Google Apps, but negotiations with Google foundered. Microsoft then walked off with the prize.

In April 2007, Google and Microsoft had the opportunity to make their pitch for Web-hosted e-mail to the country's largest university system, the California State University, which had 417,000 students spread across twenty-three campuses. The university's information technology managers (with one outsider: me) gathered in a hotel meeting room in Los Angeles to hear Jeff Keltner, representing

Google, and Walter Harp, representing Microsoft, do their best to sell to a tough crowd that arrived without showing signs of being ready to embrace Web-based e-mail systems for their campuses. Keltner and Harp were both in their thirties, both had graduated from Stanford, and both realized that before they could compete against each other, they had to first convince their audience that hosted e-mail, managed on servers beyond the campus, offered compelling benefits to their institutions. (Yahoo had also been invited to participate and had agreed to send a representative, but at the last minute canceled.)

Google's Keltner had the opportunity to speak first. Google, he said, viewed its free Google Apps, with its special ad-free version of Gmail for students, as a way of "giving something back" to universities. University information technology departments had become burdened managing their own e-mail systems, based on Microsoft's Exchange Server or similar software. These were expensive to maintain and back up, susceptible to viruses, and prone to fail. Only by historical accident had universities ended up in the e-mail business. He said, "For almost none of you is running a scalable, reliable, redundant, secure infrastructure to run massively parallel collaboration activities really a core process." Let Google handle it—and you can return to the educational technology that you know best how to provide.

Keltner reassured the administrators that the e-mail, documents, and other data managed by Google Apps would be absolutely safe because data was copied to at least three servers, creating multiple backup copies. He did not mention the problem of lost Gmail a few months earlier, and the administrators had apparently not heard of the incident. He was about to continue with his spiel when I raised my hand and asked him, How was it possible for Google's backup systems to have failed the previous December, resulting in the loss of everything that the sixty Gmail users had stored?

"Good question," Keltner said, whose normally fast-paced delivery slowed as he paused and gathered his thoughts. "We haven't talked a lot, publicly, about what exactly happened in December." He stalled for time with more flattery: "Very astute observation." He granted that e-mail had been lost for about sixty users, which was "literally about one in a million," and it was the sort of loss that happens everywhere in the computer world. It was "not a failure of any hardware, it was a failure of the brain." Regrettably, somebody at Google "hit the delete button when they shouldn't have hit delete."

Microsoft's Walter Harp did not talk about Microsoft Exchange and the benefits of using campus-based computing resources to handle e-mail. Instead he emphasized Microsoft's experience handling Web-based e-mail, which far exceeded that of Google's. Not only did MSN Hotmail have 233 million users worldwide compared to Gmail's 62 million, but also Microsoft had experience hosting corporate e-mail for Qwest, Verizon, and telecommunication giants around the world. "We don't make it into the press all the time," he said. "We're not a shiny new object. For some people, we're 'the Evil Empire.' The point being is, we're quietly doing quite well."

The administrators in the room were most concerned with the inherent problem of hosted services: messages and documents are irretrievable when systems go down. Earlier that week, BlackBerry service had failed globally and many BlackBerry users could not get their e-mail for fourteen hours. Someone in the audience asked the two representatives, "If things do fail at Microsoft or Google mail, are we failing with the rest of the world, or are we just failing in the education environment?" The two companies gave similar answers: their education customers were not segregated. As Harp explained, "There's strength in numbers here because you are failing with the rest of the world." Google's Keltner added, "The answer from us is much the same. If you're down, somebody at the Googleplex is down. That sets off a lot of alarms."

The representatives for Google and Microsoft had their sharpest exchange when Microsoft was asked about extending its education program to faculty and staff members, as well as students, as Google had done. Web-based software would be a "letdown," Harp said, for "a high-intensity productivity worker." If he himself were forced to use either Google's or Microsoft's Web-based calendar service, "I'd be pretty upset about it."

This offered the chance for Google's Keltner to pounce. Everything that Google was offering to campuses was used by Googlers themselves. He said, "This is where my e-mail is—it's a Gmail account. It's where my calendar is. All of our corporate calendar is Google Calendar. We absolutely believe this is ready for the enterprise." An old expression in the software industry, "eating your own dog food," embodied the notion that a company should never offer software that it wasn't willing to rely upon itself. In the 1980s and 1990s, Microsoft upheld and practiced "eating your own dog food," but for Web-hosted services, clearly it was Google, not Microsoft, that was committed to using its own products for its own internal needs.

Harp was not an automaton, spouting the official party line of Microsoft. In fact, he was refreshingly candid and left the best impression when he declined to criticize Google for matching ads to e-mail contents in the regular version of Gmail. I asked him whether Microsoft scanned the contents of Hotmail messages and he answered, yes, the e-mail is scanned to prepare an index for the user's searching, but was not scanned for the purpose of selling advertisements. Then he said, "Honestly? My personal opinion is I don't have a problem with that myself. I think it's neat—we can do a lot of cool stuff with that." For example, he said, the software could detect a FedEx tracking number in an e-mail message and then automatically show the user where the package was. This was merely a hypothetical use, he said, and the company had no plans to use scanning to add services.

Still, unvoiced concern about scanning seemed to linger. Google's Keltner knew from his own experience that the very word *scanning* was encumbered with negative connotations. Three years after Gmail's introduction, Keltner felt compelled to explain, once again, that scanning of e-mail was a necessity. Scanning simply meant that a machine read the contents of messages, which it had to do in order to detect spam or viruses. Talking about the topic of scanning upset him to the point that he almost lost his composure: "Anybody who says they don't scan your e-mail—point-blank, they're lying."

The day of presentations to California State University representatives ended anticlimactically: the administrators dispersed and no campus followed up with an immediate decision to use Google Apps. The next fall, Google could point to the University of Phoenix as its largest partner in education—250,000 accounts for students, faculty, and staff. But it still had too few customers to be willing to talk about the aggregate number of student accounts other than to say that it was in "the hundreds of thousands." Microsoft, however, happily provided specifics, claiming six million active accounts used by students, faculty, and alumni within three years of the 2005 introduction of Windows Live@Edu.

As time passed after the Google-versus-Microsoft meeting in Los Angeles in April 2007, Jeff Keltner's instinct that Google's competitors and critics would continue to dwell on the scanning issue turned out to be well justified. Microsoft's Walter Harp had taken the high road, refusing to use scanning to give Microsoft an advantage over Google. But Harp's ultimate boss, Steve Ballmer, did not have scruples about misstating what the competition did. In October 2007, he casually dropped a remark at a conference in the United Kingdom that was a new variation on the old falsehood, and one that was far more sinister than anything that had come before: at Google, Ballmer said, "they read your mail and we don't." The audience murmured and laughed nervously, and Ballmer paused for a moment to let the commotion subside. He resumed, "That's just a factual statement. It's not even meant to be pejorative."

Ballmer had it exactly wrong: his was not a factual statement and he most certainly meant it in a pejorative way. In fact, software analyzed the contents of each e-mail message at Microsoft's MSN Hotmail, just as Harp had explained, even though Microsoft did not do as much with the information extracted from the scan as it could have. More egregious than Ballmer's pretending that e-mail hosted by his own company was never scrutinized was his use of the pronoun *they* as the ones who "read" the e-mail at Google. Without a clarifying antecedent, the *they* left the impression that it was humans that were doing the reading of Gmail messages. With a seemingly offhand remark, consisting of just those seven words—"they read your mail and we don't"—Ballmer conjured the most frightening images that could be imagined and attached them to Google.

What was perhaps most interesting about Ballmer's comment was that he felt the need to strike out at Google, a company that had not won over significant numbers of customers for the software that competed against Microsoft's. Ballmer was not concerned about Google's inroads to date into Microsoft's core software businesses, but he was unmistakably concerned with Google's ability in the future to make cloud computing into a popular replacement for Microsoft's desktop software.

Microsoft understands that in the long term, local computing on desktop machines and in-house e-mail servers will be replaced by cloud computing. As can be seen in its marketing of Web-based e-mail to higher education customers, it has abandoned any hope of being able to sell the merits of software that is sold in packages when facing competition from the cloud. It is trying to reinvent itself as a Software as a Service company itself, ready to greet the future.

Microsoft's on-off-on bids for Yahoo in 2008 were an expression of the company's rather desperate wish to better meet the competitive challenge posed by Google by moving the place of battle from Microsoft's home ground, office applications, to Google's home ground, Web search and advertising. In May, when lack of agreement between the two companies about Yahoo's valuation led Microsoft to withdraw its offer, Microsoft changed tactics, but no one doubted that its most pressing strategic challenge remained Google. As Microsoft devotes more attention—and more of its treasury—to its online businesses, no major software company will remain to defend the notion that personal data should remain physically close to the individual and scattered among different media and devices. Centralization of data seems inexorable, and as it proceeds, the concerns about protecting individual privacy seem likely to diminish.

A parallel might be drawn to the transition in America's cities in the 1880s, when the generation of electrical power, based on alternating current, was centralized in large power plants, where electricity could be produced at much less cost, replacing the earliest, small plants, based on direct current, that were located on the premises of hotels, office buildings, and the homes of wealthy individuals. Centralization of power generation brought the need to transport electricity considerable distances, and electrocution became a risk for passersby as well as for electricians, as power lines filled the cityscape. Critics sounded alarms about the dangers, but the advantages of inexpensive electricity were too great to be ignored, even though accidental electrocutions were a frequent occurrence. Centralized power generation became so well accepted that later generations of Americans were not aware that the local mode of power generation had preceded it. In the same way, centralized computing may become ubiquitous, despite occasional data losses—the computer age's equivalent of accidental electrocutions—and later generations will not realize that there ever was a time when data was not stored at a centralized location in the cloud.

The technical advantages of moving to the cloud are clear, but the transition will be slowed by legal considerations that large corporations must weigh before they unplug their in-house servers. Unlike individuals and universities providing students with e-mail accounts, a corporation must, by law, preserve and manage every e-mail message and every internal document, maintaining absolute confidence in its ability to protect confidentiality and yet be able to retrieve whatever materials a judge may demand in the future. Compliance with the law is manageable when one uses one's own servers; relying instead entirely on Google Apps in the cloud has yet to be tried, let alone sanctioned.

In May 2008, David Berlind, an *InformationWeek* blogger, told his readership of corporate IT administrators, "Yes, It's Time to Destroy Your E-Mail Servers. What App Is Next?" Based on his experience administering Gmail for his organization, he listed many reasons why Gmail was ready to replace the Microsoft and IBM e-mail systems used within large enterprises. Or, he grudgingly added, Gmail was almost ready—the "beta" label that was still attached to the Gmail logo was a sign that the provider was not fully confident in the reliability and maturity of the service.

Google could take its time working on Gmail, preparing for the day when it could comfortably remove the "beta" qualifier. University students would supply a flow of customers who could stress test the system and also help to test out the other Google Apps that were a cloud-based alternative to Microsoft Office. Strategically speaking, Google was in a most desirable position, a company that was old enough—and large enough—to be ready to benefit more than anyone else whenever the shift to the cloud gathered momentum. But it was not so old and so large that it had a legacy terrestrial business, supplying software to organizations in-house, that would disappear. Google could greet the future in the cloud as its own.

CHAPTER 8

Algorithm, Meet Humanity

Most of corporate America develops new products stealthily. Many ideas will be tested out of public view, most will be found wanting in some significant way, and few will actually emerge from the lab. The experiments that end in failure remain unknown, the company's private business.

Google is not so reticent, however. It, too, has many projects under way that will never see light. But the company is far more willing than its counterparts to do much of its experimentation out in the open, in the marketplace. Instead of convening focus groups to gather initial impressions from prospective customers before a product's introduction, Google goes ahead and releases the product, affixing the "beta" label to warn users that the product lacks important features, and turns the general public into its focus group.

Google's reputation has not suffered. On the contrary, the company enjoys a public image that associates its brand with experimentation and innovation. Google does not have to release fully finished products; the public credits it as an inspirational achiever for merely trying out new things at a frenetic pace that its rivals cannot match. But the public's attachment to Google's culture of innovation celebrates the birth of new Google products and neglects the need for incremental improvement of older ones. Googlers themselves worry, at times, that the company has moved too fast to attend properly to making its newest offerings truly great ones. At one of Google's Friday meetings that I attended in 2007, a young woman asked Larry Page a pointed question: "We seem to be introducing a lot of products like the docs, spreadsheets, and presenting, and so on. If we're introducing those kinds of products, don't you think that they should offer more than what's already existing out there? And should we sort of complete packages? Because they seem to be, still, sort of rudimentary and not fully formed." She wondered if they were purposely designed without essential features in order to make it easier for skittish users to try the software. Her voice trailed off midsentence.

"I think that's a fair criticism," Page said. The question that Google has always wrestled with when readying new services is whether to wait until each is fully baked. It has been company policy to release products before they were polished, in order to get early feedback. If they were released in an overly buggy state, however, users would simply walk away. Page said that all of the products that she had mentioned were experiencing rapid growth, which suggested that they were fulfilling unmet needs, whatever their current shortcomings.

The rapid growth in Google Apps that he offered as exculpation began with a baseline of zero; any growth at all would appear rapid. He left important questions unanswered: How might Google's brand be tarnished by its offering Google Apps that were incomplete? Was its pursuit of personal information a strategic distraction, impeding its ability to stay ahead of the pack in search and catch up with the leaders in social networking? Was its internal culture, which lavished rewards and praise on those who conceived entirely new projects, leaving too few people to do the less glamorous work of incremental improvements needed for second, third, or fourth versions of its products?

The little-known Google Answers service is an example of a promising experiment that suffered from neglect. In 2002, Google offered users the opportunity to pose questions that would be answered by Google Answers Researchers, independent contractors who had been screened and certified by Google employees as "experts at locating hard-to-find information on the Web." The service charged customers a fee for each question answered, a radical departure from the advertising-based revenue model Google was using for its core search service. The amount a customer paid varied—customers determined for themselves the amount they were willing to pay when they submitted their questions. Google did not attempt to guarantee an answer in all cases: only if the amount offered for an answer was sufficiently high to attract the interest of one of Google's contractors would an answer be supplied.

Google retained one quarter of the fee collected by Google Answers, and the contractor received the remainder. This also was a curious departure for Google because the service did not rely on sophisticated algorithms but rather on human researchers. It was a service that would not scale, at least not quickly, in the hypothetical case that its customer base grew quickly.

Once Google unveiled the service, Google's managers gave it little thought. Despite its failing to attract customers, no one at Google bothered to tinker with the format or considered rethinking the business model. In 2005, three years after Google Answers was launched, Yahoo saw the opportunity created by Google's neglect and unveiled its own service, Yahoo Answers. It was a noncommercial service: anyone could submit a question, for free, and anyone who wished could supply an answer, though no compensation was paid. The lack of remuneration was not a problem, however. Yahoo's volunteer researchers competed for the approbation of users, who rated the quality of the answers.

Within a year, Yahoo Answers was pulling in about 14 million users monthly and had built up a database of more than 60 million answers, which were made available to all of its users. Despite Google's three-year head start, Yahoo had raced far ahead of Google. In late 2006, Google decided to pull the plug on its own Answers. Closing the business was momentarily embarrassing but not a significant blow to Google's overall revenue growth. But it did reveal a weakness at Google: the company did not know how to go about tapping the knowledge of strangers whose collective contributions were defining a new generation of online services, Web 2.0. The success of Yahoo Answers came about because Yahoo enlisted the contributions of users who enjoyed the online company of others and regarded the group's voluntary association as a community. Yahoo understood before Google how important virtual online communities were to many people.

Not only did Google fail to give consistent attention to products after they had been released, it also neglected work on bringing its disparate collections of new types of information—such as books, scholarly journals, maps, videos—together so that a single search could rummage through all of its new information silos, in addition to its database of Web pages.

Users could, of course, go to the various Google sites and do separate searches, but the sites had been developed separately, in haste, before Google could figure out how to make all of them accessible in a single search. Even when Google had only a few collections of information other than Web pages, its product managers understood that without "universal search," users were not likely to go to the trouble of searching here and there to find all of the information that Google had to offer. Either they would not think to look anywhere but on Google's home page, or they would find visiting the various sites too time-consuming. In 2001, David Bailey, a young Google engineer, did a few mockups of sample screens to show what integrated search results might look like—"Britney Spears" was called upon to illustrate how news and images could be tapped in addition to Web pages—but universal search was left on a list of desiderata.

Between 2001 and 2006, several other Google engineers briefly took on universal search as a project. But they lost interest before making progress. In Google's internal culture, engineers decide what projects are of greatest personal interest. Without champions, ideas for worthy projects sit on a shelf and gather dust. Universal search was one of those. In 2006, Bailey returned to it with what he called an "inner fire" to see the project through. It took about a year for him and his team to build the code that allowed a single search to extend to more than one silo.

The universal search algorithm had to determine whether the other kinds of information were of equally high quality as the top Web page results, which entailed developing more sophisticated software than that used for Web pages alone. The greater the variety of material, the greater the possibility that the software would make erroneous deductions. A search for "Kentucky Fried Chicken" on the Web would lead to the restaurant chain, but when the same search phrase was submitted to Google Maps, would the Algorithm know that this was not a request only for restaurants located in Kentucky? The software should be smart enough to sense that when a search term like "Wichita tornado" was submitted, what the searcher most wanted to see was not perfect matches on Web pages, which had been crawled weeks before, but rather news stories about a tornado that had just hit Wichita a few minutes earlier (a crucial clue that the news angle was most important would be the fact that in the previous five minutes more people had searched for that phrase than had done so in the entire year). In May 2007, Google was ready to announce a limited version of Universal Search.

The search results that users now saw were changed only subtly—only a few non-Web items were added to the first page of search results. Google moved with deliberate slowness, not wanting to introduce ill-chosen items that would hurt the company's reputation for trustworthy search results. For all of its innovation in new areas of information, Google remained deeply conservative in its attachment to the same basic methods that it had used for Web search since the time of its founding, and it was extremely reluctant to adopt new methodologies.

While Google clung tightly to its faith that analyzing links was the best way to sort the quality of Web pages, start-ups saw an opportunity to move beyond link analysis and develop software that organized online information by what it could understand of its actual meaning, moving well beyond word matching. Tim Berners-Lee, the inventor of the World Wide Web, has proselytized for the creation of a successor to the Web, "the Semantic Web," in which Web pages would contain code that would facilitate machine understanding of the contents of each page. His vision, which would require tremendous work on the part of every Web site editor, may never be realized. But in the meantime, new companies are springing up, like Powerset, Metaweb, and Radar Networks, to improvise new techniques for searching information on the basis of meaning extracted by software, even without the help of embedded code. In May 2008, Powerset made its first public appearance, initially searching only Wikipedia, not the entire Web. As a demonstration of proof of concept, it was quite successful; only two months later, Microsoft announced it would acquire the company. Google's dominance in the search business has not scared off entrepreneurs and venture capitalist backers. Between 2004 and 2006, no less than $350 million was invested in new companies that planned to pursue some aspect of Internet search.

Some of the challengers are attempting to write a superior search algorithm. But others have abandoned altogether the quest for a better algorithm, and look to an entirely different source for improved search results. They have turned to the approach that Yahoo used, pre-Google, at the very beginning of Web search: humans.

No one ever doubted the ability of humans to distinguish good Web pages from bad. The problem was that the Web had grown faster than Yahoo had been able to add editors to keep its Web directory current. This created the perfect opportunity for Google to supply an automated method of evaluating the quality of pages. The difference between 1997, the last year of the pre-Google era, and 2007 was that ten years later no one in the search business was trying to do as Yahoo had done, hire as many experts as needed to organize the Web. Instead every other search start-up, it seemed, was attempting to do as Wikipedia had done, harness the contributions of volunteers. A new phrase was coined—*social search*—to refer to this new category of search service, which relied not upon an engine powered by algorithms but upon the collective judgments of the group. Anyone willing to recommend Web sites that matched a particular search phrase was invited to do so. Squidoo, Sproose, and NosyJoe prepared search results based on the assumed wisdom of crowds; another little start-up, Bessed, welcomed submissions from anyone but reviewed them before making them available.

In December 2006 Jimmy Wales, the founder of Wikipedia, announced plans to introduce a search service modeled after Wikipedia, to directly compete with Google. In many cases, he said, Google "produces nothing but spam and useless crap." The spam he referred to was Web pages that used deceptive means to pull in unwitting visitors who generated revenue for the Web site, which was paid by advertisers based on the number of visitors that viewed the site's advertisements, willing or not. The most basic task of a search engine is to make a qualitative decision, he said, determining, "This page is good, this page sucks." Algorithmic search has to make a guess, using roundabout means. A human can tell with just a glance. He was confident that he could enlist a network of contributors to make those judgments, just as he had done with Wikipedia.

Mahalo, another challenger to Google, was started in 2007 and received funding from Sequoia Capital. Mahalo claimed—extravagantly—that it was "the world's first human-powered search engine." Its founder, Jason Calacanis, shared Wales's disgust with search results served up on Google that were infected with spam. He too emphasized that a human editor could produce spam-free results. Mahalo began with about thirty editors. Rather than attempting to match the comprehensiveness of Google's search index, Calacanis chose instead to have his staff prepare results for the search phrases that were most frequently submitted to Google. They began by winnowing Google's top search results to create spam-free lists of what they judged to be the best Web links by topic. Within a few months they had prepared results for five thousand terms. Soon they were also vetting submissions from users, who were paid $10 to $15 per topic for results pages that were accepted.

When Mahalo served up a list of links, a visitor benefited from what Calacanis described as "basically your own personal research assistant doing 4–10 hours of research on your search query." A hand-built Mahalo page organized links under subthemes that speeded scanning. The page on global warming, for example, had clusters of links under recent news stories, background articles, science and data, groups advocating action, groups arguing against, and other headings, including climate change humor, with videos that included online snippets of Stephen Colbert, Will Ferrell, *South Park,* and *The Simpsons.* Each link required only a single line, so the Mahalo global warming page easily accommodated eighty-five handpicked sites, far more than the fifteen that Google serves up on its usual first page of results.

Mahalo was able to ride on top of Google's algorithms: when Google made improvements, Mahalo contributors and editors, who used Google searches to compose their list of choice selections, benefited, too. Calacanis described Mahalo as a melding of human capabilities with those of the machine: "John Henry and the steam hammer versus the steam hammer alone."

Googlers were irked, however, by Calacanis's comparison of Google's search engine to the steam hammer, cold, mechanical, devoid of the human touch. As social search became more and more visible in 2007, the company's emissaries tried to humanize the Algorithm. In June, Marissa Mayer was in Paris for the company's European Press Day and did her best to place a human face on Google's core technologies. The opportunity appeared when she was asked by a British reporter why Google often prominently featured links to Wikipedia articles, without checking on the reliability of the information to be found in them. She began her answer along the old groove, stressing the value of the objectivity of an automated selection process. "Rather than trying to make individualized judgments about particular sources, like Wikipedia," she said, "we rely on automated methods, like along PageRank." She took pains, though, to point out that Web site editors made the crucial choices, in placing links to the sites that they valued most, sending the signals that Google's search engine processed. Wikipedia placed highly only because "people like the content." In her rendering, the Google algorithm was a populist instrument of the people.

Little Mahalo was hardly of a size that would make Google tremble. Yet Google did take seriously the competitive threat posed by a combination of machine algorithm and human intelligence, especially if deployed by a large rival. For an article I was preparing in June 2007 about Mahalo, I interviewed Matt Cutts, the head of Google's Web spam team, to obtain Google's official response to Mahalo's reliance on human editors. Cutts had nothing disparaging to say about Mahalo; he emphasized Google's own interest in considering new approaches to search, too. "I don't think we're ideologically bound to only computers, only algorithms," he said. The company had already taken the trouble to remove all references to "automatic ranking" in every one of its own Google help pages.

The editorial changes cleared the way for experimenting later that year with a search page that allowed its users to vote on search results, just as Digg's users vote on news stories.

Cutts shared extended thoughts on the subject in a post on his personal blog titled "The Role of Humans in Google Search." After noting that all opinions that would follow were his own, not Google's, he said that his view was that Google was perfectly amenable to social search, personalized search, or any means of "using human feedback to improve search quality." He noted that he had publicly expressed the same points the previous fall, welcoming more human input into search at Google, with the reservation that attention had to be paid to "potential abuse by bad actors," a problem he confronted daily in his battles with Web spam. He also mentioned that Larry Page had publicly expressed Google's willingness to consider alternatives to the Algorithm. Page had appeared in the midst of Jason Calacanis and a small group of fellow conferees at Foo Camp, an informal techie conference, and had remarked—in Calacanis's paraphrasing—that search engines were best for finding information, but when it came to organizing information, "Wikipedia found a better way."

Cutts, Mayer, Page—all were roving ambassadors for Google, telling the public that Google was not a frozen monolith. Indeed, the company was detaching from the Algorithm, becoming more flexible and attentive to the wisdom of the crowd, albeit slowly. Credible rumors of its interest in acquiring Digg, the social news site, swirled in 2007 and again in 2008. The notion that Google would permit users to determine the placement of items on a page was beginning to seem not just possible but likely. Still, the Algorithm remained Google's area of greatest competence.

Software, which could analyze text with ease, did not perform as well, however, when applied to the task of closely analyzing video. In 2007, after its YouTube acquisition, Google was slow to develop an algorithm for defining a video's "fingerprint," a pattern that would serve as a unique identifier. Without video fingerprints, Google would not be able to reliably automate the identification and removal of copyrighted material in videos that were uploaded to YouTube. In January 2007, Eric Schmidt pointed to Google's development work on audio and video fingerprinting as evidence of how "very concerned" the company was about respecting copyright ownership, and said that the fingerprinting technology that it was developing was "in various stages of being rolled out."

Even as it was promising the imminent release of a technical solution to the problem of copyright infringement, Google was also arguing that it did not need to release anything, that it was in full compliance with the Digital Millennium Copyright Act. The law did not require it to block the uploading of videos that infringed copyright, only that it remove videos whenever copyright holders brought to its attention instances of copyright violations. Google did not show any sympathy to copyright holders, like Viacom, that had to assign a team of employees to pore through YouTube videos, looking for unauthorized clips, sending "takedown" requests to YouTube, then repeating the same cycle endlessly as the clips reappeared almost as soon as YouTube removed them. In February 2007, Viacom submitted to YouTube a batch of more than a hundred thousand takedown requests.

At this point, Google could have made a conciliatory gesture, saying: We see the problem—it's admittedly a serious one. We have our best technical team at work on video fingerprinting, which has long been one of the most difficult standing problems in computer science. We are hopeful that we'll have technology ready soon. Instead, Google chose a more combative course, complying with Viacom's takedown requests but gratuitously adding derision, characterizing the requests as evidence that Viacom executives were too dense to understand that YouTube's hosting of their clips drew new audiences to Viacom's television programs and ultimately served Viacom's interests, too.

Viacom did not buy Google's argument. The expected lawsuit arrived in March 2007, when Viacom went to court seeking "at least" $1 billion in damages from YouTube and Google for copyright infringement. The suit argued that YouTube actively monitored uploads and removed pornographic videos, but declined to do the same for Viacom's copyrighted programs. Viacom did not take Google to task for failing to deliver the video fingerprinting technology that it had promised; instead it pointed out that Google had not even bothered to automate a simple comparison of the text in the tags that users appended to videos, or in the searches that users submitted, with a database of show titles and the names of characters of television shows and movies. Viacom asked not for perfection, but simply "exercising care," which it said "is not a Herculean task."

Google responded to the lawsuit by retreating to its interpretation of the law, which was that copyright owners did all the monitoring and Google's sole responsibility was to respond to the requests of the copyright owners. Eric Schmidt characterized the lawsuit as a form of "business negotiation" in the media industry, where, he said, one could be expected to be "sued to death."

By poking fun at Viacom's lawsuit as a negotiating stunt, Schmidt directed attention away from Google's failure to introduce software that would automatically identify and remove material that infringed copyright. A few months later, he announced at the National Association of Broadcasters meeting in Las Vegas that Google was "very close" to turning on a new service, Claim Your Content, that would "somewhat automate" the submission of requests to remove copyright-infringing videos. The new technology, he said, "is not a filtering system." Rather it was software that would come into play after the video was uploaded, looking for unauthorized copies of videos protected by copyright and deleting them if the copyright owner directed Google to do so.

Months passed, and no sign of Claim Your Content appeared. The National Legal and Policy Center, a conservative public-interest group based in Washington, D.C., made Google's lax policing of copyright infringers on YouTube and Google Video an issue of public interest and uncovered embarrassing data: random spot checks identified over three hundred full-length copyrighted movies that were available on Google Video. Google Video also ran advertisements placed by video-pirate Web sites such as MillionMoviesDownload.com. Other video Web sites had introduced video filtering technologies, but not Google. Ken Boehm, the center's cofounder, wrote Senator Patrick J. Leahy expressing puzzlement that "a company that has been largely successful in its endeavors to 'organize the world's information and make it universally accessible and useful' has apparently been unable to implement a working filtering technology to identify copyrighted content in a timely fashion."

Philippe Dauman, Viacom's CEO, sounded the same theme in October 2007, when Google finally released what it had decided to call the YouTube Video Identification Beta—six months after the company had said it was very close to releasing it. The timing was also curious because it came just two days before a consortium of content providers and Internet companies—including, besides Viacom, Walt Disney, Microsoft, NBC Universal, CBS, Fox, MySpace, and Dailymotion—announced an industry-wide copyright-protection initiative in which Google had chosen not to participate. Dauman dryly remarked, "Google is a very high quality company [with] a lot of very, very smart people. They can do things very quickly when they want to. I guess they haven't wanted to until this point." Whether Google could have moved more quickly or not, the company could hardly be surprised that its vaunted expertise in developing the most successful algorithms in the search industry would naturally lead to the expectation that it could produce industry-leading algorithms in other areas, were it genuinely interested in doing so.

The criticism that Google was deliberately holding back video fingerprinting technology seems unfounded. The evidence suggests the opposite: Google seems to have released its own video identification technology hastily, as if its executives could not stand to be embarrassed by another day of delay. YouTube was able to test the new software for only one week prior to its release, using videos supplied by only one partner. The system had found a grand total of only eighteen pirated clips on all of YouTube during the week's scouring. Shortly before Google's hasty announcement, Eric Schmidt attempted to lower the industry's expectations, saying that a system that would identify copyrighted clips with 100 percent accuracy was impossible. He suggested that reaching a target of 80 percent or 90 percent accuracy would be the best that could be hoped for.

Google claimed that its software could accurately detect an exact copy of a long clip that had not been altered. But an algorithm for matching could be thrown off by changes to the copy; the shorter the clip, the greater the difficulty in detecting a match. Even if a clip could be identified, the software could not make judgments about whether the clip was being used in a way that would fall under what copyright permitted as fair use.

Google's software required the active cooperation of the entire entertainment industry. It was designed to compare YouTube clips with a master library of all television shows and films, which Google announced it would set up and maintain on its own servers. In order for owners of copyrighted material to be able to enjoy protection, however, they had to supply Google with a copy of all works for which protection was sought. For large media companies, with deep vaults filled with programs, the requirement meant placing its most precious intellectual property into the care of Google—and by doing so, setting a precedent that would then require that they do the same thing, turning over digital copies of their entire libraries, again and again, to every Web site that hosted videos. In its haste to announce the availability of the new tool, Google could claim only that Walt Disney, Time Warner, and CBS were experimenting with the technology, but tellingly none of the three was willing to state its willingness to turn over all of their content to Google.

A more practical alternative would be the creation of an independent video repository to be used by all video Web sites, not just Google, for checking copyright status. Like most young, precociously successful companies, Google had grown too fast to bother learning how to cooperate with competitors on matters of industry-wide concern. When Google undertook book scanning, it had similarly ignored the pleas of others to join with partners to create a centralized repository. With video, Google proposed to create, once again, its own storehouse, but its plan imposed prohibitive costs and risks upon the prospective content providers.

For all of the progress that had been made in pattern recognition work in computer science, computers simply were not yet smart enough to screen video content for potential problems. YouTube was able to identify pornography and graphic violence, not because it relied on sophisticated algorithms but because it used the unpaid labor of volunteers: its users were invited to flag videos, alerting YouTube to clips that contained sexual or violent content. Once alerted, YouTube would confirm the problem and then remove the video. As YouTube cofounder Steve Chen gratefully said, "Nothing beats our community flagging." That method could not be used, however, for policing copyright problems: "We all know pornography and violence when we see them. But copyright status can only be determined by the copyright holder." Chen, however, was conveniently ignoring the presence of entire categories of material found on YouTube—beginning with thousands of clips of *The Daily Show with Jon Stewart*—whose use was notoriously unauthorized and impossible to miss.

YouTube could have adopted other means of screening for copyright problems, approaches that were labor-intensive and expensive, at least compared to free. YouTube competitor Revver was paying humans to check every single video upload for infringement, as well as for pornography and hate speech. For its punctiliousness, Revver was rewarded with obscurity in the marketplace. Carefree YouTube, meanwhile, continued to grow faster than any other online video site. By March 2008, Google/YouTube's share of online video watching was 38 percent, almost ten times the 4 percent share of second-place Fox Interactive. (Revver had such a small share of video viewing that it lacked sufficient share to make the list of top ten video sites.)

In April 2008, one year after Schmidt's appearance at the National Association of Broadcasters meeting at which he had announced Google's video filtering service, it was impossible for neutral observers to notice a drop in the number of unauthorized clips from televisions shows and series. One could find, for example, scenes from every one of the last five movies that received the Academy Award for Best Picture. The 10-minute limit on clips prevented one from viewing a full-length feature film such as *The Departed,* but the entire movie was available to anyone willing to watch it in twelve 10-minute clips.

When asked about the ongoing problems, Google always politely avowed its concern for copyright protection, but in practice the company did not seem much concerned. The Viacom lawsuit moved slowly and seemed so remote as not to even register as an irritant. In the meantime, YouTube continued to grow and grow. By spring 2008, 85 million U.S. viewers watched 4.3 billion videos on YouTube in a single month, about 50 per viewer. according to the Internet research firm comScore. Even while online video viewing grew, YouTube continued to gain share of the overall video market, as video contributors sought the one place in which the largest possible audience could be reached, and the growth in the number of clips that were uploaded at YouTube brought still more viewers. How Google should go about converting those billions of videos shown each month into a profitable business line was a question it could not answer, but its core business, serving up advertisements based upon text, paid all tuition costs while the company learned about this and the other unfamiliar businesses it was entering.

Conclusion

Google's ascendance has been accompanied by Microsoft's decline. No computer company has ever been able to enjoy pre-eminence that spans two successive technological eras. IBM in the mainframe era could not head off the ascent of Digital Equipment Corporation in the minicomputer era, which, in turn, could not head off the ascent of Microsoft in the personal computer era. Fully aware of this history, Bill Gates and his associates nonetheless hoped that, by dint of unceasing vigilance and wise management, Microsoft would become the first to succeed in maintaining its position of leadership into whatever era would succeed the one defined by the PC.

When the Internet spread from research labs and universities and seeped into the commercial world, the first challenger that gave Microsoft a fright was Netscape, which was undercapitalized and easily batted away. Subsequently, Google succeeded in pushing Microsoft into a defensive crouch.

Google could easily have lost the opportunity for dominance to another company, one born earlier in the Internet era: Yahoo was a more likely candidate, having had a considerable head start in growth by the time Google was founded. By relying on a labor-intensive approach to organizing the Web, though, Yahoo failed to keep up with the growth of the new medium and lost its early lead to the little company with which it had contracted to handle Web search queries.

Google was able to grow as fast as the Web itself because it relied upon hardware and software technology that was designed to scale up fast and inexpensively. It was able to acquire a market capitalization that exceeded all other Internet companies because it chanced upon text ads linked to the keywords of a search phrase, ads that turned out to be a highly efficient means for advertisers to reach prospective buyers. By 2007 it was able to acquire sufficient stature to successfully launch two industry-wide coalitions: OpenSocial, for social networks, and the Open Handset Alliance, for cell phones. Both initiatives in their first six months gathered many partners and seemed likely to dramatically reshape their respective industries. Considerable achievements all.

Along the way, however, Google was unable to lay claim to attracting the largest number of U.S. visitors to its Web sites. In its early years, when it functioned only as a site that referred its users elsewhere, Google took pride in its ability to speedily direct its visitors to the best site on the Web for whatever it was they were searching for. Later, as it added categories of information that it stored, it became a destination site itself. But in the meantime, Google's Internet predecessors—Yahoo, MSN, and AOL—had established comprehensive Web portal offerings designed to supply many kinds of information. They had also developed enormously popular e-mail services that long predated Gmail. Consequently, Google's competitors attracted more U.S. visitors to their sites in any given month than did Google.

Yet in April 2008, Google passed a milestone in its history when the number of visitors to its U.S. sites exceeded that of all competitors. Among the overall U.S. Internet audience of 190.7 million unique visitors—that is, disregarding multiple visits to a site by one person—Google drew 141 million visitors, edging past Yahoo, Microsoft, and AOL. It attained the number one position partly due to an increase in the volume of search requests, but also partly due to the continuing rapid growth of traffic headed to YouTube.

Converting that YouTube traffic into profits proved a problem resistant to solution. Even though by March 2008 YouTube was serving those 4.3 billion videos a month in the United States alone, Google had yet to report revenue of any material size from its operation. Google's other attempts to move beyond Web search similarly lacked an appreciable return on investment, at least in the near term. Each continued to do well in acquiring content—Columbia University in December 2007 became the twenty-eighth library to join Google Book Search, a second dozen cities in February 2008 acquired street views in Google Maps; the *New York Times* in April 2008 added a new layer to Google Earth. Each contributed to the Google aura of commanding the best information, regardless of type. But none individually could be declared a clear financial success (or failure) for Google.

Collectively, Google's multiplying services constitute a set of assets that no other Internet company has the means—strategical, technical, financial—to match. The intangible value to Google of having so many kinds of information under a single roof cannot be calculated precisely, but it's likely that all Google properties share a halo effect. Each appeals to more users simply because of its Google identity and the way the very multiplicity of services conveys authority. Visitors to one site are also more likely to use another Google site because of the irresistible convenience of staying within the Google family of services. Circumstantial evidence suggests that the non-Web services have strengthened the Google brand for Web search. Google's share of Web searches in the United States increased to almost 68.3 percent in May 2008 from 58.3 percent in March 2006. During the same period, Microsoft's share dropped to 5.9 percent from 13.1 percent. The quality of Google Web searches, compared with Microsoft searches, did not improve that dramatically; if anything, the qualitative gap narrowed. But Google has succeeded in strengthening the association in users' minds between Web searches and the Google brand, to the detriment of Microsoft, Yahoo, and its other search-engine competitors.

Eric Schmidt is fond of saying that Google users are merely "one click away" from leaving, as Google does not lock its users in. "One click away" may have applied in Google's early years, but as time has passed and Google has become a one-stop destination for information, and a one-stop destination to some for Software as a Service, its users have made an investment in their Google accounts that cannot be abandoned casually with a click.

All in all, Google has yet to stumble badly in undertaking new initiatives. But it has been mocked for failing to create a second profitable business in addition to search-related advertising. Microsoft's CEO Steve Ballmer likes to deride Google as a "one-trick pony." Microsoft, he says, is a two-trick pony—software for desktop computing and software for servers—that is trying to add a third and fourth trick to its repertoire. Ballmer hardly stands in a good position to criticize Google, however. Since becoming Microsoft's CEO in 2000, his company has continued to flounder in its efforts to build up its online services. In May 2008, the company's market capitalization remained $300 *billion* less than it had been when it reached its historic peak in 1999. The last year that its online services unit posted a profit was fiscal year 2005, and its online losses grew in each successive year, reaching $745 million in 2007. Losses in the first three quarters of 2008 indicated that the year's total will far surpass that suffered the year previously.

Google has no such worries about mounting losses. It has managed to generously fund its various online experiments while at the same time posting ever-growing profits. Its fiscal year is slightly different from Microsoft's, but for rough comparison, place Microsoft's losses in its online services segment against Google's $1.5 billion in profits in fiscal year 2005, $3 billion in 2006, and $4.2 billion in 2007. Google's growth has been so remarkable that Henry Blodget of *Silicon Alley Insider* predicted in May 2008 that by May of the following year, Google's search business will be both larger and more profitable than Microsoft Windows, which he described as "the most profitable and legendary monopoly in history."

Google's financial results have given its shareholders no reason to complain about imprudent outlays on YouTube or Google Book Search. In any case, Google's executive leadership does not have to contend with restive shareholders. The company has a dual-class voting structure. Brin, Page, and Schmidt control almost 40 percent of the voting power, which effectively gives these three control of the company. Public shareholders show no sign of dissatisfaction with the broadest possible interpretation of the company's mission to organize the world's information, nor with the speculative initiatives to expand beyond Web search. Page gave due warning in 2004 about their intentions in the company prospectus on the eve of its IPO: "In our opinion," he explained, "outside pressures too often tempt companies to sacrifice long-term opportunities to meet quarterly market expectations." Google would pursue its long-term interests and would not "shy away from high-risk, high-reward projects because of short-term earnings pressure." Anticipating that shareholders might become antsy if the company's "bets" do not quickly show a positive outcome, Page wrote: "We will have the fortitude to do this. We would request that our shareholders take the long-term view."

The company's fortitude has not yet been put to a genuine test, in which its core advertising business encounters serious turbulence and slips, or one of its very big bets turns into a very big failure. If, under adverse circumstances, Google reaffirms its commitment to organizing the world's information and does not scale back its ambition, then it will pass another milestone.

In 2005—when Google ran into legal difficulties by recording television programs for Google Video without obtaining the permission of television producers; when the Association of American University Presses had warned Google that its plan to digitize books would violate copyright law; and when Google was sued for Google News's unauthorized use of short excerpts from news articles and thumbnail-size photographs—it seemed that Google's attempts to do more than search the Web would be stymied on all sides. When Eric Schmidt was interviewed at what seemed to be a trying time for Google, he smoothly acknowledged the complications and conveyed the sense that Google was working hard with the aggrieved parties to resolve all outstanding issues. This was all predictably soothing.

And then Schmidt said something that was rather surprising: he gave an estimate of how much time Google would need to organize all of the world's information—"It will take, current estimate, 300 years." The combination of many centuries and crisp precision made the number seem whimsical, outlandishly distant. This is a company that likes not just to think big, but to think bigger than anyone else—"300 years" was showing off, wasn't it?

It turned out to be neither a joke nor a boast. It was merely a dispassionate calculation. The year before, Craig Silverstein, the company's director of technology, who had been the first employee hired by Brin and Page, also used three hundred years as an estimate, in his case as the upper end of a range of years, 200–300, that would be needed before an intelligent computer would be able to "understand emotions and other nonfactual information" and be able to do as well as today's human reference librarians.

In 2005, when Eric Schmidt referred to a three-hundred-year timeline, he was speaking not about artificial intelligence in a search engine, but about the amount of time that would be required for his company to organize the world's information. He mentioned the three hundred years a second time, a few months later, when addressing a convention of advertisers. In his talk, he explained that he spoke not as a person with a marketing background but only as a computer scientist. He said that only about "two or three percent" of all information in the world that could be indexed and searched had been converted into a form that made indexing and searching possible. Predicting the progress of digitization was a matter of simple calculation. "We did a math exercise," he explained, when asked to project how long it would take Google to fulfill the company's mission. "And the answer was 300 years."

Google's first ten years of organizing the world's information has taken it a considerable distance. It may not need 290 years to complete its mission.

Notes

Introduction

1 **American Dialect Society:** Society members designated *google* as the second-most-important word or phrase in the society's 2002 Words of the Year competition (it was runner-up to *weapons of mass destruction*). American Dialect Society, "2002 Words of the Year," 13 January 2003, http://www.americandialect.org/index.php/amerdial/2002_words_of_t he_y/. *Google* became a draft entry in the *Oxford English Dictionary* in 2006. "Dictionaries: The June Issue of the Oxford English Dictionary Newsletter Is Now Online; Google as a Verb Now in Oxford English Dictionary," *ResourceShelf*, 29 June 2006, http://www.resourceshelf.com/2006/06/29/dictionaries-the-june-issue-of -the-oxford-english-dictionary-newsletter-is-now-online-google-as-a-verb -now-in-oxford-english-dictionary/.

2 **multibillion-dollar game:** "An Auction That Google Was Content to Lose," *New York Times*, 4 April 2008, http://www.nytimes.com/2008/04/04/technology/ 04auction.html. Richard Whitt and Joseph Faber, "Cone of Silence (Finally) Lifts on the Spectrum Auction," *Official Google Blog*, 3 April 2008, http://googleblog.blogspot.com/2008/04/cone-of-silence-finally-lifts-on.html.

2 **spend the large sums:** Google also happily spends small sums, too, acquiring smaller companies. These transactions often involve an acquisition price that falls below the size that Google is required to disclose to its shareholders. In one especially busy two-month period in mid-2007, Google acquired seven companies: (1) GrandCentral Communications, a Web-based service for managing phones and messages that can, for example, have an incoming call ring a home number and cell phone number simultaneously; (2) FeedBurner, an advertising network for blogs and RSS feeds; (3) Postini, which provides security-related services for corporate e-mail, a capability that would make Google's e-mail more competitive with Microsoft's corporate e-mail systems; (4) Image America, which makes very-high-resolution cameras used in aerial photography, such as those used to gather images of the devastation in New

Orleans following hurricane Katrina (Stephen Chau, "Imaging America," *Google Lat Long Blog*, 20 July 2007, http://google-latlong.blogspot.com/ 2007/07/imaging-america.html); (5) Panoramio, which links photos to precise geographic locations; (6) Zenter, which provides software for creating online slide presentations, giving Google's online software package, which already had the equivalent of Microsoft Word and Excel, the missing third component: a PowerPoint equivalent (Sam Schillace, "More Sharing," *The Official Google Blog*, 19 June 2007, http://googleblog.blogspot.com/2007/06/ more-sharing.html), (7) PeakStream, which writes software for improving computer performance.

3 **visitors noticed:** Randall Stross, "How Google Tamed Ads on the Wild, Wild Web," *New York Times*, 20 November 2005, http://www.nytimes.com/ 2005/11/20/business/yourmoncy/20digi.html.

3 **Brin and Page were hostile to the very notion:** Sergey Brin and Larry Page, "The Anatomy of a Large-Scale Hypertextual Web Search Engine," April 1998, http://infolab.stanford.edu/~backrub/google.html. The authors probably had in mind Open Text as a cautionary example of what could happen if a search engine's search results were tainted by outside considerations. Open Text had introduced in 1996 a pay-for-placement experiment, permitting advertisers to be listed at the top of search results. In 1998, GoTo, later renamed Overture (and eventually acquired by Yahoo), also offered pay-for-placement to the highest bidder. Danny Sullivan, "Go To Sells Positions," *Search Engine Watch*, 3 March 1998, http://searchenginewatch.com/ showPage.html?page=2165971. For a detailed account of GoTo's brief brush with success, prior to Google's, see John Battelle, *The Search: How Google and Its Rivals Rewrote the Rules of Business and Transformed Our Culture* (New York: Penguin, 2005), 95–121.

4 **Marissa Mayer, a Google Vice President:** Stross, "How Google Tamed Ads."

4 **Brin said in an interview:** "Search Us, Says Google," *Technology Review*, November/December 2000.

4 **founders showed:** Sergey Brin and Larry Page, "The Future of the Internet," Commonwealth Club of California, 21 March 2001, http://commonwealth club.org/archive/01/01–03google-speech.html; Q&A: http://common wealthclub.org/archive/01/01–03google-qa.html. When Eric Schmidt arrived at Google in 2001 and he was shown the ads, which were producing revenue of about $20 million a year, he said, incredulously, "You have got to be kidding. People actually click on this stuff?" Eric Schmidt, "Technology Is Making Marketing Accountable," transcript of speech delivered to the Association of National Advertisers, 8 October 2005, http://www.google.com/press/ podium/ana.html.

5 **As late as 2002:** "Google's Toughest Search Is for a Business Model," *New York Times*, 8 April 2002.

5 **Yuri Punj:** "Google May Charge for Internet Search," *Telegraph.co.uk*, 10 April 2002, http://www.telegraph.co.uk/digitallife/main.jhtml?xml=/ connected/2002/10/04/ecngoog.xml.

5 **Achieving a one-to-one match:** "Google's Targeted Keyword Ad Program Shows Strong Momentum with Advertisers," Google press release, 16 August 2000, http://www.google.com/press/pressrel/pressrelease31.html; John Battelle, "Titans Column: Omid Kordestani," *Searchblog*, 26 October 2005, http://battellemedia.com/archives/001974.php.

6 **Google began a trial experiment:** Saul Hansell, "Google Tests Video Ads on Search Results Pages," *New York Times Bits* blog, 14 February 2008, http://bits.blogs.nytimes.com/2008/02/14/google-tests-video-ads-on-search-results-pages/.

6 **Yahoo in June 2006:** "Yahoo! to Strengthen Competitive Position in Online Advertising Through Non-Exclusive Agreement with Google," Yahoo press release, 12 June 2008, http://yhoo.client.shareholder.com/ releasedetail.cfm?&releaseID=316450. Financial terms were not disclosed by either company. Also see Google's announcement: "Google Announces Non-Exclusive Advertising Services Agreement with Yahoo in U. S. and Canada," Google press release, 12 June 2008, http://www.google.com/intl/en/press/ pressrel/20080612_yahoo.html.

6 **Jerry Yang:** Jerry Yang, "Our Google Deal," *Yodel Anecdotal,* 12 June 2008, http://ycorpblog.com/2008/06/12/our-google-deal/.

7 **In April 2008:** "Google App Engine," a part of Google Code, http:// code.google.com/appengine/.

7 *New York Times* **published:** "Planet Google Wants You," *New York Times*, 15 October 2006, http://www.nytimes.com/2006/10/15/fashion/15google .html.

7 **Google site located in China:** Andrew McLaughlin, "Google in China," *Official Google Blog*, 27 January 2006, http://googleblog.blogspot.com/ 2006/01/google-in-china.html; "Google CEO On Censoring: 'We Did An Evil Scale,'" *Infoworld*, 27 January 2006, http://www.infoworld.com/ article/06/01/27/74874_HNgoogleceocensoring_1.html.

8 **Some environmental critics:** Ginger Strand, "Keyword: Evil," *Harper's Magazine*, March 2008, http://harpers.org/media/slideshow/annot/ 2008-03/index.html.

8 **market capitalization:** Ranking based on closing prices on 13 June 2008. For current rankings, see the online chart "Large Caps," maintained by the Online Investor, http://www.theonlineinvestor .com/large_caps/.

9 **Michael Cusumano:** Randall Stross, "Maybe Microsoft Should Stalk Different Prey," *New York Times*, 24 February 2008, http://www.nytimes.com/ 2008/02/24/business/24digi.html.

9 **Dan Lyons:** "Monkey Boy's Three-Legged Race," *The Secret Diary of Steve*

Jobs, 2 February 2008, http://fakesteve.blogspot.com/2008/02/ballmer-im-completely-out-of-ideas.html.

9 **In May 2008:** "Google Receives 68 Percent of U.S. Searches in May 2008," Hitwise press release, 10 June 2008, http://www.hitwise.com/press-center/hitwiseHS2004/leader-record-growth.php.

9 **organize the world's information:** "Google Receives \$25 Million in Equity Funding," Google press release, 7 June 1999, http://web.archive.org/web/20000309205910/http://google.com/pressrel/pressrelease1.html. In an e-mail message to the author on 4 April 2008, Craig Silverstein, the first Google employee that Page and Brin hired, said that after checking the company's files, it appeared that this was the first time that the "organize the world's information" mission statement had been placed on Google's Web site.

9 **modest statement of company mission:** A sample page containing the first mission statement, saved by the Internet Archive's Wayback Machine, an online archive of Web pages, in a crawl done on 11 November 1998, is preserved at http://web.archive.org/web/19990221202430/www.google.com/company.html.

10 **In 2006, an unknown person:** Google Analyst Day comments in PPT file, preserved by Paul Kedrosky before Google removed the file from its site. *Infectious Greed* blog, 2 March 2006, http://paul.kedrosky.com/archives/002797.html#c44483, slides 8 and 20. Kedrosky was the executive director of the William J. von Liebig Center for Entrepreneurialism and Technology Advancement at the University of California, San Diego.

11 **the three men committed:** "Google Wins Again," *Fortune*, 29 January 2008, http://money.cnn.com/2008/01/18/news/companies/google.fortune/index.htm.

11 **see on a daily basis:** Chris Sacca, "Channeling Decision-Makers," *What Is Left?* blog, http://www.whatisleft.org/lookie_here/2008/02/for-reasons-i-w.html.

11 **When Brin was asked:** Ken Auletta, "The Search Party," *New Yorker*, 14 January 2008, http://www.newyorker.com/reporting/2008/01/14/080114 fa_fact_auletta.

11 **Google's strategic model:** Eric Schmidt, Press Day, 10 May 2006, http://google.client.shareholder.com/Visitors/event/build2/MediaPresentation.cfm?MediaID=20263.

12 **a million computers:** The possibility that Google had 1 million machines, running Linux, was mentioned as early as May 2006, in a speech delivered by publisher Tim O'Reilly: "My Commencement Speech at SIMS," *O'Reilly Radar*, 14 May 2006, http://radar.oreilly.com/archives/upcoming_appearances/index.html.

12 **in April 2007:** "Text of Wired's Interview with Google CEO Eric Schmidt," interviewed by Fred Vogelstein, *Wired*, interview conducted 23 March 2007, posted 9 April 2007, available only online at http://www.wired.com/techbiz/people/news/2007/04/mag_schmidt_trans.

13 **The company famously provides:** For a list of what Google refers to as "benefits . . . beyond the basics," see http://www.google.com/support/jobs/bin/static.py?page=benefits.html#bbb. Eric Schmidt is quoted on the page: "The goal is to strip away everything that gets in our employees' way." For an estimate of the cost of Google-provided meals, see Vasanth Sridharan, "Google's Ginormous Free Food Budget: $7,530 Per Googler, $72 Million A Year," *Silicon Alley Insider*, 23 April 2008, http://www.alleyinsider.com/2008/4/googles_ginormous_food_budget_7530_per_google_r. Sridharan's figure was not based on any hard data provided by Google; it assumed that Google's employees in Mountain View and New York ate two meals a day at the company's cafeteria and that the two meals, combined, cost the company about $30. Another estimate of the cost that was mentioned in the same article placed the daily cost at $15, not $30.

13 **Larry Page:** "Letter from the Founders: 'An Owner's Manual' for Google's Shareholders," 2004, http://investor.google.com/ipo_letter.html.

13 **Number One Best Company:** "100 Best Companies to Work For," *Fortune*, 21 January 2008, http://features.blogs.fortune.cnn.com/2008/01/21/100-best-companies-to-work-for/.

14 **emphasis on Ph.D.'s:** Brin and Page, "The Future of the Internet"; Randall Stross, "What Is Google's Secret Weapon? An Army of Ph.D.'s," *New York Times*, 6 June 2004.

15 **Kevin Scott:** "Google—Working at Google—The Faces at Google/Fast Company," *FriendFeed*, 18 February 2008, http://friendfeed.com/kevinscott. Scott was prompted to offer his thoughts after seeing Fast Company's "The Faces and Voices of Google," http://www.fastcompany.com/magazine/123/google.html, which he referred to as one of similar "unreservedly positive fluff pieces [that] really aren't doing the company a service." Scott himself had left Google.

15 **23andMe:** Google invested $3.9 million. In its filing of a form 8-K with the U.S. Securities and Exchange Commission (http://sec.gov/Archives/edgar/data/1288776/000119312507120640/d8k.htm), the company disclosed that Anne Wojcicki, a cofounder of 23andMe, was married to Sergey Brin, Google's president and a cofounder. (They were married just a few weeks earlier.) This first round of financing for 23andMe, which included Genentech's participation, was used partially to repay $2.6 million in interim debt financing that Brin had provided to 23andMe. The personal relationship between Brin and Wojcicki made Google's investment in her company suspect in the eyes of many bloggers. But Kevin Kelleher, a commentator at GigaOM, provided a clear-eyed evaluation of the transaction, arguing that "I haven't yet found a company that gives Google a better entry into a genomics-for-consumers startup." See "Google, Sergey and 23andMe: Why It All Makes Sense," *GigaOM*, 24 May 2007, http://gigaom.com/2007/05/24/google-sergey-and-23andme-why-it-all-makes-sense/.

Notes

15 **In 2005, Schmidt explained:** Eric Schmidt, Donald Graham, James Fallows, moderator, "Proprietary Information in the Age of Search," Zeitgeist '05, the Google Partner Forum, 27 October 2005, http://www.google.com/press/podium/eric.html.

16 **Schmidt was asked:** "Google's Goal: To Organize Your Daily Life," *Financial Times*, 23 May 2007, http://www.ft.com/cms/s/df7d8850-08ca-11dc-b11e-000b5df10621.html.

16 **Sergey Brin told:** Spencer Michels, "The Search Engine That Could," *NewsHour with Jim Lehrer* transcript, 29 November 2002, http://www.pbs.org/newshour/bb/business/july-dec02/google_11-29.html.

16 **the more it knows about each visitor:** Schmidt also defended the continuing expansion of the company's information storehouse on humanitarian grounds, stating in a podcast interview with the *Economist* in 2007 that giving the public access to "far more information than they can ever handle" was a very good thing: "More information crowds out bad ideas, bad governments, bad behavior." Before finishing, he had managed also to claim that increased access to information made the world faster growing, more profitable, and safer. "*Economist* Podcast Interview with Eric Schmidt," *Economist: The World in 2007*, n.d., http://media.economist.com/media/audio/world-in-2007/The_future_of_the_internet.mp3.

17 **10 percent of Facebook's employees:** Justin Smith, "10% of Facebook Employees Came from Google," *Inside Facebook*, 27 March 2008, http://www.insidefacebook.com/2008/03/27/facebooks-dna-is-10-google/. Smith identified forty-one employees who had worked at Google, listing them by name.

17 **June 2008:** Owen Thomas, "Google's Daycare Debacle: The Kinderplex Memos," *Valleywag*, 16 June 2008, http://valleywag.com/5016952/googles-daycare-debacle-the-kinderplex-memos; Thomas, "Google Daycare Now a Luxury for Larry and Sergey's Inner Circle," *Valleywag*, 13 June 2008, http://valleywag.com/5016355/google-daycare-now-a-luxury-for-larry-and-sergeys-inner-circle.

17 **Bloomberg financial news service:** "Google Trims DoubleClick Jobs in Biggest Staff Cuts," *Bloomberg*, 2 April 2008, http://www.bloomberg.com/apps/news?pid=newsarchive&sid=aHPI8hip9Zr8.

19 **few Googlers:** Today, Google employees refer to themselves as "Googlers," but it's amusing to note how usage has changed: in 1999, Michael Moritz, one of the venture capitalists who invested in Google, spoke of Google's possessing "the power to turn Internet users everywhere into devoted and lifelong Googlers." See "Google Receives $25 Million in Equity Funding."

19 **At the end of 2003:** Google Financial Tables, 2003, http://investor.google.com/fin_data2003.html, and 2007, http://investor.google.com/fin_data.html.

1. Open and Closed

23 **CERN announced:** CERN European Organization for Nuclear Research, "Statement Concerning CERN W3 Software Release into Public Domain," 30 April 1993, http://tenyears-www.web.cern.ch/tenyears-www/Declaration/Page1.html (for reproduction of first page of the two-page statement) and ~/Page2.html (for second page). "CERN" is the organization's most recognizable name, but the "C" may cause puzzlement when placed against its full English name: "European Organization for Nuclear Research." The acronym CERN was created by a predecessor organization, the French Conseil Européen pour la Recherche Nucléaire, or European Council for Nuclear Research. When the council was replaced in 1954 by the European Organization for Nuclear Research, "CERN" was retained.

24 **In June 1993:** Matthew Gray collected statistics about the Internet's traffic while an undergraduate and graduate student at MIT. See his page on the Web's growth at the MIT Web site: "Web Growth Summary," http://www.mit.edu/people/mkgray/net/web-growth-summary.html. In 1993, almost half of all Internet traffic was for file transfers, about 10 percent was for discussion groups (called, rather confusingly, "news groups"), about 7 percent was used for e-mail. Postscript: Gray joined Google in early 2007 and one month after joining, he posted on Google's Book Search blog an entry that began, "I love data. That was no small factor in my decision to join Google." Matthew Gray, "Earth Viewed from Books," *Inside Google Book Search*, 12 March 2007, http://booksearch.blogspot.com/2007/03/earth-viewed-from-books.html.

25 **Microsoft began planning:** Randall Stross, *The Microsoft Way: The Real Story of How the Company Outsmarts Its Competition* (Reading, MA: Addison-Wesley, 1996), 161–65. Ken Auletta wrote in 1997 that "Myhrvold and Microsoft [were infuriated] that the Internet was free. They saw it as a flowerchild culture that disdained profits and copyrights—and Microsoft." Auletta, "The Microsoft Provocateur," *New Yorker*, 12 May 1997, http://www.kenauletta.com/themicrosoftprovocateur.html.

25 **Netscape Communications:** At the time of its founding in April 1994, the company was named Mosaic Communications Corporation and the beta version of its browser was Mosaic Netscape. The company was forced to change its name and branding because of objections raised by the National Center for Supercomputing Applications, which had developed the Mosaic browser and sought to protect its trademark.

25 **Netscape declared itself:** Michael A. Cusumano and David B. Yoffie, *Competing on Internet Time: Lessons from Netscape and Its Battle with Microsoft* (New York: Free Press, 1998), 132–40. Cusumano and Yoffie offer a multifaceted analysis of Netscape's strategic and tactical missteps and apply the phrase *open, but not open* to Netscape.

26 **called the changes "extensions":** Perhaps the person who has written about extensions most trenchantly is a strategic consultant-turned-entrepreneur, Charles H. Ferguson, whose company, Vermeer Technologies, deliberately created extensions to standard HTML for proprietary advantage in its software for Web site creators, FrontPage. Microsoft purchased Ferguson's company in 1996. See Ferguson's memoir, *High Stakes, No Prisoners: A Winner's Tale of Greed and Glory in the Internet Wars* (New York: Times Books, 1999).

26 **had the company been founded two years earlier:** "Searchology@Google," press briefings, Google headquarters, Mountain View, CA, 16 May 2007, http://google.client.shareholder.com/visitors/event/build2/mediapresentation.cfm?MediaID=25550.

27 **This did not endear Google:** Sergey Brin and Larry Page, "The Anatomy of a Large-Scale Hypertextual Web Search Engine," April 1998, http://infolab.stanford.edu/~backrub/google.html.

27 **a piece of code:** The code is the Robots Exclusion Protocol, which was adopted as a standard in 1994. In its simplest form, two lines of text will keep all search engines that honor the protocol away from the site: *User-agent: *; Disallow.* See Martin Koster, "A Standard for Robot Exclusion," n.d., http://www.robotstxt.org/orig.html.

28 **demanding, perhaps, that Google share:** Mike Masnick, "AP: The News Gatekeeper Is Dead! Long Live the News Gatekeeper!" *Techdirt*, 2 November 2007, http://www.techdirt.com/articles/20071102/025323.shtml. Also see Tim Lee's follow-up post, "Search Engines Should Ignore Bossy Publishers," *Techdirt*, 6 December 2007, http://www.techdirt.com/articles/20071202/161208.shtml, which looks at an Automated Content Access Protocol proposed by a new consortium of Web publishers. Among the Frequently Asked Questions on ACAP's Web site is this: "Isn't this all about money?" The reply begins, "No, but no one would deny that it is partly about money." See "ACAP Frequently Asked Questions," http://www.the-acap.org/faqs.php, accessed 15 December 2007.

29 **AOL exploited:** In 2000, AOL had 24 million members, which was about 45 percent of all online users. Any company that wanted to advertise or sell its wares to AOL members had to be prepared to accept extortionate terms imposed by AOL gatekeepers. CUC International, the discount shopping service, agreed to pay AOL $50 million and a share of revenues. Barnes & Noble agreed to pay $40 million to be AOL's "exclusive" bookseller. Music retailer N2K signed a three-year $18 million deal, which included an up-front payment of $12 million, even though it had generated only $11 million in the previous year. AOL's appetite grew and grew. For new companies, AOL demanded a significant share of equity in the company, in addition to payments for access to AOL's customers. AOL acquired a reputation for being the most arrogant negotiator in the country. An executive at a start-up said that AOL had demanded a 30 percent stake in her company, "and then for good

measure, they tell us, 'These are our terms. You have 24 hours to respond, and if you don't, screw you, we'll go to your competitor.'" See Gary Rivlin, "AOL's Rough Riders," *Industry Standard*, 30 October 2000, http://www .thestandard.com/article/0,1902,19461,00.html.

29 **Vic Gundotra:** Vic Gundotra, interview, Mountain View, 18 December 2007. Gundotra worked at Microsoft for fifteen years.

29 **began declining after 2001:** AOL, Inc., "AOL Membership Surpasses 28 Million," press release, 8 March 2001; "Time Warner Inc. Reports Results for 2007 Full Year and Fourth Quarter," press release, 6 February 2008, http://biz.yahoo.com/bw/080206/20080206005597.html.

29 **In 2005, Michael Kelly:** "Free Internet Site: A Portal to AOL's Future?" *New York Times*, 3 June 2005, http://www.nytimes.com/2005/06/03/technology/ 03aol.html.

29 **strategic alliance:** In addition to an advertising pact, the alliance included Google's purchase of a 5 percent equity stake in AOL for $1 billion. Time Warner Inc., "Time Warner's AOL and Google to Expand Strategic Alliance," press release, 20 December 2005, http://www.timewarner.com/corp/newsroom/ pr/0,20812,1142800,00.html.

29 **AOL finally tore down:** Time Warner, "Time Warner Announces That AOL Will Offer Its Software, E-Mail and Many Other Products for Free to Broadband Users," press release, 2 August 2006, http://www.timewarner.com/ corp/newsroom/pr/0,20812,1222063,00.html. Only weeks before AOL's announcement, however, the company maintained tight control of the exits to its garden, instructing its customer service representatives to attempt to prevent members who called to cancel their memberships from successfully doing so. For an account of one customer's ordeal, which was recorded and broadly disseminated, see Randall Stross, "AOL Said, 'If You Leave Me I'll Do Something Crazy,'" *New York Times*, 2 July 2006, http://www.nytimes.com/ 2006/07/02/business/yourmoney/02digi.html.

29 *Wall Street Journal's* **Web site:** Rupert Murdoch, the *Journal's* new owner, had initially indicated after the acquisition that he believed that removing the pay wall would greatly expand the site's audience and boost its Web advertising revenue. He directed that more material be placed on the part of the Web site that was freely available, but was persuaded to stop short of eliminating the subscription model entirely. See "Wall Street Journal Web Site to Remain Subscription-Based," *Wall Street Journal*, 24 January 2008, http://online.wsj.com/public/article/SB120119406286813757.html.

30 **42 million members:** "Microsoft to Pay $240 Million for Stake in Facebook," *New York Times*, 25 October 2007, http://www.nytimes.com/ 2007/10/25/technology/24cnd-facebook.html.

31 **exclusive advertising deal:** Google Inc., "Fox Interactive Media Enters into Landmark Agreement with Google Inc.," press release, 7 August 2006, http://investor.google.com/releases/20060807.html. The agreement obligated

Google to guarantee minimum revenue share payments of $900 million for the agreement's term, which would run through the second quarter of 2010.

31 **Steve Rubel:** "Walled Gardens and the Lesson for Social Networks," *Micro Persuasion* blog, 28 June 2007, http://www.micropersuasion.com/2007/06/walled-gardens-.html.

31 **appointed three executives:** Joe Kraus and Graham Spencer had joined Google less than a year previously, when Google had acquired JotSpot, a company that made wiki software for group collaboration. Kraus and Graham's business experience on the Web stretched back to 1993, when they had cofounded Excite, a search-engine pioneer that predated Google. Kraus was also an investor in, and active member of, LinkedIn, a social network for professionals.

31 **Kraus said:** This account draws from an interview with Kraus, 4 January 2008, in Mountain View.

33 **Facebook's maddening ability:** Nick Gonzalez, "Facebook Stealing Googlers at an Alarming Rate," *TechCrunch*, 21 November 2007, http://www.techcrunch.com/2007/11/21/facebook-stealing-googlers-at-an-alarming-rate/.

33 **Microsoft announced:** "Facebook and Microsoft Expand Strategic Alliance," Facebook press release, 24 October 2007, http://www.facebook.com/press/releases.php?p=8084.

34 **in the few days remaining:** Joe Kraus had set the date for the announcement for November 5, long before Facebook set the date for its announcement on November 6. As the date approached, Kraus's team moved the date for its announcement up by four days—it would say, unconvincingly, that it was for reasons unrelated to Facebook—which gave it more time to command headlines before Facebook stole attention back.

34 **injection of credibility:** Randall Stross, "Why Google Turned into a Social Butterfly," *New York Times*, 4 November 2007, http://www.nytimes.com/2007/11/04/technology/04digi.html.

34 **open source:** Google's search engine utilized the Linux kernel, GCC, Python, and Samba. Chris DiBona, "Three Summers of Open Source," *Official Google Blog*, 15 March 2007, http://googleblog.blogspot.com/2007/03/three-summers-of-open-source.html.

34 **free hosting site:** The site was code.google.com.

34 **a number of coders:** Among the ranks of Google employees were Andrew Morton (Linux), Greg Stein (Apache), Jeremy Allison (Sambra), and Ben Goodger (Firefox). "Google's Secret Weapon," *Redmondmag.com*, January 2008, http://redmondmag.com/features/article.asp?editorialsid=2395. Google poured tens of millions of dollars into the Mozilla Foundation, underwriting the open-source development of Firefox and Thunderbird, but this was not pure altruism; Google, in essence, purchased favorable placement as the default search engine that came with Firefox. In June 2008, Danny Sullivan pointed out that Google had fought hard to pressure Microsoft to

make sure that no single search engine provider was the default in Internet Explorer 7, and had succeeded in that campaign. But Google had turned around and arranged for favorable placement for itself in Mozilla's Firefox browser. Sullivan asked Google to stop making the user's initial search choice and ensure that "any provisions of the secret contract between you and Firefox are altered to allow for the consumer choice you're so happy to espouse should happen in Internet Explorer." Danny Sullivan, "Hey Firefox—Let Us Pick Our Own Search Engine!" *Search Engine Land*, 6 June 2008, http://searchengine land.com/080606-103041.php.

35 **Tim O'Reilly:** When O'Reilly was able to see what OpenSocial offered, he was greatly disappointed to discover that it was not so open after all, and would not provide a user with the ability to move and manage a set of friend lists from one social network to another. Tim O'Reilly, "OpenSocial: It's The Data, Stupid," *O'Reilly Radar*, 7 November 2007, http://radar.oreilly.com/archives/2007/11/opensocial_social_mashups.html. Mark Cuban proposed that his personal information be made portable not by using a new set of standards, OpenSocial's, but by having Facebook, where they currently resided, make them available for export, if the member wished to do so. Cuban wrote, "I don't want to have to publish and maintain a database for every application I want to use or happen to use. Nor do I want to have to maintain multiple social network accounts to make this information available. . . . [Google's OpenSocial is] too late . . . if Facebook opens their API [Application Programming Interface, i.e., programming standards] up further and allows for its use outside the Facebook.com domain." Mark Cuban, "An Open Facebook API vs. Google OpenSocial," *Blog Maverick*, 4 November 2007, http://www.blogmaverick.com/2007/11/04/an-open-facebook-api-vs -google-opensocial/.

35 **A week before Facebook:** Joe Kraus, phone interview, 29 October 2007.

35 **Facebook founder and CEO:** Erick Schonfeld, "Liveblogging Facebook Advertising Announcement (Social Ads + Beacon + Insights)," *TechCrunch*, 6 November 2007, http://www.techcrunch.com/2007/11/06/liveblogging -facebook-advertising-announcement/. Schonfeld was taking notes and publishing without benefit of a tape recorder; Zuckerberg's phrasing may not have been transcribed exactly.

36 **Zuckerberg had no sympathy:** "Official: Facebook Poised to 'Take Over the World,'" *Daily Brief* blog, Portfolio.com, 7 November 2007, http://www.portfolio.com/views/blogs/daily-brief/2007/11/07/official -facebook-poised-to-take-over-the-world.

36 **design was changed:** Christopher Caldwell, "Intimate Shopping," *New York Times Magazine*, 23 December 2007, http://www.nytimes.com/2007/12/23/magazine/23wwln-lede-t.html.Caldwell dryly remarked: "We used to live in a world where if someone secretly followed you from store to store, recording your purchases, it would be considered impolite and even weird."

36 **they were convinced:** Louise Story, "The Evolution of Facebook's Beacon," *Bits (New York Times* blog), 29 November 2007, http://bits.blogs.nytimes .com/2007/11/29/the-evolution-of-facebooks-beacon/.

36 **Zuckerberg publicly apologized:** Mark Zuckerberg, "Thoughts on Beacon," *Facebook Blog*, 5 December 2007, http://blog.facebook.com/blog.php ?post=7584397130.

36 *60 Minutes* **featured Zuckerberg:** Kara Swisher, "Facebook: The Entire '60 Minutes' Segment," *Boomtown*, 14 January 2008, http://kara.allthingsd.com/ 20080114/facebook-the-entire-60-minutes-segment/.

37 **own sponsors:** Coca-Cola decided to take what it called a "wait-and-see" attitude before proceeding with its participation. Louise Story, "Coke Is Holding Off on Sipping Facebook's Beacon," *Bits (New York Times* blog), 30 November 2007, http://bits.blogs.nytimes.com/2007/11/30/coke-is-holding-off-on-sipping-facebooks-beacon/. Overstock.com also suspended Its participation. See "Facebook Revamps Beacon Program Amid Protests," *Online Media Daily*, 30 November 2007, http://publications.mediapost.com/index.cfm? fuseaction=Articles. showArticleHomePage&art_aid=71880, and Erick Schonfeld, "More Facebook Advertisers Bail from Beacon, Plus, New Concerns," *TechCrunch*, 3 December 2007, http://www.techcrunch .com/2007/12/03/ more-facebook-advertisers-bail-from-beacon-plus-new-concerns/.

37 **a computer's Internet address:** Google stored a small file, called a "cookie," on a user's computer when a search was conducted, which allowed it to keep track of a succession of searches, even though the searches were conducted anonymously.

37 **a 2003 murder case:** "Petrick Googled 'Neck,' 'Snap,' Among Other Words, Prosecutor Says," WRAL.com, 10 November 2005, http://www.wral.com/ news/local/story/121729/; "Petrick Prosecutors to Reopen Case with New Computer Evidence," WRAL.com, 28 November 2005, http://www .wral.com/news/local/story/122105/. The defendant Robert Petrick, who represented himself at his trial, did extract from the prosecution's computer expert the admission that all that could be said with certainty was that the searches had been conducted on the computer, but not who was on the computer at the time. See "Prosecution: Computers Map Out Petrick's Plan to Kill Wife," WRAL.com, 10 December 2005, http://www.wral.com/ news/local/story/121815/.

37 **defendant guilty:** "Robert Petrick Found Guilty in Wife's 2003 Death," WRAL.com, 29 November 2005, http://www.wral.com/news/local/story/ 122121/.

38 **Urs Hölzle:** Urs Hölzle, "Finding Needles in a Terabyte Haystack," talk delivered to Stanford EE380 Computer Systems Colloquium, 14 May 2003, http://stanford-online.stanford.edu/courses/ee380/030514-ee380-100.asx.

39 **automatically define:** Eric Eldon, "Dear Google Reader: Use OpenSocial to Figure Out Who My Friends Are," *VentureBeat*, 27 December 2007, http://venturebeat.com/2007/12/27/dear-google-reader-use-open-social-to -figure-out-who-my-friends-are/.

39 *Motley Fool:* Rick Aristotle Munarriz, "Google Comes Face to Facebook," *Motley Fool: Investing*, 28 December 2007, http://www.fool.com/investing/ general/2007/12/28/google-comes-face-to-facebook.aspx.

39 **foolish assumption:** Miguel Helft, "Google Thinks It Knows Your Friends," *Bits (New York Times* blog), 26 December 2007, http://bits.blogs .nytimes.com/2007/12/26/google-thinks-it-knows-your-friends/.

39 **Developers who tried:** Erick Schonfeld, "OpenSocial Still 'Not Open For Business,'" *TechCrunch*, 6 December 2007; Caroline McCarthy, "Google: Don't Give Up on OpenSocial," News.com, *The Social*, 13 December 2007, http://www.news.com/8301-13577_3-9833723-36.html.

39 **played the *open* card:** Ami Vora, "Opening Up Facebook Platform Architecture," *Facebook Developers* (blog), 13 December 2007, http://developers .facebook.com/news.php?blog=1&story=60.

40 **MySpace and Facebook made announcements:** Michael Arrington, "My Space Embraces DataPortability, Partners With Yahoo, Ebay and Twitter, *TechCrunch*, 8 May 2008, http://www.techcrunch.com/2008/05/08/ myspace-embraces-data-portability-partners-with-yahoo-ebay-and-twitter/; Dave Morin, "Announcing Facebook Connect," *Facebook Developers*, 9 May 2008, http://developers.facebook.com/news.php?blog=1&story=108.

40 **Google Friend Connect:** Mussie Shore, "A Friend-Connected Web," *Official Google Blog*, 12 May 2008, http://googleblog.blogspot.com/2008/05/friend -connected-web.html.

40 **Facebook blocked:** Charlie Cheever, "Thoughts on Privacy," *Facebook Developers*, 15 May 2008, http://developers.facebook.com/news.php?blog=1 &story=111.

40 **Michael Arrington wrote:** Michael Arrington, "Data Portability: It's the New Walled Garden," *TechCrunch*, 16 May 2008, http://www.techcrunch.com/ 2008/05/16/data-portability-its-the-new-walled-garden/. For a close and skeptical analysis of Facebook's claims to be protecting its members' privacy, also see Steve Gillmor, "Facebook's Glass Jaw," *TechCrunch*, 17 May 2008, http://www.techcrunch.com/2008/05/17/facebooks-glass-jaw/. Facebook's "walled garden" seemed to be of declining interest to software developers. See Vasanth Sridharan, "Google's OpenSocial Is Killing Facebook App Buzz," *Silicon Alley Insider*, 14 May 2008, http://www.alleyinsider.com/2008/5/ developers_googles_opensocial_killing_facebook_app_buzz.

40 **Google announced:** "Industry Leaders Announce Open Platform for Mobile Devices," Google press release, 5 November 2007, http://www.google.com/ intl/en/press/pressrel/20071105_mobile_open.html.

40 **Chris Sacca:** "Google: Mobile Operators Want to Block Our Apps," ZDNet .co.uk, 24 November 2006, http://news.zdnet.co.uk/communications/ 0,1000000085,39284850,00.htm.

41 **Google colleagues were upset:** Chris Sacca, "The Difference a Year Can Make," WhatIsLeft.org, 28 November 2007, http://www.whatisleft.org/. Sacca resigned from Google in December 2007; John Battelle, "A Brief Interview with Chris Sacca," *Searchblog*, 18 December 2007, http://battellemedia .com/archives/004157.php.

41 **In the summer of 2007:** Randall Stross, "When Mobile Phones Aren't Truly Mobile," *New York Times*, 22 July 2007, http://www.nytimes.com/ 2007/07/22/business/yourmoney/22digi.html.

41 **Verizon decided:** "Verizon Wireless to Introduce 'Any Apps, Any Device' Option for Customers in 2008," Verizon Wireless press release, 27 November 2007, http://news.vzw.com/news/2007/11/pr2007-11-27.html.

42 **Verizon did confer privately:** Russ Mitchell, "Search Mission, *Conde Nast Portfolio*, April 2008, http://www.portfolio.com/executives/features/ 2008/03/14/Google-CEO-Eric-Schmidt-Interview.

42 **Eric Schmidt declared:** "Verizon to Open Cell Network to Others' Phones," *Wall Street Journal*, 28 November 2007.

42 **Wikipedia:** Wikipedia always had a small number of topics—in June 2006, they numbered eighty-two—that were closed to public editing because of repeated vandalism or interminable editorial disputes. Another small group of topics were placed into "semiprotected" status, which were open to editing only by people who had been registered at the site for at least four days. See "Growing Wikipedia Refines Its 'Anyone Can Edit' Policy," *New York Times*, 17 June 2006, http://www.nytimes.com/2006/06/17/technology/ 17wiki.html.

42 **A 2006 study:** Jure Cuhalev, "Ranking of Wikipedia Articles on Search Engines for Searches About Its Own Articles," paper, http://www .kiberpipa.org/~gandalf/blog-files/wikistatus/wikistatus.pdf. Cuhalev provides a summary of his findings on his blog: "Seeing Lots of Wikipedia In Your Google Searches?" *Jure Cuhalev: In Pursuit Of the Idea*, 13 October 2006, http://www.jurecuhalev.com/blog/2006/10/13/seeing-lots-of -wikipedia-in-your-google-searches/.

42 **could not penetrate Wikipedia:** It should be remembered that the original Internet spirit, the one that goes back to the Internet's beginning in the defense establishment and in academe in the 1970s, was noncommercial. Commercial use of the Internet was expressly forbidden, until external pressure for change led in 1985 to the creation of the dot-com suffix. Wikipedia, which is overseen by a not-for-profit foundation, is a far better exemplar of the Internet's founding ethos than is Google.

42 **In December 2007:** Udi Manber, "Encouraging People to Contribute Knowledge," *Official Google Blog*, 13 December 2007, http://googleblog .blogspot.com/2007/12/encouraging-people-to-contribute.html.

43 **Charles Matthews:** See Matthews's post among the comments posted after Nicholas Carr's post, "Google Knol Takes Aim at Wikipedia," *Rough Type*, 13 December 2007, http://www.roughtype.com/archives/2007/12/google _knol_tak.php.

43 **Manber clearly anticipated:** Udi Manber, "Encouraging People to Contribute Knowledge."

43 **Danny Sullivan:** "Google: As Open as It Wants to Be (i.e., When It's Convenient)," *Search Engine Land*, 6 November 2007, http://searchengine land.com/071106-102435.php.

44 **an announcement in March 2008:** Frances Haugen and Matthew Gray, "Book Info Where You Need It, When You Need It," *Official Google Blog*, 13 March 2008, http://googleblog.blogspot.com/2008/03/book-info-where -you-need-it-when-you.html; Bethany Poole, "Preview Books Anywhere with the New Google Book Search API," *Inside Google Book Search*, 13 March 2008, http://booksearch.blogspot.com/2008/03/preview-books-anywhere -with-new-google.html.

44 **Dan Cohen:** Dan Cohen, "Still Waiting for a Real Google Book Search API," 31 March 2008, *Dan Cohen* [blog], http://googleblog.blogspot.com/ 2008/03/book-info-where-you-need-it-when-you.html.

45 **no company was purely closed:** In January 2008, Facebook joined an industry organization, the DataPortability Workgroup, created to establish standards facilitating the sharing of content among social networks. Becoming a member, however, did not signal the company's commitment to sharing its users' data with others, only that it wished to be present at the discussions of the topic. Scott Gilbertson, "Google and Facebook to Join the Data Portability Debate," *Wired Blog Network: Compiler*, 9 January 2008, http://blog .wired.com/monkeybites/2008/01/google-and-face.html; Duncan Riley, "Facebook, Google and Plaxo Join the DataPortability Workgroup," *TechCrunch*, 8 January 2008, http://www.techcrunch.com/2008/01/08/this -day-will-be-remembered-facebook-google-and-plaxo-join-the-dataportability -workgroup/. Tim Faulkner, in *Valleywag*'s characteristically tart voice, described the announcement as "about as historic as the intake of oxygen. The beauty of working groups is that they rarely change anything other than public perception." See "Facebook and Google Join Data-Swapping Group, Change Nothing," *Valleywag*, 8 January 2008, http://valleywag.com/342340/ facebook-and-google-join-data+swapping-group-change-nothing.

2. Unlimited Capacity

47 **In 1947:** Thomas J. Watson, *Father Son & Co.: My Life at IBM and Beyond* (New York: Bantam Books, 1990), 190–91.

47 **When a reporter:** "Never Stumped," *New Yorker*, 4 March 1950, 21.

47 **Hollywood copied its looks:** Kevin Maney, *The Maverick and His Machine: Thomas Watson, Sr., and the Making of IBM* (Hoboken, NJ: John Wiley & Sons, 2003), 345–46. Placing the company's new machine on very public display was a brilliant stroke of marketing on Watson's part, but it fell well short of redeeming Watson's disastrous decision to turn away John Mauchly and J. Presper Eckert, the inventors of the pathbreaking ENIAC computer, because Watson was put off by Mauchly's "loud socks."

49 **without precedent:** Google's rivals may wonder whether they should follow Google's path. In the meantime, they attempt in public to make a virtue out of their own decision to stick with just the software side of the business. In 2006, Kevin Timmons, a vice president at Yahoo, took a swipe at Google when he observed: "At some point you have to ask yourself what is your core business. Are you going to design your own router, or are you going to build the world's most popular Web site?" Google's answer has been consistent: it will do both. "A Search Engine That's Becoming an Inventor," *New York Times*, 3 July 2006, http://www.nytimes.com/2006/07/03/technology/03google.html.

49 **Larry Page began:** Philipp Lenssen, "Before Google There Was Backrub," *Google Blogoscoped*, 28 December 2007, http://blogoscoped.com/archive/2007-12-28-n47.html. For a ten-year tour of Google.com's home page, see Lenssen's "Google.com 1997–2007," *Google Blogoscoped*, originally posted 21 April 2006 but subsequently updated, http://blogoscoped.com/archive/2006-04-21-n63.html.

50 **gathered 26 million:** The 26 million Web pages, with software tricks, could be squeezed down to 53 gigabytes.

50 **established search engines:** Danny Sullivan, "How Big Are Search Engines?" *Search Engine Report*, 13 June 1997, http://searchenginewatch.com/showPage.html?page=2165301. Sullivan noted that "hardware limitations"—not only in hard drive storage capacity but also in processing power required to sort through the collected material—had kept the major search engines from expanding their coverage in the previous year. All were reporting the same number of pages, 25 to 50 million, that they had been reporting a year earlier.

50 **For three years:** "Search Us, Says Google," *Technology Review*, November/December 2000.

50 **$15,000 of their own funds:** "Search Us, Says Google"; Google Inc., "Google Milestones: The Search for a Buyer," http://www.google.com/intl/en/corporate/history.html.

50 **In early 1998, Google queries:** Sergey Brin and Larry Page, "The Anatomy of a Large-Scale Hypertextual Web Search Engine," April 1998, http://infolab.stanford.edu/~backrub/google.html.

50 **one query a second:** J. Bradford DeLong, "Google and Larry Page," *Semi-Daily Journal* (blog), 14 February 2003, http://www.j-bradford-delong.net/movable_type/2003_archives/000032.html.

51 **found a company:** Urs Hölzle, "How I Learned to Love Terabytes," talk at CERN Computing Colloquium, 7 July 2005. Brin and Page looked closely at prices and performance specs and discovered that by buying the same central processing units and same components as 100 million PC buyers, they were able to purchase thirty times the computing power that could be purchased for the same investment in high-performance servers. Brin's adviser, while encouraging him to start a company with the Google technology, assured him that he could return to complete his Ph.D. if the company didn't succeed. Brin said, "There was relatively little downside to trying." See Sergey Brin, talk as guest lecturer in the University of California, Berkeley, course "Search Engines, Technology, Society, and Business," 3 October 2005, http://video.google.com/videoplay?docid=7137075178977335350&q=sergey+brin %27.

52 **Performance issues:** This and the following account of improvements is based largely on an interview with Urs Hölzle, Mountain View, CA, 24 July 2007.

52 **received his Ph.D.:** Hölzle's dissertation title was "Adaptive Optimization for Self: Reconciling High Performance with Exploratory Programming."

52 **like eBay and Hotmail:** "The Lost Google Tapes: Interview with Larry Page, Part 3," podcast released 30 December 2006, *PodVentureZone*, January 2000, podcast from www.podventurezone.com.

53 **offered Hölzle a job:** Fifty years after IBM's rejection of John Machly on the basis of his "loud socks," socks again entered the history of computing, this time, however, as a footnote: Hölzle included in his official company biography a bit of color: that he is renowned for his "red socks," a predilection that did not bar his eligibility for his position at Google.

53 **largest search index:** Danny Sullivan, "Search Engine Sizes," *Search Engine Watch*, 28 January 2005, http://searchenginewatch.com/showPage.html?page=2156481. Sullivan reviews the history of the competition among search engines. See especially the section "Search Engine Size War I: December 1997–June 1999."

53 **When Marissa Mayer:** Julian Guthrie, "Googirl," *San Francisco*, March 2008 (the title for the online version was changed to "The Adventures of Marissa"), http://www.sanfranmag.com/story/adventures-marissa. *Valleywag* took great pleasure in noting upon the article's first appearance that the magazine editors apparently had failed to Google the word *googirl* and discover a most unflattering, raunchy noun in the Urban Dictionary. Melissa Gira Grant, "Marissa Mayer Not Really That Kinky," *Valleywag*, 28 February 2008, http://valleywag.com/361923/marissa-mayer-not-really-that-kinky. *Valleywag* then also took pleasure observing the magazine hurriedly replacing the original title for an innocuous one. Owen Thomas, " 'Googirl' Article Vanishes from Web," *Valleywag*, 28 February 2008, http://valleywag.com/362143/googirl-article-vanishes-from-web.

Notes

54 **Stanford computer science colloquium:** Urs Hölzle, "Finding Needles in a Terabyte Haystack," talk delivered to Stanford EE380 Computer Systems Colloquium, 14 May 2003, http://stanford-online.stanford.edu/courses/ee380/030514-ee380-100.asx. Google's software engineers built a special file system that broke a file into smaller chunks—*shards* was the technical term—and then spread multiple copies of the chunks over many machines. If the hard drive on any given machine failed and all of the bits on it were lost, it was a matter of no consequence: identical copies of those bits were readily available on other machines. Rather than purchase commercial disk drives that were built to be fault tolerant but were five to ten times as expensive as the ordinary, off-the-shelf hard drives that PCs are equipped with, Google wrote its own software to handle disk failures in inexpensive hard drives without missing a beat.

54 **settled on a standard design:** Luiz André Barroso, Jeffrey Dean, and Urs Hölzle, "Web Search for a Planet: The Google Cluster Architecture," *IEEE Micro*, March/April 2003. Hölzle believed that relying on unreliable hardware was preferable for a reason that had nothing to do with favorable economics—hardware that was likely to fail enforced discipline on software engineers, who knew they had to plan in advance how to handle failure "in a graceful manner." Purchasing the most expensive hardware available did not eliminate the need to plan for component failure: all hardware will fail. Even components certified as "five-9's" reliable (99.999 percent of the time) would experience failure somewhere every day in a sufficiently large collection of such machines. Programmers who assumed that hardware never fails are inclined to grow lazy, in Hölzle's view, and when a part fails, "it'll be a bad outcome." See Hölzle, "Finding Needles."

55 **Craigslist, Technorati, Second Life:** "Generator Failures Caused 365 Main Outage," *Data Center Knowledge*, 24 July 2007, http://www.datacenterknowledge.com/archives/2007/Jul/24/generator_failures_caused_365_main_outage.html; "Eleven Empty Hours for Craiglist Users," *Bits*, 25 July 2007, http://bits.blogs.nytimes.com/2007/07/25/eleven-empty-hours-for-craiglist-users/.

55 **Reducing response time:** Account based on notes taken of Marissa Mayer's presentation at a Google Scalability Conference by Dare Obasanjo, a Microsoft program manager. *Dare Obasanjo aka Carnage4Life*, 25 June 2007, http://www.25hoursaday.com/weblog/2007/06/26/GoogleScalabilityConferenceTripReportScalingGoogleForEveryUser.aspx. In its experiments, Google researchers sought to learn whether it should continue to display as a default ten search results on a page, the number Google had picked only because that was the number AltaVista had used, or instead display twenty search results on a page, as Yahoo did, which took a little bit longer to show. Google researchers tried a variety of different numbers of search results to display at one time and tracked what users did after seeing the first page.

56 **Eric Schmidt:** Eric Schmidt, Last Lectures Series talk, Graduate School of Business, Stanford, 13 April 2004, http://www.gsb.stanford.edu/multimedia/Lectures/LastLecture/schmidt.ram.

56 **in Schmidt's words:** Eric Schmidt interview at Bear Stearns 20th Annual Media Conference, 6 March 2007, http://www.youtube.com/watch?v=9HM-ZO21NwA.

57 **UNIVAC's five thousand tubes:** Kevin Maney, *The Maverick and His Machine*, 399. *Fortune* showed its readers in 1949 a picture of engineers surrounded by electric fans. The caption added that "it has been estimated that to operate a computer as complex as the human brain would require all the power of Niagara Falls to cool its millions of electronic tubes." See "Mechanical Brains," *Fortune*, May 1949, 110.

57 **Eric Schmidt once recalled:** Eric Schmidt, keynote at Roads to Innovation conference, Graduate School of Business, Stanford University, 14 November 2006, http://www.executivetalks.com/.

57 **As early as 2005:** Luiz Andre Barroso, "The Price of Performance," *ACM Queue* 3.7 (September 2005). With computer equipment's power consumption seeming to spiral out of control, Barroso worried about the impact on "the overall health of the planet," an issue that had never come up in the earlier years of computing history.

57 **design of the computers' power supply:** Urs Hölzle, "How I Learned to Love Terabytes." The standard power supply is 68 percent efficient; the more expensive one, 90 percent efficient.

58 **work to put the deal together:** "Port Deal with Google to Create Jobs," *The Dalles Chronicle*, 16 February 2005, http://www.gorgebusiness.com/2005/google.htm; Ginger Strand, "Keyword: Evil," *Harper's Magazine*, March 2008, http://harpers.org/media/slideshow/annot/2008-03/index.html.

58 **the city attorney:** "Hiding in Plain Sight, Google Seeks an Expansion of Power," *New York Times*, 14 June 2006, http://www.nytimes.com/2006/07/03/technology/03google.html.

58 **cost $600 million:** "Google Building Data Centres at a Quick Pace," *Computerworld*, 16 April 2007, http://computerworld.co.nz/news.nsf/news/C923353259FC2FDDCC2572BB001462F5.

58 **Pryor:** Sanders Mitchell, an administrator for the MidAmerica Industrial Park where Google's data center was to be located, said that his park used power from the nearby Grand River Dam Authority and offered rates that Google officials said were comparable to those they would pay in Oregon. See "Google," *Byte and Switch*, 4 June 2007, http://www.byteandswitch.com/document.asp?doc_id=123302.

58 **Council Bluffs:** The Council Bluffs area does not have a hydropower plant. The MidAmerican Energy Company, which will supply electricity to Google's center, had a newly expanded coal-fired plant in the city. It would not discuss with a Reuters reporter its arrangements with Google, however, citing its con-

fidentiality agreement with Google. See "Google to Build $600 Million Data Center in Iowa," *Reuters*, 19 June 2007, http://www.reuters.com/article/idUSN1916606420070619.

58 **Tommy Tomlinson:** Tommy Tomlinson, "Were We Googled or Gouged?" *Charlotte Observer*, 11 February 2007, http://www.charlotte.com/mld/observer/news/local/16674221.htm.

59 **Lloyd Taylor:** Lloyd Taylor, "Letter: Why Google Did What It Did," *Charlotte Observer*, 8 February 2007, http://www.charlotte.com/mld/observer/news/opinion/16649216.htm. Taylor ended up confirming the very criticism that large companies encourage states to participate in a "race to the bottom," each encouraged to match or outdo the lowest bid among the others.

59 **In a public talk:** Hölzle, "How I Learned To Love Terabytes."

59 **Two hundred jobs:** John Foley, "Google's Data Center Strategy Revealed . . . at the Rotary Club," *Information Week's Google Weblog*, 30 November 2007, http://www.informationweek.com/blog/main/archives/2007/11/googles_data_ce.html.

59 *Charlotte Observer*'s **Tomlinson:** Tomlinson, "Were We Googled or Gouged?"

60 **hired an IT expert:** "Inside the World of Google The Dalles," *The Dalles Chronicle*, 5 August 2007, http://www.thedalleschronicle.com/news/2007/08/news08-05-07-02.shtml.

60 **In April 2004:** Schmidt, Last Lectures Series talk.

61 **Schmidt has described:** Schmidt interview at Bear Stearns.

3. The Algorithm

64 **The company says that only a small number:** Matt Cutts's comment, 20 February 2008, http://battellemedia.com/archives/003744.php#comment_128693, to a post John Battelle had made seven months previously: "Just Asking," *Searchblog*, 19 June 2007, http://battellemedia.com/archives/003744.php. Cutts apologized for taking a long time to send in Google's official response to Battelle's inquiry about the company's privacy policies. Cutts said that he had sought and received a response from his company's officials, but that it had sat unnoticed in his e-mail inbox for more than six months.

65 **Facebook's employees:** Owen Thomas, "Why Facebook Employees Are Profiling Users," *Valleywag*, 29 October 2007, http://valleywag.com/tech/your-privacy-is-an-illusion/why-facebook-employees-are-profiling-users-316469.php. Thomas wrote, "What happens when you put twentysomethings in charge of a company with vast amounts of private information? Sheer madcap chaos, of course."

66 **unlikely to pose a competitive threat:** Chris Sherman, "Google Announces Largest Index," *Search Engine Report*, 5 July 2000, http://searchenginewatch .com/showPage.html?page=2162751.

67 **conventional wisdom of the time:** Danny Sullivan, "Microsoft's MSN Search to Build Crawler-Based Search Engine," *Search Engine Watch*, 1 July 2003, http://searchenginewatch.com/showPage.html?page=2230291.

67 **Two out of three of Yahoo's visitors:** "With Goto.com's Search Engine, the Highest Bidder Shall Be Ranked First," *New York Times*, 16 March 1998. Yahoo was the most popular site, however, for conducting Web searches. Danny Sullivan, "Lycos Transforms into Directory," *Search Engine Report*, 4 May 1999, http://searchenginewatch.com/showPage.html?page=2167171.

67 **Yahoo changed its suppliers:** Yahoo contracted with, successively, Open Text, AltaVista, and Inktomi.

67 **a major achievement:** Danny Sullivan, "Yahoo Partners with Google," *Search Engine Report*, 5 July 2000, http://searchenginewatch.com/showPage.html ?page=2162831.

68 **in a crowded field:** Sullivan, "Yahoo Partners with Google"; Sullivan, "NPD Search and Portal Site Study," *Search Engine Report*, 6 July 2000, http://searchenginewatch.com/showPage.html?page=2162791. Ninety-seven percent of 33,000 respondents reported that they found at Google what they were looking for every time or most of the time.

68 **Google was hungry enough:** Danny Sullivan, "Good for Google Does Not Equal Bad for Inktomi," *Search Engine Report*, 5 July 2000, http://search enginewatch.com/showPage.html?page=2162771.

68 **By April 2002:** "Google Is the Most Popular Search Engine on the Web According to OneStat.com," OneStat.com press release, 15 April 2002, http://www.onestat.com/html/aboutus_pressbox3.html.

68 **its own engine:** When Yahoo switched to its own search engine, it did not have to build one from scratch: it had technology from no fewer than three search-engine companies that it had acquired—Inktomi, AltaVista, and AlltheWeb.

68 **In May 2007:** "comScore Releases June U.S. Search Engine Rankings," comScore press release, 16 July 2007, http://www.comscore.com/press/release.asp ?press=1525.

68 **by January 2008:** "comScore Releases January 2008 U.S. Search Engine Rankings," comScore press release, 21 January 2008, http://www.comscore .com/press/release.asp?press=2068. Microsoft's share was 9.8 percent.

68 **Rich Skrenta:** Rich Skrenta, "Google's True Search Market Share Is 70 percent," *Skrentablog*, 19 December 2006, http://www.skrenta.com/2006/12/ googles_true_search_market_sha.html.

68 **In early 2007, Skrenta confessed:** Rich Skrenta, "Winner-Take-All: Google and the Third Age of Computing," *Skrentablog*, 1 January 2007, http:// www.skrenta.com/2007/01/winnertakeall_google_and_the_t.html.

68 **company officials offered:** "Microsoft Proposes Acquisition of Yahoo! Conference Call," transcript, 1 February 2008, http://www.microsoft.com/ presspass/press/2008/feb08/02-01Transcript.mspx.

69 **settle for what they chose:** Danny Sullivan, "Yahoo: Delays Expected," *Search Engine Report*, 3 September 1997, http://searchenginewatch.com/show Page.html?page=2165541.

69 **8 billion pages indexed:** Google Inc., "Google Milestones," http://www .google.com/corporate/history.html.

69 **When I speak about search:** Sullivan, "Yahoo Partners with Google."

70 **a blogger noted in 2004:** Robert Scoble, "Just a Little Search Comparison," *Scobleizer*, 28 November 2004, http://radio.weblogs.com/0001011/ 2004/11/28.html#a8764. Scoble left Microsoft in 2006.

70 **the defection of Microsoft developers:** "Move to Google Said to Upset Ballmer," *San Francisco Chronicle*, 3 September 2005. The case in which the affidavit was filed involved Kai-fu Lee, who had been vice president of Microsoft's Interactive Services Division. Microsoft sued Lee and Google in July 2005 for allegedly violating the noncompete clause in Lee's employment contract. The suit was settled in December 2005 with a private agreement among the parties. See "Microsoft Settles with Google over Executive Hire," *News.com*, 22 December 2005, http://news.cnet .com/Microsoft+settles+with+Google+over+executive+hire/2100-1014_3 -6006342.html.

71 **Microsoft chairman Bill Gates:** Tony Perkins, "Gates on Google," reprint of 2004 post, *AlwaysOn*, 3 February 2004, http://tuneinturnon.goingon.com/ permalink/post/706.

71 **managers encouraged employees:** Adam Barr, "Using Our Own Products," *Proudly Serving My Corporate Masters* (blog), 6 October 2005, http://www.proudlyserving.com/archives/2005/10/using_our_own_p.html. In 2000, Barr published an account of ten years of experience at Microsoft: *Proudly Serving My Corporate Masters: What I Learned in Ten Years as a Microsoft Programmer* (Writers Club Press, 2000). According to his blog, Barr was still proudly serving in June 2008.

72 **The first comment posted:** Adam Herscher comment, posted 7 October, 2005, http://www.proudlyserving.com/archives/2005/10/using_our_own _p.html. Herscher left Microsoft to start a new company in June 2007. Adam Herscher, "Leaving Microsoft," *The Road Less Traveled*, 25 June 2007, http://adamjh.blogspot.com/.

72 **Microsoft hired an outsider:** "Chief of Ask Jeeves to Lead Microsoft's Internet Unit," *New York Times*, 22 April 2006, http://www.nytimes .com/2006/04/22/technology/22msn.html.

72 **At the end of 2006:** "Looking for a Gambit to Win at Google's Game," *New York Times*, 9 December 2006, http://www.nytimes.com/2006/12/09/ technology/09msn.html.

73 **attempt to depict:** "Why on Earth Does the World Need Another Search Engine," Microsoft advertisement, *Wall Street Journal*, 27 October 2006.

73 *Searchblog* **broke the story:** John Battelle, "Microsoft Deal for Large Customers: Use Live Search, Get Free MSFT Products," *Searchblog*, 15 March 2007, http://battellemedia.com/archives/003447.php.

73 **Adam Sohn:** Randall Stross, "If at First You Don't Succeed, Write a Check," *New York Times*, 1 April 2007, http://www.nytimes.com/2007/04/01/business/yourmoney/01digi.html. Microsoft sought thirty companies with five thousand or more PCs that would "earn" $2 to $10 per employee annually in credits for Microsoft products based on the number of searches performed using MSN's search service. The year before, Yahoo had explored what appeared to be a rewards program for its search service, and had surveyed Yahoo mail customers about what reward would be sufficiently enticing to be worth designating Yahoo as their primary search engine. Free music downloads? Netflix discount? Frequent flier miles? But after the survey was completed, Yahoo decided not to start the program.

74 **removed from the position:** "Microsoft Reassigns Several Top Executives," *New York Times*, 15 February 2008, http://www.nytimes.com/2008/02/15/technology/15soft.html. Berkowitz had joined Microsoft in April 2006; his position was eliminated in February 2008, at which time Microsoft said he was expected to leave the company in August.

74 **in the spring of 2007:** "Ask.com Debuts 'The Algorithm' Brand Advertising Campaign," Ask press release, 3 May 2007, http://www.irconnect.com/ask/pages/news_releases.html?d=120812.

75 **Cory Doctorow:** "Wiki-Inspired 'Transparent' Search-Engine," *BoingBoing*, 1 January 2008, http://www.boingboing.net/2008/01/01/wikiinspired -transpa.html.

75 **Tim O'Reilly pointed out:** Tim O'Reilly, "Human vs. Machine: The Great Challenge of Our Time," *O'Reilly Radar*, 4 January 2008, http://radar.oreilly.com/archives/2008/01/human_vs_machine_google_ wallstreet.html. O'Reilly cited the comments of Eric Blossom, who had posted comments on an earlier *O'Reilly Radar* post, "Trading for Their Own Account," on 28 December 2007, http://radar.oreilly.com/archives/2007/12/google_knol_trading_own_account.html.

75 **is himself Jewish:** For a profile of Brin prepared for an independent Jewish magazine, see Mark Malseed, "The Story of Sergey Brin," *Moment*, February 2007, http://www.momentmag.com/Exclusive/2007/2007-02/200702 -BrinFeature.html.

75 **he, too, was offended:** "Google Says Anti-Semitic Site Offends, but to Stay," *Reuters News*, 13 April 2004. The primary reason Jewwatch.com turned out to rank at the top of the results for *Jew* or *Jews* was the hate groups' predilection for using *Jew* where everyone else used the adjective *Jewish* or other nouns, like *Judaism*. The site's high placement also benefited by the way the

Google formula favored sites that were in place for a long time—Jewwatch had been started in 1997—and by inbound links from other sites. The Anti-Defamation League could have been expected to call for Google to take action but the organization was persuaded that it was best that Google not interfere with the workings of its own system. It issued a letter that supported Google's use of an algorithm to determine results: "The ranking of Jewwatch and other hate sites is in no way due to a conscious choice by Google, but solely is a result of this automated system of ranking." Anti-Defamation League, "Google Search Ranking of Hate Sites Not Intentional," press release, 22 April 2004, http://www.adl.org.rumors/google_search_rumors.asp. Without giving any ground on the central question of whether it should in certain instances hand-edit results, Google executives held to their position that the algorithm should have the final say. The only concession the company made was to place on the search results page for the term *Jew* an additional link, labeled "Offensive Search Results," which provided users a full explanation of the linguistic quirk that produced high placements of hate sites on the results page for the search term *Jew* and of the company's policy to remove only sites that "we are legally compelled to remove or those maliciously attempting to manipulate our results." It closed with an apology for "the upsetting nature of the experience." Sergey Brin to Abraham H. Forman, 21 April 2004, http://www.adl.org/internet/google_letter.asp; Google, "An Explanation of Our Search Results," http://www.google.com/explanation.html. When a search for *Jew* was submitted at Google on 16 June 2008, the Jewwatch.com site appeared third, following Wikipedia entries for *Jew* and for *Judaism*.

76 **Peter Norvig:** Comments made at "The Ethics and Politics of Search Engines," panel discussion at the Markkula Center for Applied Ethics, Santa Clara University, 27 February 2006, http://www.scu.edu/ethics/publications/submitted/search-engine-panel.html.

76 **creating in such special cases:** O'Reilly, "Human vs. Machine." Peter Norvig disclosed the existence of these special cases that are "a small percentage of Google pages."

76 **human evaluators:** Marissa Mayer mentioned that Google had "10,000 human evaluators" at a Google Scalability Conference in 2007, as reported by Microsoft blogger Dare Obasanjo, *Dare Obasanjo aka Carnage4Life*, 25 June 2007, http://www.25hoursaday.com/weblog/2007/06/26/GoogleScalability ConferenceTripReportScalingGoogleForEveryUser.aspx. Peter Norvig also publicly described how contractors identified spam and other sites for Google to avoid when presenting search results. See "Q&A: Peter Norvig," *Technology Review*, January/February 2008, http://www.technologyreview.com/Infotech/19868/.

76 **manually exclude links:** Saul Hansell, "Google: There's Nobody in Our Black Box. Yet." *Bits* (*New York Times* blog), 19 December 2007, http://bits.blogs.nytimes.com/2007/12/19/google-theres-nobody-in-our-black-box

-yet/. Hansell said that Google's Matt Cutts "would not go so far as to say Google never uses this sort of distributed workforce to help flesh out parts of its formulas," and allowed that human reports of Web spam were used to clean up Google's index. But Cutts said that "Google vastly prefers a fully automated way to solve a problem."

77 **in March 2002:** The company officially launched—that is, officially announced its beta version of—Google News in September 2002, but the site had appeared months earlier. The Wayback Machine first crawled news.google.com on 25 March 2002. See http://web.archive.org/ web/*/http://news.google.com.

77 **Jonathan Rosenberg:** Jonathan Rosenberg, remarks at Google Press Day, 10 May 2006, http://www.google.com/press/pressday.html.

77 **"No humans were harmed":** Jonathan Dube, "Novel Approach to News," *Web Tips/Poynteronline*, 27 September 2002, http://www.poynter.org/ column.asp?id=32&aid=7127.

77 **questions about Google News:** "Google News Search," included in the Wayback Machine's crawl that was completed on 1 November 2002, http://web.archive.org/web/20021013214112/news.google.com/help/about_news_search.html. An earlier version of the information page had used slightly different wording, referring to selections made by "computer algorithms, based on how and where the stories appear elsewhere on the web." See the version collected in the crawl completed on 22 September 2002, http://web.archive.org/web/20021013214112/news.google.com/help/about_news_search.html.

78 **media critic Howard Kurtz:** "Robotic Journalism: Google Introduces Human-Less News," *Washington Post*, 30 September 2002. Kurtz acutely observed another reason why Google's news site referrals would likely hurt news organizations financially. Even though Google's links sent readers to the online sources of the stories it listed, Kurtz noted that "it is less lucrative for news outlets to draw readers for a single story than those who come in through the 'front door' because they're exposed to fewer ads."

78 **corporate press release:** "This Is Google News: Press Releases," CBS.Marketwatch.com, 18 December 2002, http://www.marketwatch.com/News/Story/Story.aspx?guid=%7B27C5CF0B-BB3D-411F-8341-1BAA5BAB138C%7D&source=blq%Fyhoo&dist=yhoo&siteid=yhoo.

78 **on February 1, 2003:** Staci D. Kramer, "Shuttle Disaster Coverage Mixed, but Strong Overall," *Online Journalism Review*, 3 February 2003, http://www.ojr.org/ojr/kramer/1044260857.php.

79 **filed patents in 2005:** Barry Fox, "Google Searches for Quality Not Quantity," *New Scientist*, 30 April 2005, http://www.newscientist.com/article.ns?id=mg18624975.900.

79 **New Jersey high school student:** Jim Hedger, "Google News Credibility Foiled by 15-Year-Old," *Stepforth SEO News Blog*, 13 March 2006,

http://news.stepforth.com/blog/2006/03/google-news-credibility-foiled-by
-15.php; "Google News Dumps Partner After Prank Item Appears,"
News.com, 20 March 2006, http://news.com.com/Google+News+dumps
+partner+after+prank+item+appears/2100-1025_3-6051690.html.

79 **four years after it had launched:** Bill Tancer, "Google, Yahoo! and MSN:
Property Size-Up," *Hitwise Intelligence*, 19 May 2006, http://weblogs.hitwise
.com/bill-tancer/2006/05/google_yahoo_and_msn_property.html. For the
week ending 13 May 2006, Yahoo News drew 6.3 percent of all Internet
visits to news sites, compared to Google News's 1.9 percent.

80 **In 1953, Howard Aiken:** "Will Machines Replace the Human Brain?" *American Mercury*, January 1953, 55. Faster machines were also expected to help in
the textual analysis and assembly of a concordance of the Dead Sea Scrolls.
Father Roberto Busa, who was attached to Rome's Gregorian University and
was overseeing the textual analysis of the complete works of Saint Thomas
Aquinas, was quoted in *Time*: "I am praying to God for ever faster, ever
more accurate machines." See "Sacred Electronics," *Time*, 31 December
1956, 48.

80 **The next year, IBM scientists:** "Electronic Translator," *Time*, 18 January
1954, 82; "Bilingual Machine," *Newsweek*, 18 January 1954, 83.

81 **Six years later:** "Machines Are This Smart," *Newsweek*, 24 October 1960,
86–87.

81 **extending to forty language pairs:** "Fancy Math Takes On *Je Ne Sais Quoi*,"
Christian Science Monitor, 2 June 2005, http://www.csmonitor.com/
2005/0602/p13s02-stct.htm.

82 **At a briefing in May 2005:** "Fancy Math Takes On *Je Ne Sais Quoi*," *Christian
Science Monitor*. A prepared demonstration that produced a good translation
of one headline, even if impressively idiomatic, could have been nothing more
than a parlor trick. When IBM in 1954 had given reporters a demonstration
of its Russian-to-English translation software, a sentence in Russian had been
typed in and, voilà, the "mechanical brain," with its 250-word vocabulary, had
produced "We transmit thoughts by means of speech." A scholar affiliated
with Georgetown University, Leon Dostert, predicted at the time that
machine translation could well be "an accomplished fact" within five, perhaps
even three, years. "Electronic Translator," *Time*.

82 **In 2005:** National Institute of Standards and Technology, "NIST 2005
Machine Translation Evaluation Official Results," 1 August 2005,
http://www.nist.gov/speech/tests/mt/doc/mt05eval_official_results_release_
20050801_v3.html.

84 **"We don't have":** Norvig was quoted in Tim O'Reilly, "Why Google Is
Offering 411 Service," *O'Reilly Radar*, 13 April 2007, http://radar
.oreilly.com/archives/2007/04/why_google_is_o.html.

84 **Dimitris Sabatakakis:** Gary Stix, "The Elusive Goal of Machine Translation," *Scientific American*, March 2006, 95.

85 **in 2006:** "NIST 2006 Machine Translation Evaluation Official Results," 1 November 2006, http://www.nist.gov/speech/tests/mt/doc/mt06eval_official_results.html.

85 **Franz Och, the Google engineer:** Franz Och, "Challenges in Machine Translation," talk to International Macintosh Users Group, Apple headquarters, Cupertino, CA, 19 April 2007.

85 **supplied users:** Users could not fully see what Google's machine-translation algorithm was capable of because the version used in "production" on Google's public Web site was not permitted to tie up machines for an hour working on the translation of a single sentence as the researchers' own version could.

85 **When Sarmad Ali:** "With Online Services, Foreign Texts Can Get Lost in Translation," *Wall Street Journal*, 20 December 2007, http://ptech.all thingsd.com/20071220/with-online-services-foreign-texts-can-get-lost-in -translation/.

86 **at a public talk earlier that year:** Och, "Challenges in Machine Translation." The world outside of Google and outside of the machine-translation research community does not seem particularly interested in this work. The audience for Och's talk was so small that no auditorium was needed: everyone who was interested in the subject of Google's "Challenges in Machine Translation" fit around a square of tables in a side conference room.

86 **a set of DVDs:** The data, which were released in September 2006, took up about 24 gigabytes of compressed text files, required six DVDs, and cost $150 to purchasers who were not members of the Linguistics Data Consortium. See the LDS's catalog entry for "Web 1T 5-gram Version 1," http://www.ldc.upenn.edu/Catalog/CatalogEntry.jsp?catalogId=LDC2006T13.

86 **translate texts in any language:** Eric Schmidt ventured some thoughts on the subject in 2007: "What happens when the million books in Arabic that have never been translated into any language other than Arabic are translated into English? What happens when all the English texts that have never been translated into Arabic are translated into Arabic?" He did not predict the imminent arrival of peace and harmony, nor did he predict a melding of languages into a universally shared one ("the fans of Esperanto might fight me on this"). See Schmidt interview at Bear Stearns 20th Annual Media Conference, 6 March 2007, http://www.youtube.com/watch?v=9HM-ZO21NwA.

86 **by May 2008:** Jeff Chin, "Google Translate Adds 10 New Languages," *Official Google Blog*, 15 May 2008, http://googleblog.blogspot.com/2008/05/google-translate-adds-10-new-languages.html; "Google Translate FAQ," http://www.google.com/intl/en/help/faq_translation.html.

87 **Marissa Mayer:** "Google Wants Your Phonemes," *Infoworld*, 23 October 2007, http://www.infoworld.com/article/07/10/23/Google-wants-your -phonemes_1.html. Tim O'Reilly pointed out that Eckart Walther of Yahoo had told him that speech recognition software had advanced significantly

when automated speech recognition had been used for directory assistance calls and enormous amounts of data—millions of voices and accents—could be captured. Tim O'Reilly, "Why Google Is Offering 411 Service," *O'Reilly Radar*.

87 **More data is better data:** As time passed and Google's information silos grew ever bigger and its algorithms smarter, the opportunities for dramatic improvements diminished steeply. Google's machine-translation team discovered that the law of diminishing returns severely restricted the pace of progress. Doubling the size of the monolingual training data was now improving the quality index (that 0 to 1 scale) by only 0.5 percent. If Google could double the number of pairs of texts in two languages like those prepared by the European Union or the United Nations—what was referred to in the field as "parallel data"—the 100 percent increase in the volume of training data would improve the scores by only about 2.5 percent.

4. Moon Shot

89 **Page explained:** Sergey Brin and Larry Page, "The Future of the Internet," Commonwealth Club of California, 21 March 2001, http://commonwealth club.org/archive/01/01-03google-speech.html; Q&A: http://commonwealth club.org/archive/01/01-03google-qa.html.

90 **"our moon shot":** Jeffrey Toobin, "Google's Moon Shot," *New Yorker*, 5 February 2007, http://www.newyorker.com/reporting/2007/02/05/070205fa _fact_toobin.

90 **Google Lunar X Prize:** "Google Sponsors Lunar X Prize to Create a Space Race for a New Generation," press release, 13 September 2007, http://www.googlelunarxprize.org/lunar/press-release/google-sponsors-lunar -x-prize-to-create-a-space-race-for-a-new-generation.

90 **high-volume scanning:** The engineering challenges posed in scanning books were of standing interest to Larry Page. In 2005 he said that eight years earlier he had been curious to learn how fast the speediest available scanners could scan and had visited a local electronics store to investigate. There he had discovered that all of the scanners provided information about the resolution of their scans, but none disclosed their scanning speeds. Recalling the experience later, he said he did not want a scanner that provided 2,400-dots-per-inch resolution, which was sufficiently sensitive to record "dust on your paper." What he wanted was a machine that could scan pages quickly. None made such a claim because "they were all really, really, really slow." "Continuous Innovation," Zeitgeist '05: The Google Partner Forum, 26 October 2005, http://www.google.com/press/podium/brin.html.

91 **ran an experiment:** Google, "History of Google Book Search," Google Book Search: News & Views, n.d., http://books.google.com/googlebooks/

newsviews/history.html. Another example of the tale being told is in Craig Silverstein's talk at the University of North Carolina at Chapel Hill, "Google's Vision for the 21st Century", 26 October 2006, http://www.hsl.unc.edu/google/Videos.cfm (specific video segment: "Google Books/Google Scholar").

91 **Adam Smith:** Smith was asked the question by this book's author during an interview in Mountain View, 19 September 2007. Smith's corporate biography described his position as "Product Management Director at Google with product development responsibility for Content products including Google Book Search, Google Scholar, and Google News Archives."

91 **when Larry Page visited:** Mary Sue Coleman, "Google, the Khmer Rouge and the Public Good," 6 February 2006, http://www.umich.edu/pres/speeches/060206google-print.html.

92 **started by Michael Hart:** Michael Hart, "Gutenberg: The History and Philosophy of Project Gutenberg," [1992?], http://www.gutenberg.org/wiki/Gutenberg:The_History_and_Philosophy_of_Project_Gutenberg_by_Michael_Hart.

93 **eschewed the notion:** Hart, "Gutenberg."

93 **about 6,300 works:** *Project Gutenberg Weekly Newsletter*, 6 November 2002, http://www.pg-news.org/nl_archives/2002/pgweekly_2002_11_06.txt.

93 **the library began:** Library of Congress American Memory, "Mission and History," n.d., http://memory.loc.gov/ammem/about/index.html. In 1994, the National Digital Library Program began with $13 million in donations from the private sector, and with congressional funds that added $15 million over five years and another $45 million in private sponsors between 1994 and 2000. Private foundations were willing to fund pilot programs for digitization of important historical materials, which, in some cases, did include books. The University of Michigan and Cornell University received funding from the Andrew W. Mellon Foundation, for example, to begin a project in 1995 on "Making of America," which entailed digitizing about 1,600 books and ten journals from a narrow swath of time in U.S. history—1850 to 1877. Neither foundation nor the universities, however, contemplated a moon shot, digitizing all books.

93 **$500,000 grant:** National Science Foundation, ITR/IM: The Million Book Project, award abstract #0113878, 21 August 2001, http://www.nsf.gov/awardsearch/showAward.do?AwardNumber=0113878.

93 **stepped forward:** Brewster Kahle, "Public Access to Digital Materials," talk at the Library of Congress, Washington, D.C., 20 November 2002, http://www.loc.gov/rr/program/lectures/video/kahle-press.ram.

93 **another $2.5 million:** Carnegie Mellon Libraries, "Frequently Asked Questions About the Million Book Project," revised 9 April 2007, http://www.library.cmu.edu/Libraries/MBP_FAQ.html.

94 **Kahle was talking up:** Kahle, "Public Access to Digital Materials." Four years after his 2002 talk at the Library of Congress, Kahle described the

opportunity to make all the world's information universally accessible: "This is our chance to one up the Greeks!" Quoted in Kevin Kelly, "Scan This Book!" *New York Times Magazine*, 14 May 2006, http://www.nytimes.com/2006/05/14/magazine/14publishing.html.

94 **When Google's team:** Daniel Clancy, "Google Book Search," talk delivered to Stanford EE380 Computer Systems Colloquium, 15 February 2006, http://stanford-online.stanford.edu/courses/ee380/060215-ee380-250.asx.

95 **The Google solution:** Adam Smith, interview, Mountain View, CA, 19 September 2007.

95 **The human touch:** For two instances of plainly visible fingers, see Duncan Riley, "Google Books Adds Hand Scans," *TechCrunch*, 6 December 2007, http://www.techcrunch.com/2007/12/06/google-books-adds-hand-scans/; Dan Cohen, "Google Fingers," *Dan Cohen* (blog), 26 June 2006, http://www.dancohen.org/2006/06/26/google-fingers/.

95 **Google did not disclose:** Clancy, "Google Book Search."

95 **Other companies:** Microsoft representative Danielle Tiedt put the digitization cost per page as ten cents. "Book Digitization and the Revenge of the Librarians Episode," panel discussion at SXSW Interactive Conference, Austin, TX, 11 March 2006, http://www.podcastdirectory.com/podshows/327406.

96 **Clancy answered:** Clancy, "Google Book Search."

96 **still under copyright:** Earlier book digitization projects had skirted copyright problems by working only with historical works long out of copyright, like "Making of America" and Project Gutenberg. The Million Book Project encountered copyright issues from the moment of its inception. India and China, the two countries most active in the actual scanning for the Million Book Project, passed laws that, in the project's description, "effectively circumvent the need to acquire permission from the copyright owner to digitize copyrighted works." See Carnegie Mellon Libraries, "Frequently Asked Questions About the Million Book Project."

97 **reports had surfaced:** "Amazon Plan Would Allow Searching Texts of Many Books," *New York Times*, 21 July 2003.

97 **Google invited:** Chris Sherman, "Google Introduces Book Searches," *Search Engine Watch*, 17 December 2003, http://searchenginewatch.com/showPage.html?page=3290351.

97 **soothing publishers:** "Publishers Grudgingly Cooperate with Amazon Database Effort," *Publishers Weekly*, 15 September 2003.

97 **When Amazon publicly unveiled:** Gary Price, "Amazon Debuts New Book Search Tool," *Search Engine Watch*, 27 October 2003, http://searchenginewatch.com/showPage .html?page=3098831.

98 **Google Print:** Google began to integrate references to books as early as December 2003, but was unwilling to comment on how many book excerpts were available or even how long the "experiment" would last. See "Google

Experiment Provides Internet with Book Excerpts," *New York Times*, 18 December 2003. The official launch of Google Print came at the Frankfurt Book Fair in October 2004. "History of Google Book Search," http://books.google.com/googlebooks/newsviews/history.html. The following publishers had joined at the time of the official launch: Blackwell, Cambridge University Press, the University of Chicago Press, Houghton Mifflin, Hyperion, McGraw-Hill, Oxford University Press, Pearson, Penguin, Perseus, Princeton University Press, Springer, Taylor & Francis, Thomson Delmar, and Warner Books.

98 **Adam Smith:** Adam Smith, interview, Mountain View, CA, 19 September 2007.

98 **Daniel Clancy would later say:** Clancy, "Google Book Search."

98 **In December 2004:** "Google Checks Out Library Books," Google press release, 14 December 2004, http://www.google.com/press/pressrel/print_library.html.

98 **the participating libraries:** "Google Is Adding Major Libraries to Its Database," *New York Times*, 14 December 2004. The *Times* article said that Stanford was, like Michigan, making nearly all of its library collections available, but this was not the case. See Stanford's press release, "Stanford and Google to Make Library Books Available Online," Stanford News Service press release, 14 December 2004, http://news-service.stanford.edu/pr/2004/pr-google-011205.html.

99 **Jack Romanos:** John Heilemann, "Googlephobia," *New York*, 5 December 2005.

99 **Authors Guild:** "Authors Guild Sues Google, Citing 'Massive Copyright Infringement,'" Authors Guild press release, 20 September 2005, http://www.authorsguild.org/news/sues_google_citing.htm. In addition to the Authors Guild itself, three guild members were the nominal plaintiffs: Daniel Hoffman, Betty Miles, and Herbert Mitgang. For the complaint, see http://fl1.findlaw.com/news.findlaw.com/hdocs/docs/google/aggoog92005cmp.pdf.

100 **a group of publishers:** The McGraw-Hill Companies Inc., Pearson Education, Inc., Penguin Group (USA) Inc., Simon & Schuster, Inc., and John Wiley & Sons, Inc. v. Google Inc., complaint filed in United States District Court, Southern District of New York, 19 October 2005, http://www.publishers.org/press/pdf/40%20McGraw-Hill%20v.%20Google.pdf., 3.

100 **Patricia S. Schroeder:** Heilemann, "Googlephobia."

100 **originated in 1999:** "Don't Be Evil or Don't Lose Value?" *Sydney Morning Herald*, 15 April 2008, http://www.smh.com.au/news/biztech/dont-be-evil/2008/04/15/1208025168177.html.

101 **Patel spread:** Jessica Livingston, *Founders at Work: Stories of Startups' Early Days* (Berkeley, CA: Apress, 2007), 169–70. Buchheit said that "I believe that [the meeting] was sometime in early 2000," but in John Battelle's account, his sources said it took place on 19 July 2001. See Battelle, *The Search*, 138.

101 **"ten things:** Google Web site, "Corporate Information: Our Philosophy," http://www.google.com/intl/en/corporate/tenthings.html.

101 **Critics previously had said:** Danny Sullivan, "14 'Is Google Evil?' Tipping Points Since 2001," *Search Engine Land*, 1 January 2007, http://searchengineland.com/070101-215524.php. One of Sullivan's fourteen "tipping points" was a January 2003 article in *Wired* magazine: "Google vs. Evil," http://www.wired.com/wired/archive/11.01/google_pr.html.

101 **A Thomas Friedman column:** Thomas Friedman, "Is Google God?" *New York Times*, 29 June 2003. Friedman did not refer to Google's "Don't Be Evil" motto; he discussed the company's growing international traffic as an example of how "the world is getting more integrated."

101 **Google dropped:** Jen Grant, "Judging Book Search by Its Cover," *Official Google Blog*, 17 November 2005, http://googleblog.blogspot.com/2005/11/judging-book-search-by-its-cover.html.

102 **When the lawsuits:** Toobin, "Google's Moon Shot."

102 **Mary Sue Coleman:** Coleman, "Google, the Khmer Rouge and the Public Good."

102 **Lawrence Lessig:** Lawrence Lessig, "Four Anti-Google Book Search Fallacies—All In One, Single Essay," *Lessig Blog*, 13 March 2007, http://www.lessig.org/blog/archives/003731.shtml. Another law professor, Columbia's Timothy Wu, offered another argument in defense of Google Print: that it was part of the broader shift from "the culture of authorial control" to that of "authorial exposure." Wu attempted to draw an analogy between Google's index to Web pages and to book pages: "Consider what it would mean, by analogy, if mapmakers needed the permission of landowners to create maps. . . . Imagine how terrible maps would be if you had to negotiate with every landowner in the United States to publish the Rand McNally Road Atlas." Tim Wu, "Leggo My Ego," *Slate,* 17 October 2005, http://www.slate.com/id/2128094/.

103 **three snippets:** Clancy, "Google Book Search."

103 **initiative had begun:** "In Challenge to Google, Yahoo Will Scan Books," *New York Times*, 3 October 2005, http://www.nytimes.com/2005/10/03/business/03yahoo.html.

103 **dependent upon handouts:** "Google Book-Scanning Efforts Spark Debate," *Associated Press Online*, 20 December 2006, http://www.nytimes.com/aponline/technology/AP-Digital-Library.html.

103 **The initiative was stymied:** Tim O'Reilly, "Book Search Should Work Like Web Search," *O'Reilly Radar*, 11 December 2006, http://radar.oreilly.com/archives/2006/12/book_search_sho.html. O'Reilly said that he had spoken with the American Antiquarian Society and Stanford about their willingness to lend their materials for a second scan; both organizations said that the most important rare works would have to be rescanned to attain images of archival quality, but they did say that for the present only a single scan was feasible.

103 **"We want a public library system"**: "U. of California Will Provide Up to 3,000 Books a Day to Google for Scanning, Contract States," *Chronicle of Higher Education*, 25 August 2006, http://chronicle.com/free/2006/08/2006082501t.htm

103 **Microsoft**: "Open Content Alliance Expands Rapidly; Reveals Operational Details," Information Today, 31 October 2005, http://newsbreaks.infotoday.com/nbreader.asp?ArticleID=16091.

103 **limited the scope of its scanning**: Microsoft declined to disclose the number of books that it intended to scan. In June 2006, the company announced agreements with the University of California and University of Toronto libraries, and referred to the size of the collections—34 million volumes and 15 million volumes, respectively—but did not say what percentage would be scanned. See "Microsoft to Collaborate with University of California and University of Toronto Libraries for Windows Live Book Search," Microsoft press release, 8 June 2006, http://www.microsoft.com/presspass/press/2006/jun06/06-08BookSearchPR.mspx.

103 **Thomas Rubin**: Thomas C. Rubin, remarks for the Association of American Publishers Annual Meeting, Yale Club of New York, 6 March 2007, http://www.microsoft.com/presspass/exec/trubin/03-05-07AmericanPublishers.mspx.

104 **As a participant**: "Book Digitization and the Revenge of the Librarians Episode," panel discussion at SXSW Interactive Conference, Austin, TX, 11 March 2006, http://www.podcastdirectory.com/podshows/327406.

104 **Google's Daniel Clancy**: "Book Digitization and the Revenge of the Librarians Episode."

105 **only 100,000 books**: "Google Book-Scanning Efforts Spark Debate," *Associated Press Online*, 20 December 2006, http://www.nytimes.com/aponline/technology/AP-Digital-Library.html.

105 **University of California**: "U. of California Will Provide Up to 3,000 Books a Day." For a copy of the contract between Google and the University of California, see The University of California and Google, Cooperative Agreement, August 2006, http://www.cdlib.org/news/ucgoogle_cooperative_agreement.pdf. The agreement required the university to display "Digitized by Google" on any Web page in which the university displayed any portion of its digital copy.

106 **Just one year**: "Google Book-Scanning Efforts Spark Debate," *Associated Press Online*.

106 **Microsoft was not willing**: Satya Nadella, "Book Search Winding Down," *Live Search*, 23 May 2008, http://blogs.msdn.com/livesearch/archive/2008/05/23/book-search-winding-down.aspx.

106 **In February 2006**: Clancy, "Google Book Search."

106 **Google gave users**: Adam Mathes, "Collect, Share, and Discover Books," *Inside Google Book Search*, 6 September 2007, http://booksearch

.blogspot.com/2007/08/share-and-enjoy.html; Bill Schilit and Okan Kolak, "Dive into the Meme Pool with Google Book Search," *Inside Google Book Search*, 6 September 2007, http://booksearch.blogspot.com/2007/09/dive -into-meme-pool-with-google-book.html; Brandon Badger, "Google Book Search in Google Earth," *Google Lat Long Blog*, 20 August 2007, http:// google-latlong.blogspot.com/2007/08/google-book-search-in-google-earth .html. One outside commentator noted that the scarcity of scanned books that are in the public domain and provide the full text prevented the "personal library" from being anything more than "a personal card catalog." Jeffrey R. Young, "Google Allows Cutting and Pasting from Its Library of Books," *Chronicle of Higher Education: The Wired Campus*, 20 September 2007, http:// chronicle.com/wiredcampus/article/2395/google-allows -cutting-and-pasting-from-its-library-of-books.

107 **In May 2007:** Viresh Ratnakar, "Found: More Books," *Inside Google Book Search*, 17 May 2007, http://booksearch.blogspot.com/2007/05/found-more -books.html. Ratnakar's post says little about the scope of the added listings, other than to offhandedly say that now Google Book Search includes "millions of books that we know about but that aren't yet online." He also thanks "our union catalog partners worldwide for helping make this happen."

108 **John E. Sprizzo:** U.S. District Court Southern District of New York, *The Authors Guild, et al. v. Google, Inc.,* and *The McGraw-Hill Companies, Inc., et al, v. Google, Inc.,* "Amended Case Management Order Regarding Coordination and Scheduling," 29 January 2008, https://ecf.nysd.uscourts.gov/ doc1/12714389563.

108 **In February 2008:** University of Michigan, "Million," http:// www.lib.umich.edu/news/millionth.html; Paul Courant, "One Million Digitized Books," *Au Courant*, 2 February 2008, http://paulcourant.net/ 2008/02/02/one-million-digitized-books/.

5. GooTube

109 **Google could search:** In its formative early years, Google was devoted to textual information. Even when Google researchers investigated the flow of information in daily life that took the form of a stream of speech, such as when listening to television, making a phone call, or conversing with another person, what was most interesting, from a computer science perspective, was how the constituent words in the stream could be captured and analyzed. In a paper presented at the 12th International World Wide Web Conference in 2003, three Google engineers, one of whom was Sergey Brin, along with an academic colleague, examined the design of an algorithm that would analyze the closed-captioning text accompanying a live television news broadcast and then suggest, on the fly, supplemental news articles found on the Web that would be matched to what was

said every twenty seconds or so in the broadcast. Whether anyone was really interested in such a service was a question left unexamined. But the paper showed, if nothing else, the researchers' interest in finding new text sources—in this case, the closed captioning of broadcasts—that a machine could read. Monika Henzinger, Bay-Wei Chang, Brian Milch, and Sergey Brin, "Query-Free News Search," paper presented at 12th International World Wide Web Conference, 2003, http://people.csail .mit.edu/milch/papers/www2003.pdf. The paper was subsequently published in *World Wide Web: Internet and Web Information Systems* 8(2):101–26 (2005). Henzinger, Chang, and Brin were at Google; Milch was a doctoral student in the Computer Science Division at the University of California, Berkeley, who had a summer research internship at Google in 2002.

110 **Yahoo launched:** "Yahoo! Video Search Beta," *Yahoo! Search Blog*, 15 December 2004, http://www.ysearchblog.com/archives/000060.html. The code that Yahoo suggested that Web publishers provide was an RSS Enclosure tag.

110 **"Web pages are self-describing":** "Search Spotlight Pans to Video," *eWeek*, 17 December 2004, http://www.eweek.com/c/a/Enterprise-Apps/Search -Spotlight-Pans-to-Video/.

110 **If one wanted to search:** Gary Price, "Searching Television via Closed-Captioning," *Search Engine Watch*, 5 November 2004, http://blog.search enginewatch.com/blog/041105-093901. Three companies that were credited for developing voice-recognition software were HP (Speechbot), Nexidia, and StreamSage.

111 **the day after Yahoo announced:** "TV's Future May Be Web Search Engines That Hunt for Video," *Wall Street Journal*, 16 December 2004.

111 **When CNN was told:** "TV's Future May Be Web Search Engines."

112 **A television industry executive:** "Striking Up Digital Video Search," News.com, 16 December 2004, http://news.com.com/2102-1032_3 -5466491.html.

112 **ten San Francisco Bay Area stations:** Chris Sherman, "Google Debuts Video Search," *Search Engine Watch*, 25 January 2005, http://blog.search enginewatch.com/blog/050125-000100.

112 **about two terabytes:** "Google Launches Video Search," *eWeek*, 25 January 2005, http://www.eweek.com/article2/0,1895,1743640,00.asp.

113 **Executives at CBS:** "Google Sees Content Deals as Key to Long-Term Growth," *Wall Street Journal*, 14 August 2006.

113 **Jawed Karim:** This chapter's account of YouTube's origins is based largely upon Karim's highly detailed "YouTube: From Concept to Hypergrowth," talk at Reflections/Projections conference, sponsored by the Association for Computing Machinery at the University of Illinois at Urbana-Champaign, 21 October 2006, http://www.acm.uiuc.edu/conference/2006/video/UIUC -ACM-RP06-Karim.wmv.

113 *Wired* **magazine:** Clive Thompson, "The BitTorrent Effect," *Wired*, January 2005

115 **publisher of Flash multimedia software:** The publisher at the time was Macromedia. It was acquired by Adobe in 2005.

115 **Karim knew:** "The Gurus of YouTube," *Time*, 16 December 2006, http://www.time.com/time/magazine/article/0,9171,1570721-2,00.html. In the article Chen concedes that the story of the company's founding that he and Hurley repeated often to members of the press, the version that involves an epiphany about sharing videos that occurred at a dinner party at Chen's apartment, was related to "marketing ideas around creating a story that was very digestible." He and Hurley also reluctantly, but clearly, said that Karim did deserve the credit for the original idea for the site.

115 **His presence tends to be omitted:** The "About YouTube" page (http://www.youtube.com/t/about) on display 15 March 2008 states that the company was founded in February 2005 without naming the trio, but introducing Chen and Hurley by name as the "first members of YouTube management team" after receiving funding from Sequoia Capital. It does provide a link to another page introducing "Founders," http://www.you tube.com/t/founders, which mentions that Karim was present at the time of the company's founding but "left the company to pursue an advanced degree at Stanford."

116 **historic first YouTube video:** *Me at the Zoo,* shot by Yakov Lapitsky, uploaded 23 April 2005, http://www.youtube.com/watch?v=jNOXAC9IVRw. Also uploaded that day was a sixteen-second segment consisting of Karim rolling down a snow-covered road for a few yards: *Rolling down a Hill,* uploaded 23 April 2005, http://www.youtube.com/watch?v=nGzAI5pLbMY. For inanity in its purest form, see *Why Was Steve Late?* featuring Steve Chen and anno-tated by Karim as *Chad and I Wait for a Late Steve,* uploaded 27 April 2005, http://www.youtube.com/watch?v=8hKqnBiQngA.

116 **they captured:** The video was played by Karim during his October 2006 talk at the University of Illinois.

117 **Arrington praised:** Michael Arrington, "Profile—YouTube," *TechCrunch*, 8 August 2005, http://www.techcrunch.com/2005/08/08/profile-youtube/.

117 *Matt Dances Around the World*: Arrington's title was more descriptive than the actual one, which was simply *Man Dancing,* supplied by the short film's author: http://www.youtube.com/watch?v=PaluLFfvOEI.

117 **Slashdot:** "YouTube—The Flickr of Video?" *Slashdot,* 14 August 2005, http://slashdot.org/articles/05/08/14/1320217.shtml?tid=95&tid=129.

117 **cover YouTube's competitors:** Michael Arrington, "Comparing the Flickrs of Video," *TechCrunch*, 6 November 2005, http://www.techcrunch.com/2005/11/06/the-flickrs-of-video/.

118 **would accept videos:** Google Video Beta's Video Upload Program, first posted April 2005, https://upload.video.google.com/. This post contains a link to a second page, "Video Upload Program for Major Producers," https://services.google.com/inquiry/video, which refers to the "1,000 hours

or more of video." It is not possible to tell if the current version of this page is identical to the one posted in April 2005, however, because Google blocked the Wayback Machine's crawler from preserving pages in this directory of the company's Web site.

118 **Jennifer Feikin:** Chris Sherman, "Google Wants Your Video," *Search Engine Watch*, 13 April 2005, http://blog.searchenginewatch.com/blog/050413 -163129.

118 **Larry Page:** "Google Video to Accept Public Submissions," *PC World*, 4 April 2005, http://www.pcworld.com/article/id,120284-page,1/article.html.

118 **Page later described:** Larry Page, keynote address at the 2006 International Consumer Electronics Show, 6 January 2006, http://www.google.com/intl/ en/press/podium/ces2006.html.

118 **Two months later:** "DVD Jon Modifies Google Video Viewer," ZDNet.co.uk, 30 June 2005, http://news.zdnet.co.uk/software/ 0,1000000121,39206455,00.htm.

118 **separate one-time installation:** "Google Video Viewer," http:// web.archive.org/web/20050629022820/video.google.com/video_download .html, from crawl performed on 28 June 2005.

118 **closed-captioning transcript:** Danny Sullivan, "More Q&A with Google Video Manager," *Search Engine Watch*, 27 June 2005, http://blog .searchenginewatch.com/blog/050627-125353.

119 **self-deprecatingly described:** Sullivan, "More Q&A with Google Video Manager."

119 **The only guidelines:** YouTube help page (preserved at Internet Archive, crawled 1 August 2005), http://web.archive.org/web/20050724003639/ www.youtube .com/help.php. From April to 1 August 2005, YouTube's guidelines for upload-ing did not mention copyright considerations. The Internet Archive's Wayback Machine preserves the precise day—2 August 2005—when the guidelines were expanded to include YouTube's avowal that it "respects the rights of copyright holders and publishers and is only accepting video uploads from persons who hold all necessary rights to the uploaded material." See YouTube help page preserved at the Internet Archive, crawled 2 August 2005, http://web.archive.org/web/20051001080750/youtube.com/ help.php.

119 **more than 150 online auction sites:** Randall Stross, *eBoys: The First Inside Account of Venture Capitalists at Work* (New York: Crown, 2000), 76.

119 **By November:** "YouTube Receives $3.5M in Funding from Sequoia Capital," YouTube press release, 7 November 2005, http://www.youtube.com/press _room_entry?entry=OPPIn7PRss.

119 **doubled again:** "YouTube Opens Internet Video to the Masses," YouTube press release, 15 December 2005, http://www.youtube.com/press_room _entry?entry=OcN9xXYar1g.

120 **Sequoia Capital:** When YouTube's cofounders knocked on Sequoia's door, they had better than even odds that Sequoia would be interested by virtue of

shared ties within clubby Silicon Valley. YouTube's Chen, Hurley, and Karim all were PayPal alumni, as was Sequoia's Botha, who had been PayPal's chief financial officer—and Sequoia had been a PayPal investor. The PayPal connection did not mean that funding would be assured, however. When a comment on Matt Marshall's *VentureBeat* blog suggested that the YouTube entrepreneurs enjoyed "a unique competitive advantage" when approaching Sequoia, Marshall pointed out that "Sequoia's not going to back you just because you knew one of their partners. But true, if you *do* know one of their partners, and they respect you and trust you, sure, you have an unfair advantage." Matt Marshall, "Q&A with Roelof Botha, the Web 2.0 Guy at Sequoia Capital," *VentureBeat*, 1 June 2006, http://venturebeat.com/2006/06/01/qa-with-roelof-botha-the-web-20-guy-at-sequoia-capital/.

121 **Larry Page:** Page, 2006 International Consumer Electronics Show.

121 **closed the video store:** Google did not issue a press release. It merely sent an e-mail message on 10 August 2007 to the store's customers, with the subject heading "Important Information About Your Google Video Account," which explained: "In an effort to improve all Google services, we will no longer offer the ability to buy or rent videos for download from Google Video, ending the DTO/DTR (download-to-own/rent) program. This change will be effective August 15, 2007." The company did not offer a refund, only a credit that could be redeemed at Google Checkout, a decision that brought upon the company even more opprobrium. A few days later, the company relented. Bindu Reddy, Google Video's product manager, wrote a humorous post on *Official Google Blog* to acknowledge, "We had made a mistake in the case of *Google Video's Download to Own/Rent Refund Policy vs. Common Sense*." See Bindu Reddy, "An Update on Google Video Feedback," *Official Google Blog*, 20 August 2007, http://googleblog.blogspot.com/2007/08/update-on-google-video-feedback.html.

121 **The pact with the NBA:** "Google Online Video Store Starts Without a Bang," *USA Today*, 19 January 2006, http://www.usatoday.com/money/industries/technology/2006-01-19-google-video_x.htm.

121 **further restricted:** Cory Doctorow, "Google Video Robs Customers of the Videos They 'Own,'" *BoingBoing,* 10 August 2007, http://www.boingboing.net/2007/08/10/google_video_robs_cu.html. Doctorow wrote that Google's video store and Amazon's Unbox store "claim to 'sell' you things, but you can never truly own the things they sell—they are your theoretical property only, liable to confiscation at any time. That's the lesson for DRM [digital rights management]: only the big motion-picture companies, search giants, and other corporate overlords get to own property. We vassals are mere tenant-farmers, with a precarious claim on our little patch of dirt."

121 **content delivery networks:** The content delivery network that appeared to be YouTube's principal distribution partner, but that never officially confirmed the relationship, was Limelight Networks. For a brief introduction to Lime-

light and its older competitor Akamai Networks, another CDN, see Michael Bazeley, "Video Is Hot, Continued: Limelight Raises $130 Million," *Venture-Beat*, 25 July 2006, http://venturebeat.com/2006/07/25/video-is-hot -continued-limelight-raises-130-million/; "Limelight Readies for Spotlight," *Forbes*, 23 January 2007, http://www.forbes.com/2007/01/23/limelight -youtube-broadband-tech-intel-cx_df_0123limelight.html?partner=yahootix.

121 **additional $8 million:** "YouTube Uploads $8M in Funding," YouTube press release, 5 April 2006, http://www.youtube.com/press_room_entry?entry =jwIToyFs2Lc. The press release referred only to Sequoia and omitted the participation of Artis Capital Management, whose contribution became public knowledge in a later regulatory filing. See "Hedge Fund Scores on YouTube," *PE Week,* 9 October 2006, http://www.pewnews.com/ story.asp?sectioncode=44&storycode=40625.

121 **bills were paid:** YouTube's single largest cost was paying for the bandwidth to deliver videos to its users. It apparently enjoyed a significant discount in the rate it was charged by Limelight Networks, its service provider, because of the scale of YouTube's operations, serving 200 terabytes of videos daily in April 2006. The standard charge was a penny per minute of streamed video, but YouTube was reported to pay between a tenth of a cent and half a cent per minute. See "Your Tube, Whose Dime?" *Forbes*, 28 April 2006, http:// www.forbes.com/home/intelligentinfrastructure/2006/04/27/video-youtube -myspace_cx_df_0428video.html.

122 **interviewed by *Wired*:** Frank Rose, "Are You Ready for Googlevision?" *Wired*, May 2006, http://www.wired.com/wired/archive/14.05/google.html.

122 **When a reporter:** "Inside a Web Giant's Manic Search for Staying Power," *Chicago Tribune*, 20 September 2006, http://www.chicagotribune.com/ technology/chi-0609200122sep20,1,5465696.story.

122 **YouTube began to run:** Chad Hurley, interviewed on *Charlie Rose,* 11 August 2006.

122 **Robert Tur:** "YouTube Dances the Copyright Tango," News.com, 24 July 2006, http://news.com.com/YouTube+dances+the+copyright+tango/2100 -1025_3-6097365.html.

122 **Digital Millenium Copyright Act:** Another clause in the DMCA requires Web sites to remove copyright-infringing material when it is brought to their attention, and when NBC had asked YouTube to remove *Lazy Sunday: The Chronicles of Narnia,* a hip-hop parody clip from *Saturday Night Live*, YouTube had done so—and received free national publicity in the bargain. "SNL Cult Hit Yanked from Video-Sharing Site," News.com, 17 February 2006, http://news.comSNL+cult+hit+yanked+from+video-sharing+ site/2100-1026_3-6041031.html.

122 **Revver's Oliver Luckett:** Digital Hollywood, "Building Blocks 2006," San Jose, CA, 15 August 2006, http://www.digitalhollywood.com/%231BBlk Sessions/BBTuesOne.html.

123 **Ahree Lee:** Lee's story was told by Scott Roesch, vice president at AtomFilms. Digital Hollywood, "Building Blocks 2006," San Jose, CA, 15 August 2006, http://www.digitalhollywood.com/%231BBlkSessions/BBTuesOne.html. The YouTube version is labeled *Me: Girl Takes Pic of Herself Every Day for Three Years:* http://www.youtube.com/watch?v=55YyaJIrmzo. The full version at AtomFilms is found at http://www.atomfilms.com/film/me.jsp.

123 **Chane was asked:** Digital Hollywood, http://www.digitalhollywood .com/%231BBlkSessions/ BBTuesOne.html.

124 **$10.6 million:** "Google's YouTube to Launch New Type of Ads," *San Jose Mercury News*, 21 August 2007.

124 **had yet to earn a profit:** Hurley, on *Charlie Rose*.

124 **"I was really confident on:** "Personal Journey with Steve Chen," Committee of 100's Sixteenth Annual Conference, New York, 21 April 2007, Part 4, http://www.youtube.com/watch?v=om3_nao3rZ0.

125 **Before the deal closed:** Matt Marshall, "Q&A with Roelof Botha, the Web 2.0 Guy at Sequoia Capital," *VentureBeat*, 1 June 2006, http://venturebeat .com/2006/06/01/qa-with-roelof-botha-the-web-20-guy-at-sequoia-capital/.

125 **Google executives:** "Google Q3 2006 Earnings Call Transcript," transcript of 19 October 2006 call, prepared by SeekingAlpha, http://www.seeking alpha.com/article/18858-google-q3-2006-earnings-call-transcript.

126 **how does one make money:** *Valleywag* published an unverifiable report in March 2008 that Eric Schmidt had told YouTube employees at the time of the acquisition that they need not worry about revenue but more recently told them, "Forget I said that." Owen Thomas, "Eric Schmidt Puts the Screws on YouTube," *Valleywag*, 18 March 2008, http://valleywag.com/ 369296/eric-schmidt-puts-the-screws-on-youtube.

126 **An analyst with the Yankee Group:** The Yankee Group analyst was Anton Denissov. "YouTube Looks for the Money Clip," *Fortune*, 25 March 2008, http://techland.blogs.fortune.cnn.com/2008/03/25/youtube-looks-for-the -money-clip/.

126 **In April 2008:** "Exclusive Interview with Google's Eric Schmidt," *CNBC*, 30 April 2008, http://www.cnbc.com/id/24387350/site/14081545.

126 **higher-resolution video:** "YouTube Videos in High Quality," *Broadcasting Ourselves* (the YouTube blog), 14 March 2008, http://www.youtube .com/blog?entry=ponKL3LTyr0.

126 **YouTube Everywhere:** "YouTube Everywhere," *Broadcasting Ourselves*, 11 March 2008, http://www.youtube.com/blog?entry=yFIR6EEySg8.

127 **acquire the *New York Times:*** In spring 2007, Eric Schmidt said Google was not interested in "businesses where we would own the content." "Google: No Plans to Exit Fast Lane," *E-Commerce Times*, 11 May 2007, http://www .ecommercetimes.com/story/57347.html. But one year later, when asked if Google might consider acquiring the *New York Times*, Schmidt allowed that "I'd never rule anything out." Without talking about the future, he looked to

the past and observed, "So far, we've stayed away from buying content." He added, "It's not our area of expertise. But the more strategic answer is that we'd be picking winners. We'd be disenfranchising a potential new entrant. Our principle is providing all the world's information." Russ Mitchell, "Search Mission," *Portfolio*, April 2008, http://www.portfolio.com/executives/features/2008/03/14/Google-CEO-Eric-Schmidt-Interview.

6. Small World, After All

129 **He was eager:** "Google Maps Is Changing the Way We See the World," *Wired*, July 2007, http://www.wired.com/techbiz/it/magazine/15-07/ff_maps.

130 **basement of the Pentagon:** This chapter draws heavily on two interviews with John Hanke, in Mountain View, CA, on 10 August and 21 August 2007. Google had no need for the Silicon Graphics computers that the Pentagon had depended upon to display satellite images. Silicon Graphics's story tangentially touched Google's for an entirely different reason: when the older computer manufacturer fell on hard times, it had to vacate its corporate headquarters in Mountain View. The new tenant—Google—turned this into the Googleplex.

131 **"Jane Austen layer":** "Jane Austen's Life & Works," *Google Earth Community*, 7 April 2006, http://bbs.keyhole.com/ubb/showthreaded.php/Cat/0/Number/411188.

131 **Keyhole's founders:** The team of founders included Mark Aubin, John Hanke, Michael Jones, Phil Keslin, and Brian McClendon, and Chikai Ohazama, who would end up at Google, and Remi Arnaud, Christopher Tanner, and Avi Bar-Zeev, who departed Keyhole before Google's acquisition.

134 **In March 2003:** "Tiny Tech Company Awes Viewers," *USA Today*, 21 March 2003.

134 **$400 annually:** "Google Earth Pro," Google information page at Keyhole.com domain, n.d. [2004?], https://registration.keyhole.com/choice_kh_initial.html.

136 **Keyhole agreed to be acquired:** "Google Acquires Keyhole Corp," Google press release, 27 October 2004, http://www.google.com/press/pressrel/keyhole.html.

137 **principal innovation:** Bret Taylor, "Mapping Your Way," *Official Google Blog*, 8 February 2005, http://googleblog.blogspot.com/2005/02/mapping-your-way.html.

137 **Keyhole promised:** "Keyhole2 Lt," Keyhole Web page (apparently predating Google's acquisition), http://www.keyhole.com/body.php?h=products&t=keyhole2LT.

138 **six months after its release:** Mike Pegg, "Google Maps Blog Buzz—Black-Berry, Google Maps Ads, DIY," *Google Maps Mania*, 16 January 2006,

http://googlemapsmania.blogspot.com/2006/01/google-maps-blog-buzz
-blackberry.html; Gary Price, "Still Seeing 'Blue Pins' on Some Google Maps;
Google Now Testing Paid Links in Google Earth," *Search Engine Watch*, 18
January 2006, http://blog.searchenginewatch.com/blog/060118-112211.
Google began offering the advertisements without an announcement. When
asked about ads that were appearing in a Google service that formerly had not
carried any advertising, a Google spokesperson said, "We are currently conducting a limited test of ads in Google Earth. We do not have any other
specifics to share at this time."

138 **Paul Rademacher:** "Google Maps Is Changing the Way We See the World,"
Wired, July 2007, http://www.wired.com/techbiz/it/magazine/15-07/ff
_maps.

139 **fast food restaurants:** fastfoodmaps.com, http://www.fastfoodmaps.com/.

139 **lowest gas prices:** *Times Herald-Record*, "Record Gas Watch," http://
www.thrnewmedia.com/maps/gas2.html.

139 **crime reports for Chicago:** *EveryBlock Chicago*, http://chicago.every
block.com/.

139 **news stories in the day's** *New York Times: Mibazaar*, http://www
.mibazaar.com/worldnews/index.html.

139 **thousands of other mashup sites:** One directory to Google Maps mashups is
Google Maps Mania—unaffiliated with Google: http://googlemapsmania
.blogspot.com/.

139 **Barry Diller:** "The Earth Is Ready For Its Close-Up," *Newsweek*, 6 June
2005.

139 **Eric Schmidt recounted:** Google Inc. Press Day, 10 May 2006, http://
www.google.com/press/pressday.html.

140 **correct the locations:** Ramesh Balakrishnan, "It's Your World. Map It,"
Google Lat Long Blog, 18 March 2008, http://google-latlong.blogspot.com/
2008/03/its-your-world-map-it.html.

140 **helped the Coast Guard:** "Google Annual Report 2005", 2006, http://
investor.google.com/pdf/2005_Google_AnnualReport.pdf., 2.

140 **effects of clear-cut logging:** Rebecca Moore, "Trading a Bow and Arrow for a
Laptop," *Google Lat Long Blog*, 15 June 2007, http://google-latlong.blog
spot.com/2007/06/trading-bow-and-arrow-for-laptop.html.

140 **U.S. Holocaust Memorial Museum:** "USHMM + Google Earth," United
States Holocaust Memorial Museum Web page, http://www.ushmm.org/
googleearth/.

141 **"The ability of people":** John Hanke interview, 21 August 2007.

141 **photos of the earth:** Poet Archibald MacLeish memorably described the
impact of Anders's photographs: "To see the Earth as it truly is, small and
blue and beautiful in that eternal silence where it floats, is to see ourselves as
riders on the Earth together, brothers on that bright loveliness in the eternal
cold—brothers who know now that they are truly brothers." Quoted in

Peggy Wilhide, "New Views for a New Century," *Aerospace Technology Innovation*, July/August 2000, http://ipp.nasa.gov/innovation/Innovation_84/wnewview.html.

141 **Robert M. Samborski:** "Start-Ups Try to Plot a Complete Picture," *Washington Post*, 27 November 2006.

142 **natural geologic formation:** "In Pictures: The Strangest Sights in Google Earth," *PC World*, second image, http://www.pcworld.com/article/id,134186-page,2-c,mapping/article.html. It can also be seen at Google Maps: http://maps.google.com/maps?f=q&hl=en&q=medicine%2Bhat,%2Balberta&ie=UTF8&z=16&11=50.010083,-110.113006&spn=0.009432,0.026951&t=k&om=1%20/.

142 **Arizona farmer:** "In Pictures: The Strangest Sights in Google Earth," fifth image, http://www.pcworld.com/article/id,134186-page,5-c,mapping/article.html.

142 **forty-year-old barracks:** "Navy to Alter Swastika-Shaped Barracks," Associated Press, 26 September 2007, http://ap.google.com/article/ALeqM5i8o4u2vVJILcEt_tFMtGnH_sYJ4w. The navy said that it would spend $600,000 on landscaping and structures to alter its appearance from above. The barracks can be seen at Google Maps: http://tinyurl.com/2x659b&usg=AFQjCNHivL1I0GhIhhuskrcNs1qwFgM1g. For nineteen more Google Maps images of no less interest than the swastika-shaped barracks, see the collection assembled by Chris Silver Smith, "20 Awesome Images Found in Google Maps," *Search Engine Land*, 14 January 2008, http://searchengineland.com/080114-124703.php.

142 **Sky in Google Earth:** Lior Ron, "Sky: The Final Frontier," *Google Lat Long Blog*, 22 August 2007, http://google-latlong.blogspot.com/2007/08/sky-final-frontier.html.

142 **Hanke attempted:** "Google Lets Users Spy on Satellite Images," *Advertiser*, 8 April 2005.

142 **available satellite imagery:** FAQ, *DigitalGlobe*, accessed 20 August 2007, http://www.digitalglobe.com/press/FAQ_press.shtml.

143 **the first sighting:** "Bloggers Ogle at Google Earth's Topless Sunbathers," *Daily Mail*, 28 September 2006, http://www.dailymail.co.uk/pages/live/articles/news/news.html?in_article_id=407401&in_page_id=1770&in_a_source. A Google spokesperson gave a lighthearted comment: "Things like this do happen and people will find them for a bit of fun."

143 **A9:** "The Earth Is Ready for Its Close-Up," *Newsweek*.

143 **Microsoft announced:** "New Windows Live Local Service Delivers State-of-the-Art Advances for Web-Based Mapping and Local Search," Microsoft press release, 7 December 2005, http://www.microsoft.com/presspass/press/2005/dec05/12-07NewLiveLocalPR.mspx.

143 **A year after:** John Hanke, "Happy Birthday, Google Earth," *Official Google Blog*, 12 June 2006, http://googleblog.blogspot.com/2006/06/happy-birthday-google-earth.html.

144 **flight simulator:** Marco Gallotta, "Google Earth Flight Simulator," *Marco's Blog*, 31 August 2007, http://marco-za.blogspot.com/2007/08/google-earth -flight-simulator.html. Frank Taylor, "Google Earth Flight Simulator Tips," *Google Earth Blog* (an independent blog unaffiliated with Google), 3 September 2007, http://www.gearthblog.com/blog/archives/2007/09/ google_earth _flight.html. Visitors to Google's blog interested in finding help for using the flight simulator were directed to Taylor's post. See Gerhard Wesp, "Where Do You Want to Fly Today?" *Google Lat Long Blog*, 6 September 2007, http:// google-latlong.blogspot.com/2007/09/where-do-you-want-to-fly-today.html.

144 **Rand McNally:** Lauren Weinstein noted in a People for Internet Responsibility forum the similarity of Google Street View and the Rand McNally maps. See his post on 13 August 2007, http://forums.pfir.org/main/messages/ 663/696.html. He provides an example of a page from a Photo-Auto Map that was for a trip from Toledo to Detroit: http://www.pfir.org/photo-auto .jpg.

145 **only streets in San Francisco:** Stephen Chau, "Introducing . . . Street View!" *Google Lat Long Blog*, 29 May 2007, http://google-latlong.blogspot.com/ 2007/05/introducing-street-view.html. Street views for San Diego, Los Angeles, Houston, and Orlando were added in August 2007. Chau, "More Street View Cities," *Google Lat Long Blog*, 7 August 2007, http://google -latlong.blogspot.com/2007/08/more-street-view-cities.html. San Diego images had the same high resolution as did San Francisco's.

145 **Mary Kalin-Casey:** "Google Maps Is Spying on My Cat, Says Freaked Out BB Reader," *BoingBoing*, 30 May 2007, http://www.boingboing.net/ 2007/05/30/google_maps_is_spyin.html. See also Xeni Jardin's follow-up post, "Google Street View: A Cavalcade of Reactions, Gag Pix, Paranoid Rants," *BoingBoing*, 5 June 2007, http://www.boingboing.net/2007/ 06/05/google-street-view-a.html. In April 2008, Street View again drew attention when Aaron and Christine Boring, a Pittsburgh couple, sued Google for invasion of privacy for including photographs of their home, located on a "clearly marked 'Private Road,' in Street View." "Couple Sues Google over 'Street View,'" *The Smoking Gun*, 4 April 2008, http:// www .thesmokinggun.com/archive/years/2008/0404081google1.html. Press coverage of the case led to the discovery that Google's cameras had traveled down the long, winding driveway of the home of the Borings' neighbors, Janet and George McKee: "Warning: Google Is in Your Driveway!" *The Smoking Gun*, 7 April 2008, http://www.thesmokinggun.com/archive/years/2008/ 0407081google1.html.

145 *Wired* **magazine's blog:** Ryan Singel, "Request for Urban Street Sightings: Submit and Vote on the Best Urban Images Captured by New Google Maps Tool," *Wired Blog Network*, 30 May 2007, http://blog.wired.com/ 27bstroke6/2007/05/request_for_urb.html. Another site, Streetviewr, whose tagline was "Because Seeing Is Believing," collected more than six hundred

submissions, http://streetviewr.com/. Its home page in late September 2007 indicated that submissions were no longer being accepted and the site owner was planning to bring the "experiment" to a close. Another blog that sprang up, *Google Maps Mania*, provided a guide, "6 Ways to Find Cool Google Maps Street Views," 9 June 2007, http://googlemapsmania.blogspot.com/2007/06/6-ways-to-find-cool-google-maps-street.html.

145 **it had anticipated the need:** "Google Zooms In Too Close for Some," *New York Times*, 1 June 2007, http://www.nytimes.com/2007/06/01/technology/01private.html.

146 **When Lance Ulanoff:** Lance Ulanoff, "Google Is Watching You," *PC Magazine*, 1 August 2007, http://www.pcmag.com/article2/0,1895,2165020,00.asp. In October 2007, Google added street views of six additional cities—Chicago, Pittsburgh, Philadelphia, Phoenix, Portland, and Tucson—with the "added bonus" of high-resolution images in Phoenix, Tucson, and parts of Chicago. See Stephanie Lafon, "More Street View Cities to Explore," *Google Lat Long Blog*, 11 October 2007, http://google-latlong.blogspot.com/2007/10/more-street-view-cities-to-explore.html.

146 **Peter Fleischer:** "Street View and Privacy," *Google Lat Long Blog*, 24 September 2007, http://google-latlong.blogspot.com/2007/09/street-view-and-privacy.html.

147 **In May 2008:** Andrea Frome, "Street View Revisits Manhattan," *Google Lat Long Blog*, 12 May 2008, http://google-latlong.blogspot.com/2008/05/street-view-revisits-manhattan.html. The face-blurring technology was in development for a year, but face recognition is a longstanding challenge in computer science and has yet to be fully mastered. Google's software was less than perfect in identifying faces. See Stephen Shankland, "Google Begins Blurring Faces in Street View," *News.com news blog*, 13 May 2008, http://news.cnet.com/8301-10784_3-9943140-7.html.

147 **the governments:** "Governments Tremble at Google's Bird's-Eye View," *New York Times*, 20 December 2005, http://www.nytimes.com/2005/12/20/technology/20image.html.

147 **When the RAND Corporation:** RAND Corporation, "Publicly Available Federal Geospatial Information of Little Unique Risk to Terrorists, Rand Study Says," press release, 25 March 2004, https://rand.org/news/press.04/03.25.html.

147 **government officials:** "Top Secret, in Plain View," *San Francisco Chronicle*, 18 May 2007, http://www.sfgate.com/cgi-bin/article.cgi?file=/c/a/2007/05/18/MNGR2PTFPL1.DTL.

148 **One cartoon:** *New Yorker*, 1 October 2007, 80, http://www.cartoonbank.com/item/124378.

148 **more serious criticisms:** "Google Earth Makes Some Officials Nervous," *City Room* (blog), *New York Times*, 28 June 2007, http://cityroom.blogs.nytimes.com/2007/06/28/google-earth-makes-some-officials-nervous/;

"Papers Portray Plot as More Talk Than Action," *New York Times*, 4 June 2007, http://www.nytimes.com/2007/06/04/nyregion/04plot.html.

149 **Elinor Mills:** Elinor Mills, "Google Balances Privacy, Reach," News.com, 14 July 2005, http://news.com.com/Google+balances+privacy%2C+reach/2100-1032_3-5787483.html.

149 **lashed out:** "Google's Chief Is Googled, to the Company's Displeasure," *New York Times*, 8 August 2005, http://www.nytimes.com/2005/08/08/technology/08google.html.

149 *Register* **derided:** "Google Snubs Press in Privacy Fury," *The Register*, 6 August 2007, http://www.theregister.co.uk/2005/08/06/google_privacy_snub/.

149 *New York Times* **headline:** Randall Stross, "Google Anything, So Long as It's Not Google," *New York Times*, 28 August 2005, http://www.nytimes.com/2005/08/28/technology/28digi.html.

150 **quietly restored:** Elinor Mills, "Google to Yahoo: Ours Is Bigger," News.com, 26 September 2005, http://www.news.com/Google-touts-size-of-its-search-index/2100-1038_3-5883345.html; "Google Talks to CNET Again," *The Register*, 28 September 2005, http://www.theregister.co.uk/2005/09/28/google_talks_cnet/. *The Register*'s amusing subheadline was "Sulk Cancelled."

150 **Schmidt never released:** Three years after his intemperate punishment of CNET over Elinor Mills's article, Schmidt had an opportunity to present to Mills a more cooperative, helpful demeanor. Instead he was most unhelpful, which gave Mills the opportunity to write an amusing account of her one-on-one interview with him: "My Stunted Interview with Google's Eric Schmidt," News.com, 29 February 2008, http://www.news.com/8301-10784_3-9883410-7.html.

150 **created unease:** The reach of Google's cameras was imagined by some as being ridiculously intrusive, or at least was a convenient subject for someone with a sharp sense of humor. See the Street View image of a commercial sign with letters that spelled out, as if it were a file placed on a Web site to block a search engine crawler, a four-line message for Google's camera van:

robots.txt
User-agent;
GoogleVan;
Disallow: bedroom

See "robots.txt" at "Request for Urban Street Sightings," *Wired Blog Network*, 30 May 2007, http://blog.wired.com/27bstroke6/2007/05/request_for_urb.html.

150 **excited the same reaction:** Xeni Jardin of *BoingBoing* asked a different hypothetical question: "Would we feel differently about street-level image mapping if it were done by a government agency? The FBI? CIA? NSA? DHS? Not implying that it should be, and this isn't 'backlash.' Just asking aloud."

See "Google Street View: Would It Be More/Less Evil If It Were CIA or NSA?" *BoingBoing*, 3 June 2007, http://www.boingboing.net/2007/06/03/google-street-view-w.html.

7. A Personal Matter

154 **Qualcomm calls:** "Intel Makes a Push into Pocket-Size Internet Devices," *New York Times*, 2 April 2008, http://www.nytimes.com/2008/04/02/technology/02chip.html. Intel, which introduced a family of chips that compete with Qualcomm's, has its own term for the category of devices that fall in between a laptop and a cell phone: *mobile internet devices.*

154 **providing Google Docs users:** Philip Tucker, "Bringing the Cloud with You," *Official Google Docs Blog*, 31 March 2008, http://googledocs.blogspot.com/2008/03/bringing-cloud-with-you.html.

154 **When Eric Schmidt was chief executive:** "Google Gets Ready to Rumble with Microsoft," *New York Times*, 16 December 2007, http://www.nytimes.com/2007/12/16/technology/16goog.html.

154 **acquired in 2006:** "New Beginnings," *Official Google Docs Blog*, 10 October 2006, http://googledocs.blogspot.com/2006/10/new-beginnings.html.

154 **presentations module:** Jeff Grimes, "And Now We Present . . ." *Official Google Docs Blog*, 17 September 2007, http://googledocs.blogspot.com/2007_09_01_archive.html.

155 **Eric Schmidt predicted:** "Google Gets Ready to Rumble," *New York Times.*

155 **Sergey Brin:** "Former Students Go Far with Search-Only Site," *Stanford Daily*, 12 April 2000, http://www.stanforddaily.com/article/2000/4/12/innovationGooglesOfDollarsShyFormerStudentsGoFarWithSearchonlySite; " 'HailStorm' on the Horizon," Microsoft press release, 19 March 2001, http://www.microsoft.com/presspass/features/2001/mar01/03-19hailstorm.mspx.

155 **The year before, Larry Page:** Danny Sullivan, "Google Goes Forward," *Search Engine Report*, 29 June 1999, http://searchenginewatch.com/showPage.html?page=2167311.

156 **Paul Buchheit:** Jessica Livingston, *Founders at Work: Stories of Startups' Early Days* (Berkeley, CA: Apress, 2007), 162–63. When Gmail was released two years later, on 1 April 2004, Google's press release boasted that it was the result of Google's policy of providing engineers with the freedom to devote 20 percent of their workweek on a project of their own choosing. "Google Gets the Message, Launches Gmail," Google press release, 1 April 2004, http://www.google.com/press/pressrel/gmail.html. The myth that Gmail was produced by the "20 percent" policy was repeated again in 2008 when Google produced a promotional video in which Joseph O'Sullivan, a Google engineer who had worked on the Gmail team, repeated the claim; http://www.youtube.com/watch?v=KCXxFdpsus0. Philipp Lenssen's *Google*

Blogoscoped called attention to the discrepancy between O'Sullivan's claim and Buchheit's own disavowal that Gmail came from the "20 percent" policy. Buchheit wrote: "Oh no, now even Joseph is repeating the Gmail in 20% time myth! . . . It wasn't a 20% project—it was my regular project. It predates the 20% time rule, in fact (though I always had side projects anyway)." O'Sullivan subsequently hedged his statement, and Buchheit wrote in again to emphasize that "20% is important as a concept because it gives license to work on things that other people don't think are important." See Lenssen's "Google Distorting Info on 20% Time?" *Google Blogoscoped*, 24 March 2008, http://blogoscoped.com/archive/2008-03-24-n79.html.

156 **Brian Rakowski:** Much of the material concerning the early history of Gmail is based on an interview with Brian Rakowski, Mountain View, CA, 2 October 2007.

157 **Ads are never going:** "Marissa Mayer, VP of Search Products and User Experience at Google," *iinnovate*, podcast, 31 August 2007, http://iinnovate.blogspot.com/2007/08/marissa-mayer-vp-of-search-products-and.html.

159 **AdSense was launched:** "Google Builds World's Largest Advertising and Search Monetization Program," Google press release, 4 March 2003, http://www.google.com/press/pressrel/advertising.html. AdSense revenues would soon account for more than $1 billion in revenue per quarter for Google, though it should be noted that 85 percent of the gross revenue was spent on traffic-acquisition costs, most of which was the revenue share that Google split with the sites that hosted the advertisements, so Google earned only about a 15 percent margin on its AdSense business.

160 **press announcement:** "Google Gets the Message, Launches Gmail," Google Press release, 1 April 2004, http://www.google.com/press/pressrel/gmail.html.

161 **At *Slashdot*:** "Google's Gmail to Offer 1GB E-mail Storage?" *Slashdot*, 31 March 2004, http://slashdot.org/articles/04/04/01/0038200.shtml ?tid=126&tid=95. See LostCluster's comments with the subject heading "Re: Wahoo."

161 **The confusion led:** "Google's April 1 Cock-Up," *The Inquirer*, 2 April 2004, http://www.theinquirer.net/en/inquirer/news/2004/04/02/googles-april-1-cock-up.

161 **intentionally trying to probe:** Google attempted to quell public concerns by issuing a clarifying statement about its privacy policies, but its attorneys made things worse when they said, "If you request that we delete your e-mail, it may remain on a backup system for a while," without making clear that Google would indeed fulfill the user's request. When Larry Page was asked in an interview about the policy statement's ambiguous language, he said, "You wouldn't want us to lose your mail, either. There's a trade-off." This only served to confirm the fears of critics. See "Google Guys," *Playboy*, September 2004, http://www.sec.gov/Archives/edgar/data/1288776/000119312504139655/ds1a.htm#toc59330_25b.

161 **Jen Fitzpatrick:** Jen Fitzpatrick, "The Science and Art of User Experience at Google," talk at Google, 7 June 2006, http://video.google.com/videoplay ?docid=6459171443654125383&.

162 **In January 2006:** Aaron Whyte, "It's in the mail . . . ," *Official Google Blog*, 20 January 2006, http://googleblog.blogspot.com/2006/01/its-in-mail.html.

162 **In their 2004 *Playboy*:** "Google Guys," *Playboy.*

162 **Brin tried to call attention:** "Google Guys," *Playboy.*

162 **attack on Gmail:** "California Senate Approves Anti-Gmail Bill," News.com, 27 May 2004, http://www.news.com/California%20Senate%20approves %20anti-Gmail%20bill/2100-1028_3-5222062.html.

163 **HailStorm:** Mark Lucovsky, interview, Mountain View, CA, 29 January 2007. Looking back on HailStorm in 2007, when Lucovsky was a Google employee and was asked whether he thought another company today could fill the role of the trusted central hub, unifying all personal data, he said he thought no company would ever be trusted sufficiently to succeed. "I don't think it could be a Google," he said. "I don't think it could be a Yahoo. I don't think it could be a Microsoft. It's a really hard story to tell, to say, 'We're doing this for the good of everything.' Nobody trusts that story. I think HailStorm, to some extent, ruined it for the Web. The opportunity came and went."

163 **derision:** Randall Stross, "Trust Us (Again)," *U.S. News & World Report*, 4 June 2001.

164 **a coalition of privacy groups:** Jeff Chester, of the Center for Digital Democracy, et al., letter to Federal Trade Commission chairman Timothy Muris, 23 October 2001, http://epic.org/privacy/consumer/microsoft/ftcletter 10.23.01.html. Other documents related to Microsoft Passport are available on the Electronic Privacy Information Center's Web page "Microsoft Passport Investigation Docket," http://epic.org/privacy/consumer/microsoft/ passport.html.

164 **Microsoft was unable to sign up:** "Microsoft Has Quietly Shelved Its Internet 'Persona' Service," *New York Times*, 11 April 2002. At the time of HailStorm's debut a year previously, Microsoft had placed onstage representatives from American Express, eBay, Expedia, and two other, smaller companies who showed prototypes and conceptual demos, all of whom subsequently backed out. See " 'HailStorm' on the Horizon," Microsoft press release.

165 **"Is Google reading":** Gmail Help Center, "Is Google Reading My Email?": https://mail.google.com/support/bin/answer.py?answer=6599&topic=1546.

165 **Brad Templeton:** Brad Templeton, "Privacy Subtleties of GMail," essay published online, April 2004, http://www.templetons.com/brad/gmail.html.

166 **distant fourth place:** In the United States, Yahoo Mail had 54 million users; Microsoft's Hotmail, 32 million; AOL, 31 million; and Gmail, only 12 million. "Google Buys Web Security Specialist," *San Jose Mercury News*, 10 July 2007.

166 **Justin.tv:** Michael Seibel, Justin.tv's CEO, said in October 2007 that the site received 500,000 unique visitors in its first five days after its launch, 11,500 accounts were created, and 15 percent of those account holders broadcast video. E-mail correspondence with author, 9 October 2007. For a commentary about the quality of Justin.tv's programming, see Randall Stross, "A Site Warhol Would Love," *New York Times*, 14 October 2007.

166 **John Battelle:** John Battelle, "Just Asking," *Searchblog*, 19 June 2007, http://battellemedia.com/archives/003744.php. Matt Cutts's post was composed on 19 June 2007, http://battellemedia.com/archives/003744.php# comment_122000. His follow-up post was on 20 February 2008, http:// battellemedia.com/archives/003744.php#comment_128693.

167 **Larry Dignan:** Larry Dignan, "Read the Fine Print of Google Office," *Between the Lines*, 22 February 2007, http://blogs.zdnet.com/BTL/?p=4537; Larry Dignan, "Will You Trust Google with Your Data?" *Between The Lines*, 23 February 2007, http://blogs.zdnet.com/BTL/?p=4544.

168 **In October 2006:** Adrian Sannier, "Like Technology from an Advanced Alien Culture", *Adrian Sannier Blog*, Arizona State University, 16 October 2006, https://uto.asu.edu/blog/2006/10/16/like-technology-from-an-advance-alien -culture%e2%80%a6/. For all parties, it was a decision that was made with public relations in mind. For Google, having ASU decide to adopt Apps permitted it to boast of an installation that was done on a large scale and quickly, within two weeks of the university's decision. For ASU, the association with Google was used to demonstrate the "agility" of ASU as it reshaped itself into what it called "the New American University." The university told its various constituents that the Google connection also "places ASU on Google's exponential technology development trajectory," which would automatically ensure that ASU would keep pace with "the leaders in the field."

169 **Google experienced for the first time:** Michael Arrington, "Gmail Disaster: Reports of Mass Email Deletions," *TechCrunch*, 28 December 2006, http://www.techcrunch.com/2006/12/28/gmail-disaster-reports-of-mass-email -deletions/.

169 **In the first quarter of 2007:** "Google Buys Web Security Specialist," *San Jose Mercury News*, 10 July 2007.

170 **One notable trophy:** "Student Privacy a Concern with Webmail Switch," *Daily Pennsylvanian*, 16 January 2007, http://media.www.dailypennsylvanian .com/media/storage/paper882/news/2007/01/16/News/Student.Privacy.A.C oncern.With.Webmail.Switch- 2633726.shtml; "Officials Say Google Was the First Choice," *Daily Pennsylvanian*, 20 April 2007, http://media.www .dailypennsylvanian.com/media/storage/paper882/news/2007/04/20/News/ Officials.Say.Google.Was.The.First.Choice-28 71128.shtml.

171 **without showing signs:** Not all campuses were resistant. Administrators at San Jose State University had approached Google and Microsoft about Web-hosted e-mail and decided to accept Microsoft's offer. Don Baker, a San Jose

State administrator in the university's computing services group who was a member of the selection committee, was dismayed that Google was unwilling to come to campus to make a presentation about Google Apps to the committee, even though the Googleplex was close to the university's campus. Microsoft, on the other hand, had gone out of its way to send a representative to make a presentation—and it could point to a hundred schools that were using Hotmail accounts, whereas Google could point to only a single campus that was using Google Apps. Baker said, "If it is this difficult to get the vendor's attention in order to use a product, what was their maintenance support going to be like during and after the installation?" Baker e-mail to author, 6 April 2007.

174 **an immediate decision:** San Jose State's Don Baker said in a phone interview with the author on 7 May 2008 that he was aware of four CSU campuses among the system's twenty-three that had decided to adopt Google Apps for Education. Google declined to confirm whether this tally was accurate or complete.

174 **250,000 accounts:** Brin mentioned the University of Phoenix account in passing during a quarterly earnings call. "Google Q3 2007 Earnings Call Transcript," prepared by *SeekingAlpha*, 18 October 2007, http://seeking alpha.com/article/50487-google-q3-2007-earnings-call-transcript.

174 **too few customers:** In August 2007, Google announced five schools that were adopting Google's education package: the University of North Carolina–Greensboro, Clemson University, University of Texas–San Antonio, Kennesaw State University, and Arkansas State University. But the press release did not mention total numbers, nor did the company respond to requests for the information in October 2007 and in May 2008. "Google@School—More Universities Announce Google Apps on Campus," Google press release, 16 August 2007, http://www.google.com/intl/en/press/annc/google_at_school .html.; Jeff Keltner, "One-Year Mark for Google Apps Education Edition," *Official Google Blog*, 25 October 2007, http://googleblog.blogspot.com /2007/10/one-year-mark-for-google-apps-education.html.

174 **six million active accounts:** Bruce Gabrielle, e-mail message, 12 May 2008.

174 **he casually dropped:** Ballmer was speaking at the UK Microsoft Startup Accelerator Program. See Microsoft's Lars Lindstsedt, "The Online Opportunity," *Microsoft Startup Zone: United Kingdom*, 4 October 2007, http://microsoftstartupzone.com/blogs/united_kingdom/archive/2007/10/01/ the-online-opportunity.aspx. A link to a video snippet of Ballmer's remarks is available in Lindstedt's post: http://www.mydeo.com/videorequest .asp?XID=48644&CID=133678. Ballmer's remark about Gmail is found at the two-minute point in the question-and-answer segment. Also see Ed Moltzen, "Microsoft's Ballmer: Google Reads Your Mail," *The Chart* on ChannelWeb Network, 7 October 2007, http://www.crn.com/ software/202300583.

175 **transition in America's cities:** Randall Stross, *The Wizard of Menlo Park: How Thomas Alva Edison Invented the Modern World* (New York: Crown Publishers, 2007), 172–81.

176 **David Berlind:** "Yes, It's Time to Destroy Your E-Mail Servers. What App Is Next?" *InformationWeek: David Berlind's Tech Radar*, 14 May 2008, http://www.informationweek.com/blog/main/archives/2008/05/get_over_it_for.html.

8. Algorithm, Meet Humanity

180 **In 2002, Google offered:** "Google Answers: Frequently Asked Questions," n.d., http://answers.google.com/answers/faq.html#who; "Latest from Google: For-Pay Search," *New York Times,* 25 April 2002.

181 **three years after Google Answers:** "Google Plans to Cancel Paid Service for Answers," *New York Times*, 30 November 2006, http://www.nytimes.com/2006/11/30/technology/30google.html; "If You Think You Have All the Right Answers, This Site Is for You," *Wall Street Journal*, 12 July 2006.

183 **Tim Berners-Lee:** Tim Berners-Lee, James Hendler, and Ora Lassila, "The Semantic Web," *Scientific American*, 17 May 2001, http://www.sciam.com/article.cfm?id=the-semantic-web.

183 **new companies are springing up:** John Markoff, "What I Meant to Say Was Semantic Web," *Bits,* 19 December 2007, http://bits.blogs.nytimes.com/2007/10/19/what-i-meant-to-say-was-semantic-web/. Cuill, another search engine whose product was in development in early 2008, was reportedly working on technology that "can index web pages significantly faster and cheaper than Google." Blekko was another search engine company in stealth mode in early 2008. See Cuill entry (last edited 20 March 2008) in CrunchBase, http://www.crunchbase.com/company/cuill, and Blekko entry (last edited 25 February 2008), http://www.crunchbase.com/company/blekko. Also see Michael Arrington, "Stealth Search Engine Blekko Gets Money from Marc Andreesen, SoftTech," *TechCrunch*, 14 May 2008, http://www.techcrunch.com/2008/05/14/stealth-search-engine-blekko-gets-money-from-marc-andreesen-softtech/.

183 **In May 2008:** Danny Sullivan, "Powerset Launches 'Understanding Engine' for Wikipedia Content," *Search Engine Land*, 12 May 2008, http://searchengineland.com/080512-000100.php; Chris Morrison, "Powerset: Don't Call Us a Search Engine," *VentureBeat*, 10 April 2008, http://venturebeat.com/2008/04/10/powerset-dont-call-us-a-search-engine/; "Powerset Joins Live Search," *Live Search,* 1 July 2008, http://blogs.msdn.com/livesearch/archive/2008/07/01/powerset-joins-live-search.aspx.

184 **Between 2004 and 2006:** "Looking for the Next Google," *New York Times*, 1 January 2007, http://www.nytimes.com/2007/01/01/technology/01search

.html. In May 2007, Don Dodge, a Microsoft executive who did not work with Microsoft's search group, published on his personal blog a post that showed why investors were so keen to enter the search business: Dodge calculated that every 1 percent of the U.S. search market would be worth about $100 million in annualized revenue, which, with certain assumptions, would lead to a market capitalization that exceeded $1 billion. See Don Dodge, "Why 1% of Search Market Share Is Worth over $1 Billion," *Don Dodge on the Next Big Thing*, 26 May 2007, http://dondodge.typepad.com/the_next _big_thing/2007/05/why_1_of_search.html. Also see Bernard Lunn, "11 Search Trends That May Disrupt Google," *ReadWriteWeb*, 16 June 2008, http://www.readwriteweb.com/archives/11_search_trends.php.

184 **Squidoo, Sproose, and NosyJoe:** Randall Stross, "The Human Touch That May Loosen Google's Grip," *New York Times*, 24 June 2007, http://www.nytimes.com/2007/06/24/business/yourmoney/24digi.html.

184 **Jimmy Wales:** "Founder of Wikipedia Plans Search Engine to Rival Google," *The Times Online*, 23 December 2006, http://technology.timesonline.co.uk/ tol/news/tech_and_web/article1264117.ece. Wales was overly sanguine about how quickly the project could be launched: in December 2006 he said that the provisional launch date was the first quarter of 2007, which came and went. For a critical view of Wikipedia, see Randall Stross, "Anonymous Source Is Not the Same as Open Source," *New York Times*, 12 March 2006, http://www.nytimes.com/2006/03/12/business/yourmoney/12digi.html.

185 **Calacanis described:** Jason Calacanis, e-mail to author, 19 June 2007.

186 **"John Henry":** Stross, "The Human Touch."

186 **Marissa Mayer was in Paris:** Marissa Mayer, presentation at Google European Press Day 2007, Paris, 19 June 2007, http://www.youtube.com/watch ?v=dNRE5x-V-sQ. Matt Cutts quoted an account of Mayer's answers to questions posed by journalists at the Press Day in a journalist's blog post that included an interesting exchange between Mayer and the *Guardian*'s Jemima Kiss. Kiss asked whether there was a place for human intervention in guiding Web search, like Mahalo's, expecting Mayer to say no, but she instead answered, "Up to today we have relied on automation, but I believe the future will be a blend of both, combing [*sic*] the scale of automation and human intelligence." Jemima Kiss, "Google's Press Day 2007," *Guardian Unlimited: OrganGrinder*, 19 June 2007, http://blogs.guardian.co.uk/organ grinder/2007/06/googles_press_day_2007.html. I was unable to confirm the accuracy of the account; I could not find it in the videos of the event that Google placed on YouTube.

187 **Cutts shared extended thoughts:** In his post, Cutts spared me any direct criticism and kindly referred to the article as "interesting." Among the comments that followed his post was one from Aaron Pratt that was not as gentle: "Forced myself to read that *New York Times* article and just wanted to say that human edited search engines like Mahalo suck. The article almost seemed

anti-Google as if the writer was being paid off by Mahalo. Expect many more of these types of articles in the future, everyone hates a winner." Cutts responded with a follow-up comment to Pratt's, saying that he did not think that I was "anti-Google" and regarded the basic question—will human-powered search threaten Google?—to be a fair one. He did take issue with my blurring the line he drew between spam and search engine optimization. See Matt Cutts, "The Role of Humans in Google Search," *Gadgets, Google, and SEO*, 23 June 2007, http://www.mattcutts.com/blog/the-role-of-humans-in -google-search/.

187 **expressed the same points:** John Battelle, "A Brief Interview with Google's Matt Cutts," *Searchblog*, 26 September 2006, http://battellemedia.com/ archives/002917.php.

187 **Larry Page had publicly:** Jason Calacanis, "FooCamp: OpenSearch," calacanis.com, 23 June 2007, http://www.calacanis.com/2007/06/23/foocamp -opensearch/.

188 **Eric Schmidt pointed:** "Google Q4 2006 Earnings Call Transcript," prepared by SeekingAlpha, 31 January 2007, http://seekingalpha.com/article/25717 -google-q4-2006-earnings-call-transcript.

188 **Viacom did not buy:** "Viacom Tells YouTube: Hands Off," *New York Times*, 3 February 2007, http://www.nytimes.com/2007/02/03/technology/ 03tube.html. In a tally that was by no means complete, Viacom had found 150,000 unauthorized clips of its shows on YouTube, which had been viewed 1.5 billion times. Surely, the lawsuit argued, the wide availability of that material on YouTube and the fact that YouTube had attained a $1.65 billion valuation in its short history before it was acquired were directly related: the infringing works had helped to draw the audience that propelled YouTube's growth and astounding valuation.

188 **expected lawsuit:** Viacom International Inc., Comedy Partners, Country Music Television, Inc., Paramount Pictures Corporation, and Black Entertainment Television LLC, v. You Tube Inc., YouTube, LLC, and Google, Inc., United States District Court, Southern District of New York, 13 March 2007, http://www.lessig.org/blog/archives/vvg.pdf., 1–2.

189 **Schmidt characterized:** Eric Schmidt interview at Bear Stearns 20th Annual Media Conference, 6 March 2007, http://www.youtube.com/watch?v=9HM -ZO21NwA.

189 **Schmidt directed attention away:** Google was not consistent in arguing that under the law it had no responsibility for monitoring what was uploaded. A year earlier, in early 2006, YouTube set a little-noticed precedent that it was willing to monitor uploaded videos for infringing material when it offered what it called a "producer program," which permitted uploading videos that were longer than the standard ten minutes. The videos were not made publicly available immediately. Roelof Botha, a YouTube board member, explained that when the longer videos were uploaded, "we do extra verifica-

tion, make sure copyright is actually clear." One could have asked, why go to the trouble to make sure that copyright was clear if the DCMA absolved the host video service of any and all responsibility? See Matt Marshall, "Q&A with Roelof Botha, the Web 2.0 Guy at Sequoia Capital," *VentureBeat*, 1 June 2006, http://venturebeat.com/2006/06/01/qa-with-roelof-botha-the-web -20-guy-at-sequoia-capital/.

189 **he announced:** "A Conversation with Eric Schmidt," interviewed by John Seigenthaler, National Association of Broadcasters 2007, Las Vegas, 16 April 2007, http://www.youtube.com/watch?v=gAaBVUpLJ10. Also see Schmidt's description of Claim Your Content in "Google Q1 2007 Earnings Call Transcript," 19 April 2007, prepared by SeekingAlpha, http://seekingalpha.com/article/32897-google-q1-2007-earnings-call-transcript.

189 **National Legal and Policy Center:** Ken Boehm to Patrick J. Leahy, 25 September 2007, http://www.nlpc.org/pdfs/Letter%20HSCJ.pdf.

190 **Philippe Dauman:** "Viacom Chief Jabs Google's Antipiracy Effort, Talks Up Copyright Guidelines," *Computerworld*, 18 October 2007, http://www .computerworld.com/action/article.do?command=viewArticleBasic&article Id=9043252.

190 **a consortium:** "Disney, Microsoft Lead Copyright Pact," *Wall Street Journal*, 18 October 2007, http://online.wsj.com/public/article/SB11926978872 1663302.html.

190 **test the new software:** "Nabbing Video Pirates: Who Needs Google?" *BusinessWeek*, 16 October 2007, http://www.businessweek.com/technology/content/oct2007/tc20071016_876447.htm.

190 **Eric Schmidt attempted:** "Google Takes Step on Video Copyrights," *New York Times*, 16 October 2007, http://www.nytimes.com/2007/10/16/business/16video.html.

191 **Google claimed:** Liz Gannes, "YouTube Finally Launches Video ID Tool," *NewTeeVee*, 15 October 2007, http://newteevee.com/2007/10/15/youtube -finally-launches-video-id-tool/.

191 **In its haste to announce:** "Nabbing Video Pirates," *BusinessWeek*.

192 **Steve Chen gratefully said:** Steve Chen, "The State of Our Video ID Tools," *The Official Google Blog*, 14 June 2007, http://googleblog.blogspot.com/2007/06/state-of-our-video-id-tools.html. In March 2008, another weakness of YouTube's vaunted "community flagging" was exposed: its operation is slow. A clip that was posted in England showing what appeared to be a young mother being gang raped by three teenage boys was watched six hundred times before being removed. When Kent Walker, Google's general counsel, was called before a parliamentary committee to explain how such a clip could have been allowed to have been posted, he said it would be "inefficient" to screen every minute of footage. "You do not have a policeman on every street corner to stop things from happening, you have policemen responding very quickly when things do happen," he said. "Google Admits YouTube Rape Video Was 'a Mistake,'" *Times*

Online, 1 April 2008, http://technology.timesonline.co.uk/tol/news/tech_ and_web/article3662228.ece. The case took an unanticipated turn when the woman who had appeared to be a rape victim was subsequently arrested "on suspicion of underage sex and perverting the course of justice." "YouTube 'Rape Victim' Arrested," *Register*, 1 April 2008, http://www.theregister.co .uk/2008/04/01/alleged_youtube_rape_victim_arrested/.

192 **Revver:** Digital Hollywood, "Building Blocks 2006," San Jose, CA, 15 August 2006, http://www.digitalhollywood.com/%231BB1kSessions/ BBTuesOne.html.

192 **By March 2008:** "Number of Online Videos Viewed in the U.S. Jumps 13 Percent in March to 11.5 Billion," comScore press release, 12 May 2008, http://www.comscore.com/press/release.asp?press=2223.

192 **impossible for neutral observers:** Greg Sandoval, "YouTube's Filtering Issues Still Not 'Moot,'" *News.com News Blog*, 18 April 2008, http://www .news.com/8301-10784_3-9921916-7.html.

193 **By spring 2008:** "Number of Online Videos Viewed in the U.S.," comScore press release.

Conclusion

196 **Yet in April 2008:** "comScore Media Metrix Ranks Top 50 U.S. Web Properties for April," comScore press release, 15 May 2008, http://www .comscore.com/press/release.asp?press=2229.

196 **by March 2008:** "Number of Online Videos Viewed in the U.S. Jumps 13 Percent in March to 11.5 Billion," comScore press release, 12 May 2008, http://www.comscore.com/press/release.asp?press=2223.

197 **Columbia University:** Gabriel Stricker, "Columbia University Joins the Google Book Search Library Project," *Inside Google Book Search*, 13 December 2007, http://booksearch.blogspot.com/2007/12/columbia-university -joins-google-book.html.

197 **second dozen cities:** Vaibhav Vaish, "A Dozen More Cities in Street View," *Google Lat Long Blog*, 12 February 2008, http://google-latlong.blogspot .com/2008/02/dozen-more-cities-in-street-view.html.

197 *New York Times:* Wei Luo, "All the News That's Fit to Print on a Map: The New York Times in Google Earth," *Google Lat Long Blog*, 7 April 2008, http://google-latlong.blogspot.com/2008/04/all-news-thats-fit-to-print-on -map-new.html.

197 **Google's share:** "Google Receives 68 Percent of U.S. Searches in May 2008," Hitwise press release, 10 June 2008, http://www.hitwise.com/press -center/hitwiseHS2004/leader-record-growth.php.

198 **Steve Ballmer likes:** Ballmer made the remarks at a talk he gave at Stanford University. "Microsoft CEO Says Google a 'One-Trick Pony,'" cbs5.com, 15

March 2007, http://cbs5.com/business/local_story_074175502.html. He returned to the "one-trick pony" characterization of Google in October, at the Web 2.0 Conference. "Ballmer: Search Like 'Precocious' Tot," *Associated Press*, 18 October 2007, http://ap.google.com/article/ALeqM5grlwt32po MtIMBrxig_ocloy2LNgD8SBRNV04. He said the two new tricks that Microsoft was trying to learn were "devices and entertainment, and advertising and the Web."

198 **Henry Blodget:** Henry Blodget, "Google Search To Surpass Size of Microsoft Windows in 2009," *Silicon Alley Insider*, 13 May 2008, http://www.alley insider.com/2008/5/google_to_surpass_size_of_microsoft_windows_in_2009.

199 **"outside pressures":** Larry Page, "Letter from the Founders: 'An Owner's Manual' for Google's Shareholders," 2004, http://investor.google.com/ipo _letter.html.

199 **When Eric Schmidt was interviewed:** "For Soaring Google, Next Act Won't Be as Easy as the First," *Wall Street Journal*, 30 June 2005.

200 **Craig Silverstein:** "Google's Man Behind the Curtain," News.com, 10 May 2004, http://www.news.com/2008-1024_3-5208228.html. Silverstein made the same point six weeks earlier, but instead of referring to the local reference librarian, which was clearly his intended meaning, he was quoted as saying it would be 300 years before computers were as good as "your local reference library." See "Inside the Wide World of Google," *CBS News*, 28 March 2004, http://www.cbsnews.com/stories/2004/03/25/sunday/main608672.shtml.

200 **a second time:** "Google ETA? 300 Years to Index the World's Info," News.com, 8 October 2005, http://www.news.com/Google-ETA-300-years -to-index-the-worlds-info/2100-1024_3-5891779.html; Eric Schmidt, "Technology Is Making Marketing Accountable," transcript of speech delivered to the Association of National Advertisers, 8 October 2005, http://www .google.com/press/podium/ana.html.

Acknowledgments

This book would not have been written were it not for Elizabeth Kaplan, my stalwart literary agent for almost twenty years. I began the book with a wisp of an idea and some hesitation about whether it was a feasible project. Elizabeth supplied the encouragement I needed to lace up my shoes and start, and when I ran into difficulties at the end and became wobbly, she knew exactly what I needed in order to finish.

At Google, Karen Wickre was liaison extraordinaire. She was on duty around the clock, it seemed, responding immediately to my requests with exactly the information or referrals I was looking for and adding a good dash of humor, too.

Karen worked closely with her colleagues in Google's corporate communications group, who did their part to persuade other Googlers to make themselves available. For their efforts on my behalf, I am indebted to group head David Krane, and to Sean Carlson, Erin Fors, Jason Freidenfelds, Courtney Hohne, Rachael Horwitz, Meghan Hughes, Michael Kirkland, Jon Murchinson, Megan Quinn, Oscar Shine, Gabriel Stricker, Katie Watson, and Larry Yu.

I'd like to thank the following individuals at Google for making time for interviews: David Bailey, Peter Chane, Matt Cutts, Vic Gundotra, John Hanke, Urs Hölzle, Joe Kraus, Mark Lucovsky, Franz Och, Brian Rakowski, Eric Schmidt, and Adam Smith. Craig Silverstein was helpful, too, filling in some holes in my understanding of Google's early history.

Acknowledgments

Bruce Gabrielle of Microsoft helped bring his company's portion of the story up-to-date.

In reporting that I did for various *New York Times* assignments that pertained to Google, I received the help of Marissa Mayer of Google, Jason Calacanis of Mahalo, Michael Cusumano of MIT's Sloan School of Management, Adam Jusko of Bessed, Kristen Roby of Microsoft, Michael Seibel of Justin.tv, and Allan R. Adler of the Association of American Publishers.

At San Jose State University's College of Business, William Jiang and Anne Lawrence, who served as chair and vice chair, respectively, of the Department of Organization and Management, cleared the way for the book, lightly tossing aside bureaucratic obstacles so that I could take a yearlong leave to work on the project.

Don Baker, who oversees San Jose State's computing services group, kindly allowed me to join him when fielding sales presentations by Google and Microsoft.

In 2006–2007, I was a postdoctoral fellow of Stanford Law School's Center for Internet and Society. Thanks in particular go to Lauren Gelman, who was then the center's associate director, and to the law school's librarians.

For arrangements that enabled me to hear Google executives present talks off campus, I wish to thank Roger Sherman of the International Macintosh Users Group and Dennis Wharton and Kathy Roberts of the National Association of Broadcasters.

At the Free Press, Emily Loose was an active editor who did not wait idly for me to send her the first pages; from the start, she debriefed me regularly and helped shape my research agenda. When I finally did begin to write up my discoveries, she was demanding, pushing me to make improvements after I was ready—*more than ready*—to declare the narrative complete.

Danielle Kaniper of the Free Press deftly handled sundry arrangements. Chuck Antony and Edith Lewis supplied sharp eyes as copyeditors.

Gail Hershatter, Lee Gomes, Pamela Basey, and Gary Rivlin read the manuscript with tough love and delivered the detailed criticism that I both hoped for and dreaded. Addressing their suggestions served to greatly improve the work.

Most of all, I would like to thank my wife, Ellen Stross, who supplied indispensable encouragement, perspective, and counsel on all questions. With her at my side, I am the most fortunate of authors.

Index

Index

Index

Index

Google (*cont.*)
  second source of profits, elusive, 126,
    166, 196–197, 198
  secrecy, 58, 61–62, 219–220
  and Sequoia Capital, 120
  share prices, 3, 16
  silos, information, 106–107, 166, 182
  site visitors, has most, 196
  social-networking features, 38–39
  Software as a Service, 8, 197
  spam-infected search results, 184–185,
    187
  spider, 27, 28, 30, 51, 109
  Stanford origins, 4
  stock options, 16–17
  Street View, 144–147, 150, 197, 246
  Summer of Code, 34
  systems failure, 172
  and Systran, 81
  Talk, 39, 155
  terms of service, 167
  text advertisements, 3, 4, 5
  TGIF meetings, 12–14, 179–180
  translation, statistical machine, 82–87,
    227
  trustworthiness of, 35, 166–167,
    167–168, 249
  twenty-percent time, 247–248
  unfavorable impression of, prospect's,
    250–251
  universal search, 182–183
  users' satisfaction, 221
  valuation, 3
  venture-capital financing of, 9
  Video, 112–113, 117–119, 121–122,
    124–125, 189, 199
  video fingerprints, 187–192
  video search, problems with, 109, 110
  Video Store, 120–121, 238
  and Web 2.0, 24, 181
  Web page index, size of, 50, 51, 53, 69,
    89
  and Wikipedia, 42–43
  wireless-spectrum auction, 2, 40, 41
  and Yahoo, 4, 6, 65–68, 155
  YouTube acquisition, 2, 124–125,
    187

Google Blogoscoped, 247–248
Google Earth Hacks, 139
Google Sightseeing, 139
Goose Creek, SC, 58
Gore, Al, 158
GoTo, 202
Grand River Dam Authority, 219
Gray, Matthew, 207
Greenstein, Daniel, 105
Gregorian University, 226
Grouper, 117
Guardian, 253
Gundotra, Vic, 29

HAL 9000, 16
Hanke, John, 133–136, 142–143
Harp, Walter, 171, 172, 173, 174
Hart, Michael, 92
Harvard University, 98, 99
  Computation Laboratory, 80
Henry, John, 186
Henzinger, Monika, 235
Herscher, Adam, 72
Hi5, 34
Hoffman, Daniel, 231
Holocaust Memorial Museum, 140
Hölzle, Urs, 38, 52–55, 59, 217, 218
Horowitz, Bradley, 110
HOTorNOT, 114
Houghton Mifflin, 231
HousingMaps, 138
Houston, 244
HP, 103, 235
Hurley, Chad, 113, 115–116, 120, 124,
    236, 238
Hyderabad, India, 94
Hyperion, 231

IAC/InterActive, 139
IBM
  Almaden Research Center, 28
  culture compared with Google's, 98
  data center operations, 56
  e-mail, 176
  machine translation, 80, 81, 83, 226
  in mainframe era, 195
  Mark I, 81

Index

Index

Index